Dream Dictionary

Interpretations with
NUMEROLOGY

BY EVAD ARAS

FIRST EDITION

TABLE OF CONTENTS

Published by the: House of Collectibles, Inc.
773 Kirkman Road, No. 120
Orlando, FL 32811

Printed in the United States of America

ISBN: 0-87637-015-6

INTERPRETATION OF DREAMS

What is a dream? The library shelves are heavy with scholarly books describing dreams in sophisticated and elaborate manner. Poets have been writing about dreams in lyrical terms. But to get a simple definition, I looked into a recently published dictionary and found: "DREAM. A train of thought or images passing through the mind in sleep."

A dream is a personal matter; it occurs exclusively in the sleeper's mind and is not shared with anyone else. Many reasons are expounded by students of psychology as to the cause of dreams. Some say the dreams are due to physical reasons such as overeating or being hungry before going to bed, or the bedroom is either too hot or too cold, or the experiences of the day or night preceding the sleeping hours worried or excited the person and brought on the dreams. But other students of dreams say they are not due to physical (outside) causes; their contention is that the dream is an expression of the unconscious mind of the sleeper which may be (or seem to be) in contradiction to the conscious mind. They say the dream, in such case, is a wish-fulfillment of something the person unconsciously strives for, but may not be able to achieve while conciously awake. Those who are interested in the field of parapsychology, especially in the study of E.S.P. (Extra-sensory perception), look upon dreams as a matter of precognition—the foretelling of events to come.

Everybody dreams. You may hear someone say, "I never dream." However, it's hardly likely the person does not have any dreams; it may be that he or she doesn't want to remember the dream, or just cannot remember it. It is possible that a person who is not inclined to analyze his own emotions or thoughts does not want to analyze his dreams, so he just conveniently and consciously forgets them as soon as he awakens from sleep. On the other hand, if a person is inclined to introspectively analyze every one of his thoughts and emotions he will remember the dream in detail, and be curious about why he dreamed it and what it may mean to him.

If a person is under psychiatric treatment, he may be instructed by his analyst to keep a written report of each dream and its details, so that the dream may be interpreted later on by the psychotherapist.

1

Each person has his or her own "pattern" of sleeping and dreaming. Many scholarly studies have been made (especially at the "sleep laboratories" at Duke University, New York University, Cornell University and University Chicago, among others) and many books on the subject of sleep have recently been written. The scientific studies were done on men and women under controlled conditions; to their skulls were clamped electrodes which registered (during their sleep) on the EEG (electroencephalograph) tapes. Of course other tests were included at the same time. One of the interesting results of these sleep-and-dream tests was that each person who was a subject participating in the test did dream. So it is not likely that there are people who don't have dreams.

Over one hundred years ago, in Vienna, Dr. Sigmund Freud (regarded as the father of psychoanalysis) brought into the medical (and mental) diagnoses of patients the concept of dream interpretation. He had many followers (and dissenters) to his theories; but to this day his book, *The Interpretation of Dreams* is the bible of those psychologists and other workers in the field of human behavior who go along with what is known as the Freudian theory. He interpreted the dreams of his patients in terms of images and symbols; for instance, a person or an animal or a flower or a building in a dream was not just that. The object or the person in a dream might be a sex symbol and not what actually appears in the dream. In fact, Freudians are inclined to see a sex symbol in almost everything in a person's dream, and much (perhaps too much) stress has been laid upon interpreting everything in a dream to have its origin in a desire for sex-fulfillment, overlooking the fact that a human being has other motivations besides a sex drive.

As an example of the Freudian interpretation of dream symbols, the phallic symbol (the male sex organ) is denoted in the dream's inclusion of such elongated articles as a pen or pencil, a baseball bat, a tall narrow tower, a knife; even in the tails of animals, or a long fish or a snake; and fruits such as bananas and cucumbers.

In interpreting the female sex symbol, the Freudians are interested in rounded objects in the dream. For instance, fruits like the apple, fig and peaches, as well as plants like roses and cabbages (which are full blown), are taken to show the dreamer's interest in the female sex organs and her breasts. Openings in the body (eyes, mouth, ears or other openings) and in boxes or other objects which have openings, are indicative (to the Freudian concept) of the opening into the female womb.

These are but a small list of interpretation of sex symbols in dreams; but they serve the purpose of showing how the psychoanalyst bases his interpretation of the person's suppressed sex desires or whatever his or her sex attitudes might imply in the dream (which is unconscious) and may not be shown (or even known) by the dreamer in his conscious waking hours.

The interest in dream interpretation did not commence with Freud; it is not a modern concept. You merely have to go back to the Holy Bible, Genesis Chapter 40, wherein Joseph interprets for Pharaoh his dream about the three branches of the vine as a symbol of three days in these words, "Yet within three days shall Pharaoh lift up thine head, and restore thee unto thy place. . . ." Also, Chapter 41, Joseph interprets Pharaoh's dream about the seven leanfleshed kine devouring the seven fat kine, and the seven withered and thin stalks of corn devouring the seven good ears of corn, in these words, "The seven good kine are seven years; and the seven good ears are seven years; the dream is one." Joseph went on with his interpretation of the seven lean years which would follow the seven good ones and which helped Pharaoh provide for those lean years. To students of dreams and their symbolic meanings, the biblical story has much significance.

The Greek philosopher, Aristotle, deals with dreams and their interpretation in his writing. The ancients (both civilized and non-civilized) usually thought the dreams were manifestations of the wills and the punishments of their various gods and idols. Let us say that so long as man has existed on this earth, so long has he dreamed and been puzzled by these unconscious "pictures" in his mind during his sleeping hours. Primitive man and contemporary civilized man is not immune to dreams; but the way in which the dream is either ignored or accepted or interpreted depends on the scientific or the emotional approach to it.

Some people fear dreams, due to their misconception of what a dream really expresses. A dream should be accepted as a part of one's own mind, expressing itself unconsciously during sleep. Actually a dream can add interesting new dimensions to a person's mind and life, if considered as an "extension" of the mind and not as something disctinctly apart from the mind and something that has to be feared.

3

VARIOUS KINDS OF DREAMS

There are all types of dreams; some may be puzzling and seem to have no relationship whatsoever to the dreamer's mind and life style; some may be serene and lovely and very calming; others may be exciting, perhaps frightening, or even nightmares. Generally dreams fall into the following categories (although you may have some dreams which are so unique that they don't belong in any one of these):

HAPPY DREAMS. The dream is about pleasant people and places and activities; the dream may be frivolous and full of fun (in which you participate, or are not there but see other people in happy situations). A dream of this sort may not occur with regularity but when it does you wake up with a feeling of joy.

FREUDIAN (or PSYCHOLOGICAL) DREAMS. As told heretofore, these may be dreams which are symbolic of sex suppression or of wish-fulfillment. These may be happy or unhappy dreams, and may provoke much serious thought in the dreamer when he wakes from sleep.

IN SPACE (or ASTRAL) DREAMS. In the dream the spirit leaves the body and it travels in space, or the dream may be that you are falling from a great height and into space (without landing anywhere). It may also be a dream where physically (not the spirit leaving the body) you are in some new place which is not familiar to you and which may be a long distance from where you are or want to be. In these "distance" and "travel" dreams, the strange thing is that upon waking the dreamer may not be able to immediately orient himself to reality and may think he is still in "space travel." People who have an interest in parapsychology usually find such dreams interesting as a basis of interpretation.

PRECOGNITIVE DREAMS. These are the prophetic dreams, and are usually a subject of much controversy. The Freudians reject the concept of prophecy in dreams; whereas the people who interest themselves in parasychology (especially in the field of ESP) generally interpret dreams as foretelling what may happen in the future. In this category of precognitive dreams are the interpretations by Joseph of Pharoah's dreams. After huge and earth-shaking events take place (especially disasters) newspaper editors and radio and television news editors get bombarded with stories from people who tell of their dreams of precognition about that certain event. In the case of the assassinations of John F. Kennedy and his brother Robert and Dr. Martin Luther King, after each event countless number of people told of their dreams (which they had before the events) in which either actually assassination was spelled out or they had symbolic warnings of the impending killings. This takes place after shipwrecks, floods, earthquakes and other natural disasters occur. There is no actual proof that dreams of precognition do work out; but many people think of them as portents of what's going to happen. The scientific students of sleep-and-dreams reject the theory.

UNHAPPY DREAMS—NIGHTMARES. These may sometimes be due to actual physical discomfort, rather than expressions of the unconscious mind. The dreamer might have an ailment and be in pain, which causes fretful sleeping and dreaming, or he may be overly tired and worried. He may have eaten too much, or gone to bed feeling hungry. The room may be too cold or too hot, or he may use too many blankets to cover himself (and so he may dream he is smothering). However, if one can rule out such physical discomfort as contributing to an unhappy dream or a nightmare, then the dream and its symbols are taken into consideration when the interpretation is made. Some people suffer actual fright and pessimism when waking out of a nightmare or an unpleasant dream. Such fear could be easily dispelled when the person can objectively tell himself, "It was only a dream" and then put his mind and energies to more productive matters.

Researchers in the field of dreams have come up with a fact that on a basis of three-to-one the unpleasant dreams occur more than the happy dreams. Another finding is the origin of the term "nightmare." It may be only theoretical but it's an interesting story that ancient Romans and Britons blamed bad dreams on an immense mare (female horse) which would lie down across a sleepers' chest. This caused the person to feel he was being suffocated, so the dream would depict him as being strangled and he would struggle against it.

DREAMS UNDER HYPNOSIS. Freud and others report cases where a hypnotist could command a person to dream of a certain person or action, and that dreamer (when later waking up and describing the dream) would relate that the theme of the dream followed the suggestion given by the hypnotist. For example, a hypnotist commanded a young woman to dream of having a sex

5

relationship with a male member of her family. She dreamed not of the actual act of intercourse, but of many articles of long, narrow size (such as a snake and long keys) which were phallic symbols. It is not known whether she had such symbolic dreams before or after that incident, but the dream immediately following the hypnotic suggestion carried out the order she received from the hypnotist.

DREAMS NOT RELEVANT TO DAILY LIFE. A dream does not necessarily reflect the person's tastes, intelligence and abilities. For instance, a housewife does not necessarily dream about home and family life; a doctor or a lawyer may not dream about his profession; an actor or a business man does not necessarily have dreams relating to his work; students may not dream about school.

COLOR IN DREAMS. An interesting finding by scientists who study dreams is that people generally do not dream in color. About two out of three dreams are in black and white (the way the movies and television appear, except when they are deliberately filmed in color). No psychological conclusion has been reached by researchers in the study of dreams as to any special meaning for dreaming in color.

DREAM WITHOUT A THEME. Some dreams have definite patterns; they are like small one-act plays you see in theatre or on television; they have a beginning, a middle plot and an ending. But many dreams are completely without any pattern and without any theme; all the components of the dream are unrelated to one another. To interpret the meaning of these dreams, one has to approach each separate part or symbol in that dream as if it were a code word and then try to decipher and decode whatever meaning the dream may have. Sometimes such a dream without a theme may have multiple meanings in the interpretation.

CHILDREN'S DREAMS. A very young child may have fears when waking from a dream, not being old enough to separate the reality of the waking hours from the dreams during sleeping hours. But when the child has sufficiently matured to be able (after explanation to him by some adult) to understand that the dream is an unconscious thing which is transmitting a message to the conscious mind, he may then be able to remember the dream and relate it to an adult (who may be interested in interpreting the dream). Children's dreams are mainly wish-fulfillments, as they are not yet beset with the problems and tensions of adult life.

6

HOW TO INTERPRET YOUR DREAMS

When you wake up from a dream (or someone else is relating his or her dream to you) do not be in a rush to run to the meanings of the details of the dream (which are listed in this book). Take your time, relax, then jot down on a paper all that you can remember about the dream—who besides yourself was in it, where it took place, what happened in it, a description of the surroundings, and any other detail you can remember. What you might think is a trifling detail in your dream might actually be of much significance; so write down everything you can remember about it.

Sometimes the things and places and people appearing in your dream may seem to be completely unrelated to the pattern of your life and to your thoughts and abilities and desires. However, the very fact that they did became a part of your mind, while you were asleep, signifies they must have some meaning for you and in some cases they may help you to better understand yourself and to better chart your future course.

The dreams which are outlined in this book are listed in alphabetical order. Therefore, if you dream of an angel you turn to the listing of ANGELS and find out what your dream signifies.

Also, if you dream of flowers, you turn to the listing of FLOWERS as well as to the listing of the special flower about which you dreamed (for instance, ROSES or DAISIES). If you dream about jewelry you turn to the listing in this book marked JEWELRY; if it is about a specific piece of jewelry you might also turn to the listing of the special article (for instance, BRACELET or NECKLACE).

The purpose of this book is to help you. In some cases you will be made happy because of a joyous meaning and prediction attributed to the subject of your dream. In other cases you might find an interpretation of the dream to be a warning that something unpleasant might happen. However, do not accept this as a dire prophesy; use this warning as a means for you to prepare yourself for any such incident, and you will be able to avert running into trouble. There is a time-honored saying that "to be forewarned is to be forearmed" and you can be forearmed and prepared to handle a difficult situation when the meaning of the dream is pointed out to you and you might be able to avoid it.

Use this book as a means of helping yourself to keep a strong, optimistic attitude toward life, and to be on guard to avoid troublesome things and people.

Do not discard the paper on which you noted the details of your dream. Mark a date on it, and keep it. You may have this same dream many times; if so, it is an emphasis of how your are thinking or for what you are wishing. Sometimes you might have a dream that never recurs, and sometimes you might even forget the dream. But you can train your memory to work for you, if you are interested in your dreams and what they may mean to you in their interpretation. This can become an interesting way for you to understand the inner you, which may not be too apparent in your outer manner.

NUMEROLOGY—THE LUCKY NUMBERS

The three numbers which follow each dream listing are compiled through the occult art of numerology. Jot down these numbers on your note pad, as they should be lucky for you for the two days following your dream (that is, from twenty-four to forty-eight hours after you wake up).

SIX NUMBER COMBINATION

You might want to double the lucky numbers, turning them into six figures instead of the three which follow the listing of the dream category. For example, following the word ABANDONMENT is the number 540. So you reverse the three figures to 045, then you add them to the original 540, and the combination makes 540-045.

AARDVARK

AARDVARK—181. If you dream about this ant-eating animal, you will have to work harder to achieve your ambitions.

ABANDONMENT—540. If you abandon a close relative, the dream means you may run into trouble. But if you are the one who is abandoned by a relative or friend, there may be sickness in the family.

ABBATOIR—598. See Slaughter House.

ABBREVIATION—954. When you abbreviate the words you write and speak in your dream, or someone else does it and you notice it, it signifies you may break up a friendship or maybe lose your wages.

ABDICATION—954. If you dream that a member of a royal family abdicates the throne, you will be successful in social life.

ABDUCTION—954. See Kidnapping.

ABILITY—905. Admiring another person's ability to do things well, means you are going to get some money unexpectedly. If you dream that you are the one who shows ability, you will be happy in some new accomplishment.

ABNORMALITY—905. When you dream of an animal or person with physical or mental abnormalities, it is a sign of your worries disappearing and you will be made happy.

ABORIGINES—459. You will soon be able to pay off your debts if you dream of these primitive people.

ABORTION—959. This dream, whether the abortion is your own or someone else's, means you will be disappointed in matters of money and love.

ABRASION—954. You will succeed in many small things if you dream you scrape the skin on any part of your body.

ABROAD—514. See Travel.

ABSCESS—599. If you dream of some other person who has an abscess, you will soon go to another place. But if you have an abscess, beware of real estate or stock market deals.

ABSENCE—435. If in your dream you are looking for some person who is absent, you may receive bad news from a distance.

ABSINTHE—085. If you drink this liquor in your dream, a false friend is talking behind your back.

ABSURDITY—905. Silly situations which occur in a dream signify your love affairs will flourish.

ABUNDANCE—435. When you dream of large quantities of food and other possessions, you better be cautious and try to save money.

ABUSE—195. Should someone be abusive to you in your dream it shows you will have a slight illness, but if you are abusing someone in the dream, you will soon be better off in money matters.

ACCENT—540. See Brogue.

ACCEPTANCE—405. If you accept from someone else a valuable item or money, you will find happiness in love and good luck in business. But if you refuse to accept it, you will stand in your own way of happiness.

ACCIDENT—540. You must guard against doing anything that caused the accident in your dream; for instance, if you dream of getting cut with a knife, or being in an automobile crash (or whatever caused the accident) you have to avoid handling a knife or driving in a car for a whole day.

ACCOMPANIMENT—540. When you dream you are musically accompanying a singer, you will find happiness in the person you love.

ACCORDIAN—914. If you play the accordian, look forward to a pleasant love affair. But if the accordian is out of tune, you may have to work harder for the things you want to achieve.

ACCOUNTANT — 140. If a girl dreams she is in love with an accountant she may not find happiness in marriage, but she will be otherwise financially taken care of.

ACCOUNTS — 409. When you figure accounts and they come out right the first time, you can make a business profit. If you cannot make your figures come out right, you will go through some business anxiety.

ACCUSATION — 954. If you dream of being accused of doing something wrong, be careful about listening to people who flatter you.

ACE — 135. The ace of clubs shows lack of friendship from others; the ace of hearts will bring you happiness in love; the ace of diamonds foretells you will get money; the ace of spades means you will work hard and not get paid enough.

ACETYLENE FLAME — 135. If you see the glaring white flame of an acetylene torch you will make a change for the better, but if in your dream you smell the bad odor of the flame, you must be careful not to go into debt.

ACHE — 385. See Pain.

ACHIEVEMENT — 540. In whatever field you achieve success, in your dream, you will find life happy and peaceful.

ACNE — 345. See Pimples.

ACORNS — 849. If you see acorns by themselves, or growing on oak trees, your plans will soon be fulfilled.

ACQUITTAL — 012. If you dream of being acquitted in a jury trial, you must relax in facing problems and they will be solved soon.

ACROBAT — 210. See Contortionist.

ADAM AND EVE — 525. When you see this couple in the Garden of Eden, you must be prepared to face some family problems and illness, but to dream only of Eve, you will be lucky with good children.

ADDICT, DRUGS — 179. See Dope.

ADENOIDS — 949. If you dream of being operated on the adenoids, you will find satisfaction in working in the community with other people.

11

ADJOURNMENT—540. When you are at a meeting and it is adjourned, take care in choosing food as you might have indigestion.

ADMIRAL—812. If a girl dreams of marrying an admiral, she is going to be pursued by a wealthy older man. If a man dreams of being an admiral, or talking with one, he will find good results in his work and in friendships.

ADMIRATION—954. To admire someone else in a sincere manner, means you will one day be rich. When you dream someone is admiring you, it shows you may be disappointed in some undertaking.

ADOPTION—954. If in your dream you adopt a child, you will reap good returns from an investment.

ADULTERY—585. If you commit adultery in your dream, you should avoid quarreling with family and business people. If you resist someone who is trying to seduce you, you will win out over people who try to blacken your reputation.

ADVANCEMENT—540. You will find your life easier if you dream you got a promotion in business or in school.

ADVENTURE—185. The kind of adventure you dream about will influence you in real life. If it is a funny adventure, you will find fun in what you do, but if the dream adventure is a harsh one, you might go through disappointment in real life.

ADVENTURER—858. A girl who dreams she is being wooed by an adventurer, should be hesitant about forming new friendships with strange men.

ADVENTURESS—599. If a man dreams he is being pursued by an adventuress, he may soon have to face some embarrassing situations.

ADVERSITY—905. If you go through adversity in a dream, it is a good sign you will soon overcome pressing difficulties.

ADVERTISEMENTS—409. Reading newspaper advertisements that are illustrated, means you will be financially better off, but if the ads do not have pictures, you will need to work hard for quite a while.

AERIAL—912. See Antenna.

AFFECTION—954. If you are exchanging signs of affection in your dream with some other person, you can look ahead to happiness in love and marriage.

AFFLICTION—954. Should you dream that you have a physical affliction of some kind, it is a sign you will enjoy good health.

AFRICA—931. If you are in the Sahara Desert, or any other part of the African continent, you will be instructed to serve on a jury.

AFTERNOON—554. When you dream of events that happen in the afternoon, things will be bright for you in the near future.

AGATE—105. Whether the agate is set in a ring or some other kind of jewelry, you will be asked to settle some differences between two close friends.

AGE—175. Guessing a woman's age in a dream, foretells you may have some trouble with one of the opposite sex.

AGENT—540. If yvu dream you deal with an agent, if you are married, you may be deceived by your mate.

AGNOSTIC—093. See Atheist.

AGGRESSIVENESS—599. See Arrogance.

AGONY—545. Suffering great agony in a dream, shows you will soon meet a friend who is very poor, but if you dream that someone else is suffering agony, you may change your place of residence or work.

AGUE—715. A woman who dreams she suffers from this ailment may soon bear a child, but if a man dreams of this ailment, he will enter a new business field. A girl who dreams this should be getting a new lover.

AIRPLANE—145. If you dream you fall from a plane, you may have a short duration of hard luck, but if you are a passenger on the plane, expect to receive a raise in pay. If you are the pilot of the plane, you are in line to receive success in something new you will start. If you dream the plane is taking a quick nosedive, you will have pleasant experiences with one of the opposite sex.

AISLE—925. When you are in the aisle of some public building, you will soon have to make an important decision.

ALARM CLOCK—531. You can look forward to a stimulating

13

and profitable good time, if you hear an alarm clock in your dream.

ALBUM—213. Looking at photographs in an album may tell you to be cautious or you may run into a small accident.

ALCOHOL—852. (Also see Drinking.) If you dream you are drinking to excess, you might soon have a failure, but if you dream you are using alcohol for medicinal purposes, the sign is a good one as things should come out right for you.

ALE—125. If you drink ale in your dream, you should enjoy some good times socially.

ALGEBRA—281. Solving algebraic problems in your dream means you may have some slight argument over an unpaid bill.

ALIBI—929. Giving an alibi for yourself means you may suffer some misunderstanding in your marriage. When another person gives an alibi you will receive honorable recognition.

ALIMONY—545. If you dream you are paying out alimony, you may be indulging in pleasures which will be costly, but if you receive alimony in your dreams, you will suffer some slight ailment.

ALLEY—255. Being chased by a bad person through an alley is a sign of impending disgrace coming your way. If you walk alone through an alley, you may have a quarrel with the one you love. If you dream you come to a dead end of an alley and cannot go ahead, you will not be able to put your plans into motion.

ALLIANCE—435. Dreaming of an alliance made through marriage or in some other way with someone who is wealthy and well-known, predicts you will argue with the person you love.

ALLIGATOR—085. Watching alligators in a zoo means you will take a short vacation trip, but if you dream an alligator is attacking you, people who do not care for you may make fun of you.

ALLOWANCE—435. If a man dreams he is receiving an allowance from his wife or sweetheart, he will find his social companions unfriendly toward him. If an allowance comes from parents or a husband, such a dream spells happiness.

ALLSPICE—935. Using or smelling the aroma of allspice signifies a love attachment which will be very pleasant.

14

ALMANAC—413. (Also see Calendar.) If a man dreams he is referring to an almanac, he will find good results in business. A woman who looks for information in an almanac may have to break some interesting engagements.

ALPHABET—250. If you dream of seeing separate letters of the alphabet, you will be able to do good work as a librarian, or writer, or actor.

ALTAR—018. Praying before an altar foretells you will have relief from tension and worries.

ALTAR BOY—255. If you dream you are doing your duties in church, you will receive unexpectedly good news.

ALTITUDE—145. If you are uncomfortable while in high altitude, you will be in danger of committing some foolish mistake.

ALUM—213. To dream of having your tongue or lips puckered by tasting alum shows you may go through some misunderstanding with the one you love, but if the alum is agreeable to your taste, and does not cause puckering, then such misunderstanding will turn out agreeably.

ALUMINUM—413. If you use aluminum kitchenware, which is bright and clean, you will find happiness in love; but if the aluminum is dirty and dull, you may suffer frustrations in love.

AMATEUR—518. When you perform some amateur thing in your dream, as an actor or artist, and do not charge for your work, it foretells you will be rewarded well for your kindness to an elderly person.

AMBASSADOR—458. If you dream you are your country's ambassador to another country, you must be very cautious about making an investment, but if you talk to some ambassador who came here from another country, you may expect someone you trust to prove treacherous toward you.

AMBITION—954. When you dream you are following your ambitions, you can look forward to a higher position and increased wages.

AMBULANCE—435. If you are being taken to a hospital in an ambulance, you need to use great care about saying or doing the wrong thing, but if you see an ambulance, though you are not in it, it is a warning to you to be more discreet in dealing with the opposite sex.

AMBUSH — 198. Hiding in an ambush in your dream means you can look forward to some happy surprises.

AMMONIA — 491. When you dream you use ammonia to do house-cleaning, it foretells you will enjoy good health. If you just smell the ammonia fumes, you have to guard against drinking too much.

AMMUNITION — 954. To buy and store a lot of ammunition for a hunting trip, you will need to explain why you failed to do certain things. If you dream you lose ammunition, you may have an argument with one of the opposite sex.

AMPUTATION — 954. Should you dream that part of your body is surgically cut off, you can await a raise in salary very soon.

AMUSEMENT — 540. Enjoying yourself with some kind of amusement foretells your future will be much better. If you dream you are not enjoying yourself and are bored with the amusements, you are warned to watch out for some trouble.

ANAGRAMS — 139. If you dream of playing anagrams, you will find a happy way out of annoying love situations.

ANARCHIST — 990. When you dream you are an anarchist, it is a sign that you have to curb hasty actions and be more careful in planning.

ANCESTORS — 589. Dreaming of old ancestors, but not your mother or father, signifies you will find yourself accepted in your community.

ANCHOR — 858. If you are on a ship and raising the anchor, it means you will soon have a fairly dangerous adventure which will turn out all right. If you just see an anchor, without touching it, you can look forward to good opportunities coming your way.

ANCHOVIES — 959. Eating this small fish means you will receive a reward for some good effort you exerted for some other person.

ANEMIA — 391. Suffering with this blood disease, in a dream, is a happy sign that you will have good health.

ANESTHESIA—991. If you smell ether or other anesthesia, it means you will soon meet with good luck. Should a doctor administer anesthesia to you, you will enjoy good health, but if, in your dream, you object to being given anesthesia, you may be heading for a long illness.

ANGELS—523. (Also see Cherubs.) Dreaming of seeing angels is a sign that you and some of your friends will have a short illness.

ANGER—758. If you express yourself in anger because of temper, you may become embarrassed through some love affair. If your anger is against some injustice being done, it foretells happiness with the opposite sex.

ANIMALS—129. See various animals, listed under their separate species. (Also see Zoo.)

ANKLES—259. A man who looks leeringly at a woman's ankles, in his dream, is headed for an exciting love affair. If you dream you sprain an ankle, you are going to lose out in a money deal.

ANNIVERSARY—185. Any anniversary or birthday celebration, in a dream, predicts happy get-togethers with members of the family.

ANNOUNCEMENT—540. Receiving a social or business announcement predicts good news to come your way, but if the announcement card is edged with black, you can look ahead to bad news.

ANNULMENT—540. To dream of getting a marriage annulled is a sign of peace and satisfaction coming to you.

ANTARCTIC—093. When you take a trip to the South Pole, in your dream, your new plans may not turn out too successfully.

ANTELOPE—565. (Also see Deer.) To see this animal in a zoo foretells you will suffer a disappointment. If you shoot the antelope, you may be bothered by an enemy. If you see the animal in an open space, you may soon get an increase in money.

ANTENNA—441. If you are putting up an antenna for a radio or television set, you can succeed in something you thought might be too hard to do.

ANTIDOTE—505. (Also see Poison.) If you are given an antidote for poison in your dream, you need to be careful in dealing with others.

ANTIQUES—159. Looking at lovely old pieces of furniture, bric-a-brac and other antiques, signifies you will enjoy a happy family life.

ANTISEPTIC—093. Applying any kind of antiseptic to a wound is a prediction that you should watch out about getting into an automobile accident.

ANTS—409. If ants come into your home or on your clothes, it is a sign of trifling annoyances in your personal life. If you dream of watching ants being busy and not touching people, it shows you may get scolded for not working as hard as you should.

ANVIL—292. See Blacksmith.

ANXIETY—505. If you dream you are suffering anxiety about something or someone, it shows you will feel pangs of loneliness.

APARTMENT—540. When your dream shows you living in an expensive and large apartment, you will be blessed with more money, but if you are in a tiny, inexpensive apartment, you may soon have an argument with members of the family.

APE—165. See Monkey.

APOLOGY—575. Should someone offer you an apology, in your dream, watch out you don't get hurt in a small accident. If you apologize to someone, you will soon get an apology from someone who has hurt you.

APOPLEXY—545. If you have a sudden attack, it foretells you will be criticized by close relatives. Should someone else have an attack, it shows you will go on a large journey.

APPENDICITIS—099. (Also see Belly, Pain.) An attack of appendicitis is a warning to you not to talk too much so that you may receive financial gain.

APPETITE—905. If you lose your appetite in your dream, you may go through a short time of sadness. If your appetite is good, you will be blessed with good food to satisfy your tastes.

APPLAUSE—195. When you applaud another person who is performing, your health will be good from now on. If you are being applauded by others, your new plans will work out successfully.

APPLE—625. If you see green apples in your dream, you may hear bad news. If the apples are ripe, you will soon do something to bring you happiness. When the apples are baked, or in a pie, or applesauce, you can hope for an honorable reward.

APPLEJACK—131. Drinking this stimulating beverage is a sign you may do or say something that will place you in a false light.

APPOINTMENT—540. Making a date to meet one of your friends foretells that you must be careful your secrets are not discovered by others.

APPRECIATION—954. If you show appreciation to another person, you should have good luck coming your way. When someone shows appreciation towards you, you might displease some people by your type of clothes.

APPRENTICE—935. To dream of learning a job while you are an apprentice, shows you will be lucky in love and business matters. If you have an apprentice working for you, you will have a chance to make some money.

APPROVAL—212. When you show approval of someone, you will have much happiness. If you show approval of someone who does not deserve it, you will suffer some disappointment.

APRICOT—350. When you dream of eating this fruit, you will be lucky in love but unlucky in finances.

APRON—854. (Also see Pinafore.) If a woman dreams of wearing pretty aprons, good things will happen to her, but if a man is wearing an apron, he will be bossed by some woman.

AQUARIUM—913. (Also see Fish.) If you see fish swimming in an aquarium, be cautious in avoiding accidents.

AQUEDUCT—130. Water running through an aqueduct predicts you will be lucky in love and enjoy good health, but if the aqueduct is dry, watch out for depressing worries.

ARABS—129. If you visit Arabs in their own land you should have some romantic adventures, but if you see Arabs riding on horses, beware of jealousy from the opposite sex.

ARBITRATE—105. If you want to have some dispute arbitrated by others, you will gain in some new plan, but when you take part as an arbitrator between others, you may find it hard to get out of an unpleasant situation.

ARBOR—258. Talking to a member of the opposite sex, while under an arbor, foretells good results in doing something artistic.

ARCADE—145. To walk through an arcade means you may find it hard to get rid of some temptations coming your way.

ARCH—838. If you dream of going under an arch, you may hear gossip about yourself. If the arch is broken, you are using too much energy in a needless manner.

ARCHBISHOP—856. When the archbishop you meet in your dream is dressed in full vestments, you will quarrel with members of the family.

ARCHERY—585. When you hit the bull's-eye in an archery contest, you will be able to reach your ambitions. If you don't hit the bull's-eye or if the dart falls down, disappointment will occur for you.

ARCHITECT—530. (Also see Blueprint.) If you dream of making plans for some structure, you will find success through hard work.

ARCTIC—093. Pushing through the ice to reach the North Pole is a sign of reaching your high goals.

ARENA—541. (Also see Stadium.) Watching a sports event in an arena is a sign you will be considering the offer of a new job.

ARGUMENT—540. (Also see Debate.) If you dream you are hot-tempered in an argument, you will have to guard against hasty decisions. If you argue in a reasonable manner, good luck is coming your way.

ARISTOCRAT—810. A dream in which you are being snubbed by an aristocrat means your possessions will multiply.

ARITHMETIC—093. (Also see Accounts.) When you dream of trying to solve arithmetical problems, you will be faced with personal problems that will be solved through hard work.

ARMCHAIR—198. Whether you or someone else in your dream sits comfortably in an armchair, it predicts pleasant travel for you. If the chair is empty, you may be faced with a puzzling situation that is hard to solve.

ARMHOLE—525. If you put your arms through wrong armholes, in your clothes, it is a sign of someone trying to hurt your reputation with the opposite sex.

ARMISTICE—935. The ending of armies fighting, when experienced in your dream, points to good future conditions for you.

ARMOR—358. If you dream you are wearing a knight's suit of armor, you must be cautious about handling money matters. If you see the armor on display, you may soon receive honorable mention.

ARMORY—585. See Arsenal.

ARMS—839. See Guns.

ARMY—835. If you dream of a military battle, you will need to keep quiet to avoid a scandal. If the army is marching, you may become disturbed about unusual happenings around you.

AROMA—531. Smelling an unpleasant odor, foretells you may find it hard to attract someone of the opposite sex. If the odor is a pleasing one, the one you love will be most agreeable to you.

ARREST—590. If you are being arrested by a policeman, in your dream, you must be careful not to take reckless chances. If you are a policeman and arresting someone, you will soon find a way to clear up your troubles.

ARRIVAL—212. To watch people arriving at a depot or terminal, is a sign you will enjoy good health. If you dream you are arriving at a destination, you will find satisfaction in your work.

ARROGANCE—435. Should you meet people who are being rude and nasty to you, your dream means you will find much pleasure and success.

ARROW—853. If you shoot an arrow in your dream, it is a warning that the one you love will be unfaithful. An arrow shot by someone else and striking you means you will hear gossip about you.

ARSENAL—412. Ammunition and soldiers inside an armory or other military building predicts you will succeed in your work. If you are alone in the arsenal building, you may suffer disappointment.

ARSON—954. See Fire.

ART—180. (Also see Gallery, Museum, Painting, Statue.) Viewing objects of art, and talking about art with others, foretells a job promotion.

ARTERY—585. (Also see Blood, Vein.) If you dream you cut an artery, you will win the admiration of people, if you play fair with them.

ARTHRITIS—099. Dreaming of suffering with pain is a happy sign you will have good health.

ARTICHOKE—515. When you dream you are eating this vegetable, it is a sign you are going to act in some foolish manner.

ARTISAN—914. See Craftsman.

ARTIST—990. If you dream you are an artist, it is a warning of business losses. If you watch someone else painting, you will enjoy pleasurable leisure. If the artist is painting a nude model, you will attend some wild parties.

ASBESTOS—053. Wearing protective clothes or gloves made of asbestos, in a burning building or forest, is a warning to avoid family quarrels.

ASCETIC—093. See Holy Person.

ASHES—809. If you dream you are clearing ashes from a furnace or stove, you will suffer some embarrassment. If someone dumps ashes on you, it shows some difficulties in the future.

ASP—196. See Snake.

ASPARAGUS—719. Eating asparagus in a dream means you will need to make the first move to make up with someone with whom you had an argument.

ASPIC—693. See Gelatin.

ASPIRIN—894. If you take aspirin in a dream, someone is going to spread gossip about you. If you give aspirin to another person, you will have to keep yourself from gossiping about others.

ASSASSIN—994. An important person, being assassinated in a dream, is a warning you will receive shocking news, but it will clear up soon.

ASSAULT—120. Dreaming that you are assaulted is a sign there will be family quarreling. If another person is assaulted, you will receive upsetting bad news.

ASSEMBLY—225. (Also see Speech.) If you dream you are in a peaceful assemblage, your private affairs will improve, but if the assemblage is an angry mob, you will suffer personal disappointment.

ASSISTANCE—435. Giving assistance, financial or physical, to someone else is a happy sign of success for you. If you are assisted by another, you may need to ask for help in financial matters.

ASTHMA—831. If you are an asthmatic person, and dream of having an attack, there is no actual meaning to the dream. If you are not an asthma sufferer, but you dream about it, it is a warning to be careful about new plans.

ASTROLOGY—575. (Also see Horoscope.) Studying a book on astrology in a dream foretells financial success and happiness if you persist in your plans.

ATHEIST—990. Whether you dream that you or somebody else is an atheist, it predicts you will not have as much success as you expect from investments. It may also mean you will have disappointing dealings with the opposite sex.

ATHLETICS—939. Winning athletic events is a sign of good fortune coming your way. If you are injured in athletics, you can look forward to being praised by people of importance.

ATOM BOMB—532. If you see a bomb explode in your dream, you will find one of your friends to be a liar.

ATONEMENT—540. To dream you are doing penance or otherwise atoning for a wrong, means you will lose or break a treasured heirloom.

ATROCITY—905. See Brutality.

ATTACK—131. See Assault.

ATTAINMENT—540. See Achievement.

ATTIC—093.

ATTORNEY—455. See Lawyer.

AUCTION — 309. Dreaming that you are an auctioneer will bring you a little hard luck. If you are attending an auction, you will receive a salary increase.

AUDIENCE — 435. If you are facing an audience, in your dream, you will receive some satisfactory social stimulation. If you sit in the audience, you will aid a friend in need.

AUDITORIUM — 913. Hearing music while you are in an auditorium is a sign of accomplishment on your part, but if the music is out of tune, you will not succeed in all your plans.

AUNT — 140. Dreaming about an aunt or an uncle is a good omen of receiving money and being in pleasant surroundings.

AUTHOR — 858. (Also see Writer.) If you dream you are an author, you may run short of money. Having a good discussion with an author means you will enrich your mind and your social standing. Should you dream an author wants you to lend him money, it foretells you will receive money in a will.

AUTOBIOGRAPHY — 685. Dreaming of writing your own life's story is a sign that your mate or sweetheart is not trusting you. If you dream of reading another person's autobiography, you will rise in business and social life.

AUTOGRAPHS — 683. If someone, in your dream, asks you for your autograph, you can look ahead to high accomplishment in your work. If you are collecting autographs, you will gain by studying the lives of people who became famous through their achievements.

AUTOMOBILE — 925. Not being able to get to the top of a hill when driving a car, is an omen of you being jilted by the one you love. If you run out of gasoline, you may have to work very hard for your money. Driving on the left side of the road foretells you may travel abroad. If any parts of the car break, you must guard against accidents.

AUTOPSY — 695. Attending an autopsy, in your dream, means you will have some stimulating things happen to you, but not much money.

AUTUMN — 134. If you walk where there are trees with beautiful autumn-colored leaves, you will receive an unexpected gift from someone not too close to you.

24

AVALANCHE—385. Dreaming that you are caught in an avalanche is an omen that you must be careful with your health.

AVIATOR—058. A woman who dreams she is in love with a flyer can look forward to an early marriage. A man who dreams he is a flyer is going to receive high praise.

AWAKENING—144. To dream of suddenly waking up (even though you do not actually wake up) means you will gain much happiness.

AWARD—184. If you receive an award for some good work or deed you achieved, it is a sign that good luck is on its way to you.

AWNING—947. If you lower an awning in front of a window, you will find a much better job or business. To raise the awning is a sign of children coming to the one who is married; or if you are not married it means you will find happy companions among the opposite sex. If you dream you are sitting underneath the awning, you will have a narrow escape from being hurt.

AXE—145. Dreaming about a shiny, sharp axe is an omen of receiving a promotion in your job. If you dream you are using a dull axe, you need to be more careful in your clothes and general appearance.

BEETLE

BEARD

BABY—125. A pretty, smiling baby is a sign you will find satisfying love and friendship. A crying baby is an omen of disappointment and illness. If a woman dreams she is breast-feeding a baby, she must not confide too closely in anyone, as she might have some false friends. A walking baby means you will be able to think and act on your own. A sick baby, in a dream, foretells petty worries to come.

BABY CARRIAGE—175. If you dream of a baby carriage you can look forward to much enjoyment of sincere companions.

BACHELOR—258. When a woman dreams of a bachelor, she may find the one she loves is being fickle to her. A man, when he dreams he is a bachelor, must regard this as a sign he must be careful in dealing with women.

BACK—131. If you dream you see another person's bare back, it is a warning that you must not lend assistance or money to everyone who asks it. To dream that your own back is bare, you will meet with grave disappointment.

BACKBONE—545. Dreaming that you see someone else's backbone is a prediction of you reaching a peaceful long life. If you see your own backbone (maybe in a mirror) you will succeed in your goals.

BACKGAMMON—354. See Cards.

BACON—355. If you dream you eat good quality bacon, you will get more money. If the bacon is spoiled, it is a warning that you will be very disappointed. Dreaming that you are smoking or curing the bacon shows someone will be ill.

26

BACTERIA—891. See Germs.

BADGE—475. Dreaming that you wear a badge is a happy sign of your rise on the social scale.

BADGER—758. To dream of seeing a badger is a prediction that your present worries will soon disappear.

BADMINTON—054. See Athletics.

BAG—217. If you dream of a paper bag, you must be very careful to avoid sudden danger. A bag made of leather is a sign you are going on a trip. A cloth bag means you will succeed in work and other plans.

BAGGAGE—175. (Also see Suitcase, Trunk.) If someone carries your luggage, you will have some interesting things happen to you. Many pieces of baggage grouped together predict traveling to distant places. If you dream some baggage is being dropped, you will suffer disappointment.

BAGPIPE—365. When you hear the bagpipe played, it is a sign of good things happening to you. If the bagpipes are not in tune, you may suffer some discomforting incident.

BAIL—192. To dream you are going bail for a person in trouble, is a warning for you to resist making any contracts unless you are sure of yourself. If you are seeking bail for your own self, you may meet with an accident.

BAILIFF—166. See Sheriff.

BAIT—190. If you dream of bait used for fishing, you may hear that one of your friends is ill.

BAKERY—585. To dream of bakers and of bread and cakes on the shelves of a bakery, predicts a new baby will be born to a young couple.

BAKING—947. If you are baking bread or cakes, you can look forward to financial betterment.

BALDNESS—599. To dream of a man with a bald head is a sign that some tricky people will try to make you cooperate with them, and a warning for you to be very careful in the near future. If you dream of a bald-headed woman, you have to be very careful in dealing with the opposite sex.

BALES — 259. If you see large bales of paper or cotton or other materials, you will be able to get rid of an unsatisfactory situation.

BALLET — 250. To dream you are watching the ballet, or dancing in one, it is a warning that you may run into jealousy and failure in many areas of your life.

BALLOON — 554. Going up in a balloon predicts an unpleasant journey for you. Seeing a balloon, but not being in it, means you will have some set-backs in business.

BALLROOM — 553. (Also see Dancing.) A ballroom filled with dancers shows you will be happily surprised. If there are no dancers in the ballroom, it is an omen of sadness coming into your life.

BAMBOO — 255. If you find bamboo shoots, either growing or cut, you can hope for pleasurable social life with someone you adore.

BANANA — 141. Dreaming about a banana tree means you will be disappointed in someone whom you admire. If you eat a banana, you may suffer some illness.

BAND — 144. See Orchestra.

BANDANA — 146. If you wear a bandana on your hair, you will become pessimistic because of too much work to do. If you see an older woman with a bandana, it foretells a satisfactory family life.

BANDIT — 490. If you dream you are accosted by a hold-up man, you are going to have trouble with indigestion. If you are the bandit, you will soon need to offer someone an apology.

BANISTER — 058. Sliding down the banister, in your dream, means you are going to have small worries about finances.

BANJO — 405. If you play the banjo, you will have good times socially. If you dream an old man is playing the banjo, you will quarrel with your loved one.

BANK — 241. To dream you are in back of a bank teller's window, receiving gold coins, it is an omen that you will become wealthy. If you are giving out the gold coins to someone, you may be reckless in some of your actions. If there is nobody at the teller's window, you may suffer some business set-backs.

BANK BOOK — 551. If you lose your bank book, it is a sign you must

28

be cautious about participating in politics, or in listening to others' gossip.

BANKER—615. Dreaming about a banker is a prediction you might suffer financial loss if you are not careful.

BANKNOTES—413. Handling dollar bills (or higher denominations) which are new and crisp is an omen of your financial state becoming much better. If the bank notes are old and dirty, you may get some money but it will also bring you trouble.

BANKRUPTCY—627. Whether you or someone else goes through bankruptcy in your dream, it is a good sign that you will get money through an inheritance.

BANNER—380. See Flag.

BANQUET—257. If you attend a lavish banquet, you will find better success in social and financial affairs. If the banquet guests' faces are ghostlike, or no guests are at the tables, you will get into confusing situations with people.

BAPTISM—763. To undergo baptism, in a dream, means you may not show enough self-confidence in certain demanding situations.

BARBARIAN—815. See Savage.

BARBECUE—210. If you attend a barbecue meal, it means you will be misunderstood or insulted by people who are close to you.

BARBER—507. Dreaming of a barber foretells you will be rewarded through your work, if you concentrate on giving your best efforts to it.

BARGAIN—777. If you get something good at a bargain sale, you will be able to fulfill your newest plans with success.

BARMAID—072. A man who dreams he is being attentive to a barmaid will find himself in the company of people of low standards. A woman who dreams she is working at a bar is also inclined to seek men who are not of high standards.

BARN—343. If the barn in your dreams is overflowing with harvested farm crops and healthy cattle, it is a prediction of good financial conditions for you. An empty barn, however, shows struggle for financial reward.

BAROMETER—846. To dream of a barometer shows you will experience a satisfactory result in your present situation. A broken barometer foretells you will have to undertake serious matters to keep your business affairs in good shape.

BARREL—950. In your dream, if you see a barrel that is full of a liquid or solid material, you will enjoy good luck in money matters. If the barrel is empty, you may have to undergo some bad times.

BARRIER—353. (Also see Fence.) To be kept from entering some place because of closed doors or other kinds of barriers, you will find it hard to fulfill your projects.

BARROOM—882. Dreaming of drinking at a bar shows you will receive much devotion from those who are close to you. If you get drunk, you can expect to hear some unpleasant things. If you see women drinking at a bar, it means you may desire some companionship which is not worthy of your good taste.

BARTENDER—433. (Also see Bar Maid.) If you tend the bar, you may be tempted to do things that you would be wise to avoid.

BASEBALL—232. (Also see Home Run.) To dream of seeing a baseball game is a prediction of your being able to maintain an optimistic attitude toward life. If a woman dreams she participates in the game, she will derive much satisfaction in social matters.

BASEMENT—361. See Cellar.

BASIN—542. If you see a basin of cold water, in your dream, you may encounter some difficulty in family life. A basin of warm water shows you will enjoy a happy home life. Dirty water in a basin foretells serious family quarrels. If you pour the contents out of the basin, you will gain financial success.

BASKET—129. If you carry a basket filled with good things, you will be offered the chance of a much better-paid job. If the basket is empty, you will not have your plans fulfilled.

BASKETBALL—869. Watching the game in process predicts you will not be able to achieve all you go after. If a woman dreams she is participating in the game, she will have to contend with rivals in attracting the man she wants.

BASSOON—811. If you dream you are playing this instrument, you will work too hard and not achieve much.

BASTARD — 446. To be called a bastard by someone is a good sign that you will achieve an advancement in your work, but if you call someone by that name, it is an omen that you will run into hard luck. If you dream you are a bastard, you are due to receive money and recognition.

BAT — 780. A bat flying around in your dream and making you feel scared shows you will be depressed over disappointments, but if the flying bat does not scare you, it is an omen for new things in your life which will turn out satisfactorily for you.

BATH — 584. If you dream of taking a bath by yourself or with others in the tub, you will have to be cautious about intoxicating liquor or temptation from people who are not well-meaning. If you dream of bathing in the ocean or other body of water, you may look forward to getting money. If you bathe in dirty or muddy water, beware of people who gossip.

BATON — 078. Seeing in your dream a drum major (or majorette) with a baton leading a parade, means you will have some petty arguments in the family. A baton in the hand of an orchestral conductor shows you can achieve your high aspirations.

BATTLE — 932. See Army.

BATTLESHIP — 321. Dreaming of a fleet of ships is a good omen of money through business matters, but if you see only one Battleship, you will be able to gain more but need to work less. If the ship is firing its guns at an enemy vessel, you will meet with opposition in your plans.

BAYONET — 818. If you dream you are being stabbed by someone with a bayonet, the omen is that you may suffer financial loss. If you stab someone with your bayonet, you will have to be very cautious about how you deal with the opposite sex.

BAY WINDOW — 900. To dream you are gazing out of a bay window, you will enjoy many peaceful, relaxed times. Should the window panes be broken, it shows you will move to a new place.

BEACH — 472. Lying on the beach, in a nude state, foretells of an interesting, new project you will start. If you are wearing a bathing suit, it will be necessary for you to give an account to some people

31

about something you did. Should you dream of pulling a small boat onto the beach is an omen of your needing to ask someone for help in money matters.

BEACON LIGHT—339. If you dream of a beacon light, you will enjoy whatever you set out to do in life.

BEADS—797. (See also Rosary.) Dreaming of stringing beads is a sign that you will unexpectedly get some money. Counting the beads means you will find peace within yourself. If you drop some beads, you may suffer disappointment and annoyance about small matters.

BEAGLE—492. If you see a beagle hound on a busy thoroughfare you will hear good news from some distant friends.

BEANS—817. Growing beans (any sort of bean) in the ground foretells money worries will be over. If you eat baked beans, in your dream, you must guard against friends spreading gossip about you.

BEAR—170. To dream of a bear is a sign that you will meet with challenges in business matters. If you kill the bear, you will be able to get rid of people you do not want to have on your social list. A girl who sees a bear in her dreams may have to be in conflict with unpleasant people who stand in her way.

BEARD—122. (Also see Goatee.) If you dream you have a beard (whether you have one, or not) and somebody pulls hairs out of your beard, it is a warning you may suffer a loss of something you own, and there may be unpleasantness with friends. A beard on a woman shows you will have to beware of false friends.

BEATING—116. To dream someone is beating you is an omen that you will have disputes within your family. If you dream a child is being beaten, you will be anxious to win out over the other person in all situations.

BEAUTY—176. Dreaming of a beautiful child foretells love and marriage mutually beneficial to you and the one you love. To dream of a beautiful woman means you will gain business and social success.

BEAVER—873. Seeing a beaver is a sign of good earnings for you if you work carefully. If you kill a beaver, in your dream, someone will try to prove you are not a reliable person.

BECKONING—916. When a friend beckons you, in your dream, you will have good financial rewards in the near future. If you are beckoned by someone who is a false friend, you will suffer financial loss.

BED—254. (Also see Sheets.) If you dream you are in bed with a stranger (of the opposite sex) you will need to make decisions for some new venture. If the person in bed with you is of your sex, it means you will need to apologize why you failed to carry out a promise to someone. To dream you are in bed in an unfamiliar room, is a sign you will have a visit from distant friends. Should you dream your bed is outdoors, there is a likelihood you will earn a good deal of money. If the bed has no occupant in it, but it is white and covered with a pretty spread, it predicts you will be rid of annoyances very soon.

BED BUGS—468. Seeing bed bugs in a dream indicates you will receive an unpleasant message. If you kill the bed bugs, it is a sign you will overcome bad luck.

BED PAN—130. If you see a bed pan in your dream, it is a happy sign of good luck.

BEEF—014. Cooked beef seen in your dream, is a warning for you to try to avoid pessimism and family quarrels. If the beef is bloody and raw, it is an omen to be careful not to cut yourself and cause bleeding.

BEER—566. When you see beer with a foam on the top, whether you are drinking it or pouring some for another person, it is a sign of finding joy with people who are close to you. Should the beer become stale and have no head on it, it shows you will suffer some setbacks in relationship to the one you love.

BEES—331. See Hive.

BEESWAX—497. (Also see Wax.) To rub beeswax on a hot iron, while pressing clothes, foretells better relationship in marriage. If the wax starts to burn, there may be financial need.

BEETLES—164. Dreaming of beetles which crawl over you, shows you will go through some money hardship. If you kill the beetles, money matters will become much better.

BEGGAR—474. (Also see Pauper.) If you give money to a beggar,

33

you will experience good fortune for yourself. To refuse the beggar's plea, you will go through unpleasant social and financial relationships.

BEHEADING—825. If you dream your head has been cut off, you will have to work very hard to put through your plans, but to watch another person being beheaded, someone may be sent away or die.

BELCH—488. Sounding off with a belch at an elegant dinner shows you will need to be very careful or you will lose a close companion.

BELIEF—744. To dream that belief in God no longer exists, is a warning that you will meet hardships in the future.

BELLOWS—365. To dream you work the bellows, in and out, is a sign you will win out over hard financial times. To see bellows, but not touch them, means old friends are planning to visit you.

BELLS—280. (Also see Doorbell.) The Liberty Bell, if it is seen in your dream, shows you will have business advancement. If you hear tolling bells, you may hear of the death of someone who is far away.

BELLY—874. (Also see Stomach.) If you have a pain in your abdomen, you will enjoy good health. Something crawling on your belly means you will go through a humiliating experience. If you dream your belly is swollen, it predicts a slight illness.

BELT—607. If you dream you wear a new belt, you will meet someone who will stand in your way of full financial attainment. If the belt is old style, you might be too hasty in dealing with some people and they will expect you to apologize.

BENCH—184. If you sit on a bench, do not tell your innermost secrets or lend money to people you don't know too well. If you see a bench, but do not sit on it, it shows you will renew old friendships.

BENEDICTION—138. See Blessing.

BENEFACTOR—481. If someone acts as a benefactor toward you, it is an omen for you to be careful that your reputation doesn't get ruined. If you are the benefactor, your work and your investments will bring you good results.

BEREAVEMENT—706. See Death.

BEST MAN—840. When a bachelor dreams he is functioning as best man at a wedding, he will be married before the year is over.

BET—446. To bet at cards is a warning that some tricky people will try to get money from you. Betting at the race track is a prediction that you should avoid new plans unless you are sure of yourself.

BEVERAGE—923. See Drinking.

BEWILDERED—860. If in your dream you act in a bewildered manner, you will receive a letter which you will find hard to understand.

BEWITCHMENT—430. A man who dreams of a bewitching woman should be on the alert for impending money worries.

BIBLE—100. Dreaming of the Holy Bible foretells you will be given a chance to accept a position where you will have to take responsibilities. To dream of arguing against the Holy Bible's teachings, means that you will be influenced by someone who is not to be trusted.

BIBLICAL CHARACTERS—305. If you dream you are in the presence of the men and women mentioned in the Holy Bible, you will be approached to give service to people in need.

BICARBONATE OF SODA—510. Drinking this for medicinal purposes means you will soon go on a short journey.

BICYCLE—669. Riding downhill on a bicycle is a warning for you to cautiously take care of your reputation and to avoid any accident. Going uphill on the bicycle foretells successful results for your plans.

BIER—690. See Coffin.

BIGAMY—373. (Also see Polygamy.) A man who dreams he has two wives is warned he may lose some of his sex appeal and intelligent thinking. A woman who dreams she is a polyandrist (having more than one husband) has to be cautious or she may lose her reputation.

BIGOTRY—271. If you dream you are disclosing a biased attitude toward people whose politics, race and religion are not like your own, means you will suffer a humiliating experience from a person who may be much less intelligent or successful than you are.

BILIOUSNESS—130. See Nausea.

BILL—206. Receiving bills for things you bought, or for rent or other items, means there is good luck in store for you.

BILLBOARD—499. To look at billboards, in your dream, shows that you will get pestered by someone who will scold you. If you hide behind a billboard, you will run into temporary dissension with a friend.

BILLIARDS—403. Playing billiards in a dream foretells arguments and going to court over some property or possession. If the billiard table and balls are not being used, someone is lying about you and accusing you.

BINGO GAME—186. See Raffle.

BINOCULARS—189. Looking through binoculars at a race track is a sign of good luck coming to you. If you use binoculars to spy on people, you are warned that false accusations will be hurled at you.

BIOGRAPHY—614. See Autobiography.

BIRCH BARK—723. Stripping the bark off a birch tree foretells you will be made very tense and uneasy because someone will nag you needlessly. To eat the bark of the birch means you will go through failure of small plans.

BIRDS—400. (Also see Cage.) Dreaming of beautifully feathered birds foretells a rich and congenial marriage. Birds without feathers and who do not sing are warnings that you may be dominated by someone who is richer than you. Flying birds show prosperity. If you catch a bird in your dream, you will have good fortune. To shoot a bird is an omen of loss of business deals, or loss of crops if a farmer has this dream. If a bird has an over-sized beak, you may be the subject of a scandal.

BIRD'S NEST—944. Dreaming of a nest full of eggs portends success in all meetings with people. An empty nest means business worries and pessimism. If the nest contains young birds, you will go on a pleasant trip. If the little birds are deserted and crying, you will be worried about someone in the family.

BIRTH—320. (Also see Childbirth, Obstetrics.) If you dream you are present when the baby is delivered, you will enjoy financial success. If a married woman dreams she gives birth, she will derive much contentment. A single girl who dreams she gives birth may suffer gossip spoken about her, and she may lose her sweetheart.

Should a man dream he is having a baby, he will go through hard times in his work and in social life.

BIRTH CONTROL—606. If married people dream about this, they will have children who will be a source of pride to them.

BIRTHDAY GIFTS—218. To dream of receiving gifts shows you will be able to carry out your plans. To give someone else a gift means you will be invited to an important event.

BIRTHDAY PARTY—444. When you dream of attending a birthday party, if you are a young person, you may find yourself in financial difficulties, but if you are an older person who has this dream, you will meet with loneliness and with obstacles which may be hard for you to handle.

BIRTH MARK—942. If you dream you have a birth mark on your body, you are going to meet people who will be interesting and helpful to you.

BISHOP—387. To meet a bishop in your dream shows that you will have to work very hard to achieve your aims.

BISON—999. To see this animal in your dream is a sign of good fortune coming your way. If you kill the bison, you will have hard luck. Seeing the bison in a zoo foretells a happy marriage for people who are close to you.

BITE—809. If you are bitten by a person or animal or insect, it is an omen of hardship coming to you through some person who is against you for some reason.

BLACKBERRIES—670. To gather blackberries in your dream is a sign you will go through some disappointing loss.

BLACKBIRD—275. Flying blackbirds, in your dream, reveal you will bring ill fortune to yourself. If you dream someone is blackmailing you, it is necessary for you to be careful in how you treat people of the opposite sex.

BLACKBOARD—426. If the blackboard has a lot of chalk writing on it, be prepared for bad news about risky investments.

BLACKJACK—687. Hitting someone with a blackjack, in your dream, foretells you must practice calmness and self-control so as not to do anyone harm (even an enemy).

BLACKMAIL—778. If you are blackmailing another person, you will bring ill fortune to yourself. If you dream someone is blackmailing you, it is necessary for you to be careful in how you treat people of the opposite sex.

BLACKSMITH—334. When you see a blacksmith and his workshop, in your dream, you will start some new projects which will materialize in success.

BLADE—251. (Also see Cut, Knife, Razor, Sword.) If you see a rusty blade (without a handle) in your dream, you will have a slight sickness. If the blade is sharp and shiny, you are warned that someone will disapprove of the way you conduct yourself and will gossip about it.

BLAME—515. To dream of a person who is assuming blame for an incident, be on guard against insincere friends. If you are the one who is blamed, you will have success in business. If you lay the blame on another, you will become very upset and tense.

BLANKET—968. Clean and new blankets, in your dream, show you will overcome failure and will forestall an illness. Torn or dirty blankets are an omen of treachery on the part of someone who wants to hurt you.

BLASPHEMY—684. If someone is expressing blasphemous remarks, it is a sign you will mistake an enemy for a friend. If you dream that you are doing the blaspheming, you will bring bad luck down upon you. If someone is cursing you directly, you will find money worries easing up.

BLAST—869. Dreaming that you set off a blast is a sign that you will enjoy more comfort and contentment than you ever had.

BLAST FURNACE—961. To dream that you are feeding fuel into the furnace to keep the blast roaring, signifies you will make quick progress in your new enterprise.

BLAZE—021. (Also see Bonfire, Fire.) A house that is on fire and blazing away is a sign that you will have difficulty in convincing your friends they may trust you. A blaze in a fireplace means you will enjoy a peaceful home and family life.

BLEEDING—101. See Blood.

BLEMISHES — 251. (Also see Scar.) If you dream you have blemishes on your legs, you will be the subject of gossip. If you have blemishes on your face, the opposite sex will find you attractive.

BLESSING — 161. A blessing bestowed upon you by a clergyman, or by a very poor person, foretells for you a happy future. If you dream you are giving a blessing to another person, you will have to deal with many frustrating disappointments.

BLINDFOLD — 381. To dream someone puts a blindfold over your eyes is a warning to avoid worrying over petty annoyances in your life.

BLIND MAN'S BLUFF — 491. Playing this game in your dream shows you will be drawn into some plans which are not wise, and could make others ridicule you.

BLINDNESS — 611. To see blind people in your dream reveals that a fine person will make a bid to you for help in money matters. If you are the one who is blind, you may have to give up some of the good things you have and settle for less.

BLINKING — 671. If you meet a person, or see an animal, with eyes that are blinking in your direction, it will be necessary for you to use discretion in some puzzling situation.

BLOCKADE — 176. To dream you are in a region which is being blockaded, you may suffer some money worries. If you are blockading the enemy's land, some people may not give you credit for the intelligence you possess.

BLONDE — 180. A man who dreams he is pursuing a blonde woman may suffer much disappointment in his undertakings. If a girl dreams she is blonde and is being admired by men, it is a sign that she may go through a temporary ailment.

BLOOD — 183. If you dream of blood on your hands, you are warned to be overly cautious as hard luck may be on its way in your personal affairs. Blood flowing from a wound is an omen thay you may suffer an illness, or some business losses. If you see clothes that are stained with blood, some bad friends may want to keep you from success in the new plans that are open for you.

BLOODHOUND — 187. (Also see Hounds.) If the hounds are friendly, in your dream, they are a good sign that you have sincere friends.

If they are chasing you, one of your good friends has turned unfaithful toward you.

BLOOD SUCKER—448. (Also see Leech, Vampire.) If you are the victim of a blood-sucking animal, your dream predicts you may not be able to trust all your friends.

BLOSSOMS—231. To dream of blooming shrubs and trees, is a sign of peace of mind and good health and financial ease.

BLOT—056. When you write with a pen in your dream and you make blots, you will have some temporary sorrow.

BLOTTER—914. Dreaming of a blotter is an omen of secrets being told which might hurt a deserving friend. To dream of a dirty old blotter is a sign of arguments between friends and family.

BLOWGUN—429. If you dream of a savage handling a blowgun, you can gain a good deal by doing some work with your hands. If you see a school child using a toy blowgun, you will be invited to many social activities.

BLOWOUT—104. Should you dream of one of your automobile tires having a blowout, it is a sign that an accident may happen to you.

BLUEPRINT—414. If you dream you are studying plans you have made for a house, it is an omen you must be careful in any deals about buying land. If you discuss the plans with an architect or builder you are soon going to buy some fashionable clothes.

BLUSHING—974. To dream you are blushing, it shows you will be embarrassed by scandalous tales about you. If you see someone else blush, you may say some sarcastic things which will annoy your companions.

BOA CONSTRICTOR—020. See Snake.

BOAR—707. If you dream about this animal, be discreet in business matters.

BOARDWALK—843. Dreaming of walking on the boardwalk with someone of the opposite sex means you will inherit money.

BOASTING—644. To dream you are boasting to anyone is a sign of your tendency to do rash acts which you could regret. If another person brags to you, you will be able to overcome difficulties.

BOAT—255. (Also see Deck.) A ship sending out signals foretells your future dealings will come out fine. If you are on a ship in stormy waters, or the boat is leaky, you will be burdened with many small worries. If you are on a sailboat, you will receive needed cooperation from others. Dreaming you fell overboard is an omen of annoying incidents in your life.

BODY—100. To dream of seeing a beautiful woman's body means you will gain admiration from others. A man's body shows promotion in your job.

BODY SNATCHER—727. If you see someone robbing a body from a grave, you will be blamed for things you did not do, but if you rob the grave, you must avoid arguments with friends or family.

BOG—967. Walking through a bog in your dream, means you will go through hard times but you can overcome them if you try.

BOILER—732. To see a boiler in a cellar shows you may have a short illness or lose something. If the boiler is old and rusty, you will have many petty annoyances.

BOILS—411. If you pick on a boil on some part of your body, you will quarrel with relatives. If the boil is lanced, it means you will have to do work which is irritating.

BOLL WEEVIL—865. To dream of boll weevil in a cotton field is an omen of enemies talking about you in a scandalous way.

BOLONEY—941. If you eat boloney in your dream, you can expect sudden changes in your way of life.

BOLTS—223. Dreaming of seeing or working with bolts, is a sign you will have to work hard to overcome opposition.

BOMBPROOF SHELTER—910. To be in a shelter while bombing is going on, is a good omen of a future without worries.

BOMBS—550. Exploding bombs foretell you will move to a new place. If the dropped bombs fail to explode, you might lose your job.

BONDS—094. If you are investing or are being given bonds or stocks, this foretells good cooperation from people in construction trades.

BONES—140. (Also see Skeleton.) To see a big stack of bones in your dream is a prophecy of sneaky friends who want to hurt you.

If you see bones sticking out of the flesh of a body, be cautious about confiding in others.

BONFIRE—261. (Also see Blaze, Campfire.) Watching a bonfire in your dream means you will overcome your worries. If sparks fly out from the bonfire, you will have small irritations.

BONNET—836. See Hat.

BONUS—290. If you get extra money above what is coming to you, you will prosper in your work.

BOOKCASE—330. An empty bookcase shows you are in danger of losing your job, but a filled bookcase means good results in your work and in hobbies.

BOOKKEEPER—412. See Accounts.

BOOKS—602. (Also see Library.) Reading books in your dream foretells happiness and money to you provided you do more studying. If you see children reading books, you will be satisfied with behavior of youngsters who are close to you.

BOOKSTORE—415. To dream you work in a bookstore shows you will have good friendships with intelligent people. If you buy books, you may find satisfaction in writing as a hobby.

BOOMERANG—145. If you dream you tossed out a boomerang and it came back and hit you, it means you have to be careful about what you tell to others.

BOOTBLACK—190. Earning a living by shining shoes in your dream, is an omen of pleasant days to be enjoyed by you.

BOOTLEGGER—447. If you talk to a male bootlegger, you will make new plans and they will turn out all right, but if the bootlegger is female, you will suffer depressing disappointment.

BOOTS—509. (Also see Galoshes.) Dreaming you see others wearing boots, is a sign that the one you love will be fickle. If you wear new boots, you will have good luck in business. If you see or wear old, torn boots, it foretells worries and illness.

BOOTY—500. If you discover booty which was hidden by thieves or pirates, you will soon find money matters easing up.

BORDERLAND—868. If you dream of being on the border between two countries or states, it is a prophecy of worrying over which way to proceed in your plans.

BORROWING—696. To dream you borrow from another person, shows you may have some money worries. If someone borrows from you, you have sincere friends who will help you in time of need.

BOSOM—090. See Breast.

BOSS—963. Dreaming that you and your boss are on congenial terms shows you will be happy in your job provided you do your work well.

BOSTON TERRIER—149. Seeing this dog in your dream signifies you will have more money provided you don't get too careless or extravagant.

BOTTLES—739. A full bottle is a prophecy of good luck in love and in work. Empty bottle means you will face an emergency but can overcome it by good thinking.

BOULEVARD—480. If you dream you are walking or driving on a brightly lit boulevard, you will travel to a far place. A poorly lit or dark boulevard shows you will be frustrated in some new attempt.

BOUNTY HUNTER—886. To dream you hunt people or animals to get paid with a bounty, is a prophecy that some false friends plot against you.

BOUQUET—924. Dreaming of a beautiful floral bouquet shows good celebration with friends, also you may get a legacy from a rich person. A bouquet of faded flowers foretells sickness which may be fatal.

BOWL—498. A bowl filled with food is a sign you will not suffer poverty. If the bowl is empty, you may have some money problemsz

BOW LEGS—127. To dream you have bow legs shows you will soon receive a legacy. If you make fun of someone who is bow legged, you will suffer ridicule from people who are close to you.

BOWLING—300. Whether your dream shows you bowling in indoor alleys or outdoors, you will succeed in earning good wages.

BOX—011. Empty boxes are an omen that you will not succeed in all your work aspirations. Money-filled boxes show you will be prosperous and have no worries. Boxes filled with furniture or clothes or other articles are a sign of a pleasant journey in store for you.

BOXER—092. If you dream you are in the boxing ring as a fighter, or are watching other fighters, you will succeed in your aims if you persist in them.

BOY—928. Dreaming of a boy at play or work is a good sign that you will find joy in work and home life.

BOY SCOUT—304. If you dream of scouts going through their activities, your wishes will be granted.

BRACELET—666. To find a bracelet means a legacy will come to you. Losing a bracelet predicts you may have some petty troubles. A bracelet worn on the arm shows you will get a gift and will have a happy marriage. An ankle bracelet is an omen of unpleasantness due to gossipy friends.

BRAGGART—196. See Boasting.

BRAID TRIMMING—639. If you see uniforms or other garments trimmed with shiny or gold braid, you are in line for a better job.

BRAIDED HAIR—228. See Hair.

BRANCHES—173. Tree branches in bloom are a sign you will find life more relaxed and happier. If the branches are buffeted by a strong wind, you may suffer disappointment but only of a temporary nature.

BRANDY—667. If you drink or serve brandy to others, you will be wealthy but you may not be considerate of others.

BRASS—256. To dream of brass objects is a prophecy that your worries about finances wil be over and you will prosper.

BRASSIERE—004. If a woman dreams she forgets to wear her brassiere, she will have an argument with a close friend. To dream the strap breaks on the brassiere means good times at a party. If a man dreams he is wearing a brassiere, he may have misunderstandings with women.

BRAVERY—658. To dream of being brave in emergencies means you will be called upon to do some brave deed.

BRAWL—789. See Fight.

BREACH OF PROMISE—514. To dream of being sued for breaking a promise to marry someone, you must act in a way so that people will not point with ridicule at you.

BREAD—579. If you dream of eating fresh bread, you will be assured of good friendships and comfort in your life. Stale bread is an omen of sickness and social annoyances.

BREADLINE—940. Dreaming of someone else standing on a breadline, is a sign of loss of friends and money. If you stand on such a line, you will enjoy good health.

BREAKAGE—470. If you break something in a house or other articles, you will have arguments with people you love. To break a window pane is a prophecy of a fatal illness.

BREAKFAST—830. To eat breakfast with others at the table means you will find success in your undertakings. If you eat alone, some friends might prove false. Lots of good food on the table is a prediction of many interesting changes in your life.

BREAST—296. If you see a bosom that is well-developed with lovely skin, it foretells money coming your way. An underdeveloped bosom with wrinkled skin shows you will be disappointed in the person you love.

BREAST FEEDING—149. See Milk.

BREATH—133. To lose your breath and have to gasp is an omen of disappointment over something you are working on. If your own breath or the breath of another person is fresh and sweet-smelling, you will gain in some financial deal. Bad-smelling breath means you will have a mild illness.

BREEDING—709. If you dream you are breeding cattle or horses or other animals, you will have a lawsuit to collect a legacy.

BREEZE—706. See Wind.

BREWERY—585. Dreaming about a brewery portends you will have some trouble with people in high office, but you can overcome this by exerting yourself.

BRIBES—259. If you accept a bribe you will go through a long sickness. If you are offering someone a bribe, it is an omen that some people will try to take advantage of you.

BRICKS—319. Dreaming about making bricks is a warning that you will be faced with emergencies in your personal and business matters. If you are laying the bricks in some construction work, you will get some money but must wait for it.

BRIDAL WREATH—108. If you dream of a beautiful floral wreath your chances for a happy marriage are very good.

BRIDE—945. (Also see Wedding.) A girl who dreams about being a bride can expect to receive a legacy of money. If the bride is indifferent to the bridegroom, she may not find her husband completely to her taste. To kiss a bride means you will make up with estranged friends.

BRIDEGROOM—200. If a man dreams he is a bridegroom he will find some money. If he is nervous during the ceremony, it is an omen he will be faced with certain decisions he may not be able to make.

BRIDESMAID—434. A girl who dreams she is a bridesmaid can look forward to an early marriage for herself. To see a bridesmaid with a torn dress means you will be annoyed at some relative who hides facts from you.

BRIDGE—365. To dream of an old, unsafe bridge structure is a sign of worry over lost articles. Crossing a safe bridge means you will overcome present troubles. If the bridge breaks and falls, watch out for insincere admirers.

BRIDGE GAME—135. See Cards.

BRIDGEWORK—581. See Dentures.

BRIDLE—428. If you dream of putting a bridle on a horse, you will have to handle some unpleasant situations caused by dishonest people.

BRIEF CASE—194. To dream of carrying a new brief case is a sign of disappointment due to your own carelessness. If the brief case is old, you will have a satisfactory short trip.

BROADCASTER—058. To dream that you are broadcasting on radio or television programs predicts that people will carefully listen to your ideas.

BROCADE—612. Wearing clothes or seeing household decorations made of beautiful brocade material, is a warning that someone close to you is not being entirely sincere.

BROGUE—989. To dream of someone or yourself speaking with an accent or a brogue shows you will achieve an influential post.

BROKER—373. If you dream of a broker you must not rush into making investments without first studying the market.

BRONCHITIS—040. Dreaming that you or someone else suffers from bronchitis is an omen of your needing to work very hard to achieve your ambitions.

BRONCO—182. See Rodeo.

BRONZE—547. Any articles made of bronze which appear in your dream are a sign that you may not feel too secure in your personal or business affairs, and people may be envious of you.

BROOM—070. If you sweep with a new broom, you will have good luck if you practice thrift. An old broom foretells loss in investments.

BROTHEL—701. (Also see Prostitute.) To dream of being in a brothel predicts pleasant home life and a position of prestige in your activities.

BROTHER—858. To dream of being cooperative with a brother predicts good luck in social and business life.

BROTHER-IN-LAW—213. If you dream of a brother-in-law, even if you do not have one, some man you trust may prove to be insincere.

BRUISE—995. An accidental bruise on the leg is a warning to be careful while out walking, but a bruise on any other part of the body means you will win praise for your actions in emergency situations.

BRUSH—198. Using a hairbrush or toothbrush with sturdy bristles is a sign of good things coming to your home as well as prosperity in business. If the bristles are worn out, the dream means you will not achieve all you desire.

BRUTALITY—905. If you are the victim of brutality, it is an omen of financial gain to you. If you are an onlooker when someone else is being brutalized, you will have a reunion with some old friends.

BUCKBOARD—184. To dream of riding in a buckboard is a prophecy of security and serenity in your old age.

BUCKET—150. If you dream of carrying a bucket full of liquid, you will enjoy thinking about good past events. Tripping over a bucket is an omen of severe illness.

BUCKLE—828. To dream of seeing or wearing a buckle means you will be asked to participate in social activities provided you will not be careless about your work or church loyalties.

BUCKSHOT—850. If you load your gun with buckshot, you will get into trouble, if you don't keep your temper from blowing up.

BUCKTOOTH—508. Dreaming of your own tooth or teeth protruding in a conspicuous manner, is a sign of you becoming pessimistic, but if you see such teeth on another person, you will go on a long journey.

BUDGET—759. (Also see Thrift.) If a man dreams he is sticking to a tight financial budget, he has a good chance to advance in business, but a woman who dreams of budgeting may not find men sufficiently attentive to her.

BUGLE—725. (Also see Reveille.) To dream of you or someone else blowing a bugle, predicts good fortune coming to you as well as happy news from an old friend. If "taps" is sounded on the bugle, it foretells an unhappy event in your life.

BUGS—179. If your home has bugs running all over the place, it is an omen of sickness or other unhappy events. If you dream you clear the bugs out of the house, you will be able to overcome current difficulties.

BUILDINGS—479. To dream of large and luxurious buildings is a sign of pleasant journeys for you. Small, clean buildings mean you will enjoy comfort in family and job situations. Badly maintained, old buildings show you will go through some unpleasantness.

BULL—122. A white bull seen in a dream prophesies advancement in your work. Being chased by a bull means you have to be cautious in business deals. To see a bull goring someone (perhaps in a bullfight), you must try not to borrow money from others.

BULLDOG—457. If you dream you are chased or bitten by a bulldog who is guarding someone's property, is an omen of being approached by an officer of the law, should you be tempted to evade some legal regulations.

BULLET — 007. To dream of a bullet, whether you fire it or someone else does, is a prophecy of illness and misfortune.

BULLFIGHT — 220. If you dream you are happy at a bullfight, you will have some worries in your home life. If you are annoyed at the bullfight, you will go on a long journey.

BULLSEYE — 555. Hitting the bullseye only one time, with any kind of weapon, shows you will have good luck. If you hit it with every shot you make, you have unfaithful friends.

BULLY — 225. To bully someone else shows you are in for some worrisome times. If you dream you come to the defense of someone being bullied, you will gain high recognition.

BUM — 213. (Also see Tramp.) If you give food or money to a bum, your social life will be advanced. To refuse help to a bum, means you will be involved in unpleasant situations.

BUNDLE — 338. See Package.

BUNGALOW — 408. To dream of a bungalow is a sign of happy times in friendship and business.

BUNION — 453. If you dream of a bunion on your foot, you will find peace and security in your later years.

BUNK — 141. Dreaming of going to sleep in a bunk, whether it is on a ship or a cabin in the woods, predicts financial worries.

BUREAU — 840. If you dream you are putting things into bureau drawers, you can look forward to good relationships with other people. If you can't find what you seek in the drawers, you will meet with many petty irritations.

BURGLARS — 189. Dreaming about burglars is a prediction of money matters becoming better for you.

BURIAL — 912. (Also see Undertaker.) Attending a funeral in good weather portends you will soon go to a wedding. But if the funeral is in the rain, you will suffer some job difficulties. If you dream you are being buried alive, you may make some serious mistakes in your actions in the near future.

BURLESQUE — 715. To dream you are watching a burlesque show, is a sign you will make some foolish mistakes.

BURNS — 640. If you burn any part of your body, in a dream, you will be lucky in taking care of some responsible jobs.

BURRO—890. Dreaming of a burro is a prediction of a pleasant home life.

BUS—330. Riding on a bus, in your dream, means you will undergo some money worries.

BUSH—629. If you hide behind a bush, you may be put into an embarrassing situation. To see a burning bush in your dream means you will suddenly hear some shocking news.

BUSINESS—487. To dream about your own business is a sign you may be part of some difficult discussions with others.

BUSINESS MACHINES—148. If you dream you are operating a business machine, you will find advancement in your work. If the machine breaks or stops, you may be blocked in your ambitions.

BUST—293. (Also see Breast.) To dream of looking at a bust made by a sculptor, is an omen of the death of someone you know.

BUSTLE—906. If a woman dreams she is wearing a dress with a bustle, it is a prediction of a pleasant relationship with an attractive male.

BUTCHER—643. Watching a butcher slaughter an animal is a prophecy of serious illness in your home. If you dream he is slicing meat, it means you must be careful to avoid scandal about yourself.

BUTLER—984. If you dream you are a butler, you will soon be free of money worries. If you are waited on by a butler, you may have to be cautious in handling finances.

BUTTER—058. To dream you see or eat butter, shows you will be able to keep out of debt and that you will have good health.

BUTTERMILK—921. If you dream about seeing or pouring or drinking buttermilk, you will have to avoid arguments with friends and spending money foolishly.

BUTTERFLY—456. Dreaming of a butterfly is a sign of good luck and happy marriage.

BUTTOCKS—123. If someone kicks you in the buttocks, you may run into an accident. To dream you kick another's buttocks, you may get a higher position but have difficulty in supervising those who work under you.

BUTTON—345. To dream you lose a button means you will have to apologize to someone. Metal or bright-colored buttons on a uniform are a sign of marrying someone very desirable. If you dream of cloth or unattractive buttons, you will have some worries about finances and health.

BUTTONHOLE—997. If you dream of neat buttonholes, you will gain in achievement. Torn buttonholes show discouraging situations.

BUZZARD—418. To see this bird in your dream is a prophecy of people talking about you in a malicious manner.

BUZZER—380. (Also see Doorbell.) If you dream you hear a buzzer it is a prediction of satisfaction in your work and among your friends.

CELLO
Man Playing
a Cello

CAB—701. To dream you are driving a taxicab, or riding alone in it, shows you will find life pleasant in all areas. If you are being driven by someone in a cab, you may have petty annoyances.

CABARET—679. Whetver you dream of being a performer or a guest at a cabaret, the sign is that you are going to have dissention among your friends.

CABBAGE—337. If you dream you are cooking cabbage, you will receive good luck, but if you dream of eating cabbage, you may go into debt because of careless spending.

CABINET—801. See Bureau.

CABLE—463. To dream of wire or rope cable being stretched across some space is an omen of risky work you will undertake. If your dream shows you did the cable job well, you will be rewarded with money and recognition.

CACTUS—120. Dreaming of a cactus plant signifies petty arguments with friends. If the cactus has flowers on it, good fortune is on its way to you.

CAFETERIA—450. If you eat well from a filled tray in a cafeteria, you will receive an inheritance. If you drop the tray, you may be sick for a short time.

CAGE—331. (Also see Birds.) A cage with birds in it foretells happiness in money and family matters. If the cage is empty, you will be witness to an accident.

CAKES—454. Delicious cakes eaten in a dream portend good luck in all areas of your life, but if a girl dreams she is eating her wedding cake, she may not have good luck for a while.

CALENDAR—728. (Also see Almanac.) If you dream you are checking off certain dates on a calendar, you will have less to worry about than you now have.

CALF—126. (Also see Cattle.) To see a calf nursing at the cow's udder means you will achieve your ambitions, but a calf being slaughtered predicts you will suffer disappointments about some of your ideals.

CAMEL—352. When you dream of a camel, it is a prophecy of better things coming into your life.

CAMEO—355. If you see someone wearing a cameo ring or earrings or pin, you will soon find life less tense for you.

CAMERA—370. (Also see Photograph.) When you see or use a camera, you may have some difficulties in maintaining calm relationships with your friends.

CAMP—961. Dreaming of being in an outdoor camp is a sign of you or some of your friends taking a long journey.

CAMPFIRE—665. (Also see Blaze, Bonfire.) When you see a blazing campfire in your dream, you will find improvement in finances and your home will be happier.

CAMPFIRE GIRL—596. To see a campfire girl in your dream foretells joy in home and family life.

CAMPUS—092. If you dream of being on a college campus with someone of the opposite sex, your marriage may be a stormy one.

CANAL—300. Whether you dream of swimming in a canal, or are on a boat on the canal, your love life may become complicated.

CANARY—185. A cheerful, chirping canary in your dream is an omen of pleasurable social life. If the canary is scared, or is dead, you may go through temporary worries and sickness.

CANCAN—314. Whether you watch this dance, or perform it, you may run into some uncomfortable situations with people at social events.

CANDLES—259. Unlighted candles show you will have some disappointments. Candles which are lighted are a sign that family life will be made more pleasant.

CANDLESTICK—931. Lighted candles in the candlestick portend happy celebrations. Unlit candles or no candles in the candlestick predict some worries which need attention.

CANDY—224. If a man dreams he is eating candy, he will have troubles to contend with. If a girl dreams she makes or eats or receives candy as a gift, she will have good times with the opposite sex.

CANKER SORE—606. To dream you have sores in your mouth or on your lips is a prediction you will go through some annoying situations.

CANNED GOODS—439. If you open a can of food or beverage, in your dream, you may be embarrassed by someone you trust. If your shelves are stocked with lots of canned goods, you will have good times on vacation.

CANNIBAL—212. (Also see Savage.) To be the victim of a cannibal, or to see someone else be eaten by him, prophesies some bad news coming close to home.

CANNON—454. If you dream a cannon is being fired, it is a sign of you receiving recognition for some of your deeds. If the cannon balls are seen on the ground, you will have pleasant relationships with others.

CANOE—455. To dream you are on a calm stream in a canoe predicts success in love, but if the canoe upsets in the water, you may quarrel with one of the opposite sex.

CANOPY—565. If you see or walk under a canopy, you will find happiness in marriage.

CANTELOUPE—165. To dream of seeing canteloupes on the vine is an omen of gain in money. If you eat the melon, you will go through a temporary illness.

CANTEEN—554. Whether you drink from a canteen, or it is empty of water, you are going to have some bad luck with friends.

CANYON—558. To fall into or be lost in a canyon or chasm, or riding horseback through a canyon, are all signs of impending troubles and depressing news. If you walk through a canyon alongside a stream, you will have good luck with the opposite sex.

CAP — 306. (Also see Hat.) If you dream you are wearing a cap, you will have financial gain and will be able to meet difficulties and win out over them.

CAPE — 941. To dream you are wearing a cape, is a sign you can overcome troubles if you use good sense to study them.

CAPITOL — 052. Seeing a capitol building (state or government) is an omen that you may suffer indecision and take unnecessary risks.

CAPSULE — 420. If you dream you are swallowing a capsule as medication, your love life and business life will be successful.

CAPTAIN — 306. Dreaming you are a captain of a vessel or in the army means you will come into some money. If a girl dreams she is in love with a captain, she must not put too much trust in her friends.

CAR — 514. See Automobile.

CARAVAN — 201. Being a member of a caravan which is going across a desert predicts you will take a long voyage with someone you love.

CARDINAL — 412. If you dream of a Cardinal in his church robes, you will have to make plans to move to a new place.

CARDS — 812. (Also see Ace, Joker.) Winning at a game of cards shows you will be free of money worries. If you lose at cards, you will have an argument with your loved one.

CAREER — 396. A man who dreams he has a satisfactory career can look forward to success in business matters, but a woman dreaming of being successful in a career means she will have difficulty with a husband although better luck in love with several men.

CARESSING — 540. See Petting.

CARGO — 280. Loading cargo onto a vessel or a freight train or truck predicts traveling. If the cargo is thrown overboard or meets with disaster in some way, it means an accident is going to occur.

CARICATURE — 139. To see yourself drawn in a caricature means you may receive insults from other people. If you are drawing a caricature of someone, you have to watch your tongue and not gossip about others.

CARILLON — **192.** Hearing chimes played from a tower of a church or other building is an omen of good times and fun. If you play the carillon in your dream, you will come into a legacy. If chimes are out of tune, you may suffer disappointment from those you love.

CARNATION — **807.** Seeing or wearing fresh carnations is a sign of being lucky in love and enjoying exciting times. Withered carnations are an omen of family quarreling.

CARNIVAL — **212.** Watching or joining in the festivities of a carnival means you will accept lots of party invitations.

CAROUSEL — **952.** See Merry-go-round.

CARP — **830.** See Fish.

CARPENTER — **796.** If you dream you are a carpenter, it is a happy omen of good luck in finances and friendships.

CARPET — **213.** See Rug.

CARRIAGE — **691.** To dream of a horse-drawn carriage portends you may run into some difficult situations with relatives.

CARROTS — **509.** Dreaming of carrots is a sign of a comfortable state of finances, also having a large happy family.

CART — **181.** If you drive a horse cart, your plans will materialize with success. If you dream you are a passenger in the cart, you will need to struggle hard to provide for your family.

CARTOON — **177.** (Also see Caricature, Comic Strip.) If you are pleased with cartoons that show much humor, you will be lucky in love but not so lucky in business matters.

CARVING — **947.** To dream you are carving meat, you may have to get a new job because of money losses due to the risks you took. If you carve fowl, you will be unlucky in friendships and in money.

CASCADE — **727.** See Water Fall.

CASH — **198.** If you handle or receive cash, you will experience good results in business matters.

CASHIER — **958.** To dream of being a cashier, you will have to guard against someone trying to get what belongs to you.

CASKET—159. See Coffin.

CASTANETS—400. If castanets are being used in a Spanish dance, you will have to contend with adverse situations in your home as well as some slight ailment.

CASTLE—306. To dream of walking through or living in a castle, you will go on interesting journeys and have enough money to enjoy them.

CAT—310. A mewing cat, in your dream, is a sign of friends talking behind your back. If a cat scratches or bites you, you will find some of your friends unfaithful to you. If the cat is calmly sitting or sleeping, you will have good luck with the opposite sex.

CATACOMBS—329. If you see skeletons while walking through catacombs, good health and money will come to you.

CATALOGUE—293. To dream you are reading a catalogue, or ordering goods from it, you can look forward to increased finances.

CATASTROPHE—715. If you dream of an accident or other situation that turns into a catastrophe, you might be hurt if you take chances.

CATECHISM—993. Dreaming of discussing the catechism, you will have to decide whether to accept a new job offered to you.

CATERPILLAR—218. To see a caterpillar in your dream predicts you have to watch out for friends who might put you in a disrespectful situation.

CATFISH—998. If you catch or eat catfish, you will soon have good fortune.

CATHEDRAL—812. To see a cathedral in your dreams portends you will work very hard to achieve your aspirations.

CATTLE—225. (Also see Calf, Cows.) If you dream of lean, unclean cattle, you will need to strive hard to get to your goals, but if the cattle are well-fed and clean, you will find joy with interesting friends. Watching a cattle stampede is an omen of money coming your way.

CAULIFLOWER—358. To dream of cauliflower growing is a prophecy of overcoming your money worries. If you eat cauliflower, you must pay more attention to your work if you want to succeed in it.

CAVALRY—285. If you dream of charging cavalry, you will get a promotion in your work and win respect from others.

CAVE—122. Whether you dream of being in or out of a cave, you will find things difficult for a short while in work and friendships.

CAVE MAN—314. If a girl dreams of being captured by a cave man, she will enjoy happiness in her marriage.

CEDAR—418. If you dream of smelling the pleasant aroma of cedar wood, you will find satisfaction in writing letters or articles.

CELEBRATION—954. (Also see Holiday, Party.) To attend a celebration in your dream is a sign of your future being lucky.

CELEBRITY—905. To meet a charming celebrity in your dream is a prediction you will receive a happy surprise. If the celebrity is unfriendly, you will be disappointed in your desires.

CELERY—585. Crisp, fresh celery is a sign of your achieving wealth and importance. If the celery is wilted and old, you may receive unhappy news through relatives.

CELIBACY—125. If you dream you do not have any sex life, you will be disappointed in some plan you hoped to achieve.

CELL—522. See Jail, also Warden.

CELLAR—218. Any dream about a cellar predicts you must guard against meeting people who might try to involve you in insincere activities.

CELLO—225. To listen to a tuneful cello in your dream shows you will go through some interesting experiences. If the cello is out of tune, or is broken, you may have an illness and have to make some disagreeable decisions.

CEMENT—540. Using cement to stick together any two objects is an omen of advancement in your work and better pay.

CEMETERY—219. If the burial ground is well-kept, or if you put flowers on the grave, you will share happiness with friends and family. If the burial ground is neglected and barren of any grass or other growth, it is a prophecy of loneliness and pessimism.

CENSOR—952. To dream you are functioning as a censor, or if you get a letter stamped "Censored," you will be betrayed by someone who knows your innermost secrets.

CENSUS—919. If you dream you are giving information to a census-taker, you will change your place of residence. To dream you are a census-taker, your marriage partner will be an efficient person.

CENT—786. (Also see Penny.) To dream of a shiny new coin is a warning someone you trust will prove unfaithful.

CENTENARIAN—915. If you dream you are a hundred years old is a sign of congenial friends and a happy long life.

CENTERPIECE—535. A lovely embroidered or lace centerpiece laid across the table shows you can expect money matters to improve.

CENTIPEDE—545. To dream of this insect portends many disappointments to you, which you may avoid if you plan things carefully.

CEREAL—512. If you eat cold cereal you will suffer through neglect of duties you ought to perform. If the cereal is hot, you will be able to put through some good business transactions.

CEREMONY—555. If you dream of a fraternal or religious ceremony, you will find satisfaction with good friends.

CESSPOOL—552. A cesspool in your dream is a prophecy of unpleasant relationships with the opposite sex.

CHAINS—949. To be bound by chains signifies you will have to assume serious responsibilities. If you break the chains and free yourself, your money problems will soon be lightened.

CHAIR—198. Sitting in a comfortable chair is an omen of your life becoming easy to handle. If the chair is not comfortable, you will undergo some petty annoyances with others.

CHAIRMAN—261. If you dream you are being the chairman (or chairwoman) of a meeting, you will receive respect for your sincerity toward other people. If you listen to a chairman, you will have a chance for job betterment.

CHALK—121. Using chalk to write on a blackboard or any other place, you are warned about disappointments in business plans. If the chalk squeaks while you are writing with it, be careful when you see a strange animal.

CHALLENGE—475. If you challenge someone to a fight, you will argue with someone of the opposite sex. If someone issues a challenge to you, you will have to be more humble in getting out of your difficulties.

CHAMBER POT—650. A chamber pot in your dream is a happy sign of more money and happiness in the family.

CHAMELEON—554. If you dream of this animal changing color, you must watch out not to be the victim of unfaithful friends.

CHAMPAGNE—745. To dream of drinking champagne at a big party is a prophecy of careless handling of finances. If you drink a toast to a bridal couple, you will have good luck in love.

CHANDELIER—958. A lighted chandelier predicts higher status in social and business life. If the chandelier falls, you will need to avoid making silly decisions. To hang on to a chandelier portends you will get into unpleasant social situations.

CHAPEL—652. Praying in a chapel is a sign you will try to make up for any insincere things you said and did. If you are in a chapel, without saying a prayer, you will find contentment of mind and heart.

CHAPERONE—854. To be accompanied on a date by a chaperone is an omen of disagreements with people you find annoying.

CHARCOAL—512. If you dream of a fire in which charcoal is the fuel, you will be lucky in being saved from accidents or worries. Dreaming of using charcoal to sketch pictures is a sign of pleasurable, lazy living.

CHARITY—905. (Also see Contribution.) To dream of having to receive charity from others is an omen of better times coming to you. If you give charity to another, you will have better luck in all things, but if you refuse to give charity, you will encounter hardships in the near future.

CHARLOTTE RUSSE—995. If you dream you are eating one, or if some of the cream gets smeared on you, you will argue with friends and will have to pay up your debts.

CHARM—183. Wearing a charm on your bracelet or watch chain foretells good health and financial betterment.

CHARMING—947. To dream of being with charming people and acting charming yourself is a prediction of all things in your life becoming better for you.

CHASE—195. Being part of a chase in your dream reveals you will have financial security in old age although you will have to do hard work to achieve it.

CHASM—193. See Canyon.

CHASTISEMENT—596. If you dream you are spanking or otherwise chastising anyone, you will have money worries and slight illness. If you are being chastised by someone, you will have better money conditions.

CHEATING—940. To call some person a cheat foretells you will get a traffic or other kind of ticket from a policeman. If you are called a cheat, your luck is going to rise.

CHECKS—319. If you write out checks in your dream, you can look ahead to earning and inheriting good sums of money.

CHECKERS—585. Playing checkers is a sign of embarrassing quarrels with relatives which you could avoid by keeping your temper.

CHEESE—595. Whether you buy or make or eat cheese in a dream, the signs point to financial matters being eased up and to happiness with your mate. If the cheese should have too strong an odor, you will go through some embarrassing situations.

CHEF—856. See Cook.

CHERRY TREE—855. To chop down the tree foretells you are in danger of loss of your good name and loss of money. If you pick cherries off the tree, you will make slow recovery from money worries.

CHERUB—812. If you dream of pretty little baby angels, you will find happiness in the presence of children.

CHESS—599. Dreaming of playing chess is a sign of friction between yourself and others in marriage and business matters.

CHEST, HAIRY—985. If a girl dreams of seeing a man with a hairy chest, it is an omen of criticism if she does not act properly in male company.

61

CHESTNUT — 410. To pick or roast or eat chestnuts in your dream shows good results if you do handwork, and a harmonious relationship with those of the opposite sex.

CHEWING GUM — 713. To dream of chewing gum in your own house shows you will be happy in family and friendly relationships. If you chew gum in public, you will be scorned by some old friends.

CHICKEN — 154. See Hen.

CHICKEN POX — 654. If you dream you have this ailment, you will go through some trifling annoyances. If a child whom you know has this illness, it prophecies the child will reach high accomplishment.

CHIFFONIER — 811. See Bureau.

CHILBLAINS — 045. If you dream of getting frostbite and suffering itchy chilblains, you will be freed of current worries.

CHILDBIRTH — 895. (Also see Birth, Midwife.) If a woman dreams she is giving birth, she will find life much easier than it is now, but a man dreaming he is giving birth will find difficulty in his work and friendly relationships. To dream you are watching someone giving birth, is a warning you must take care of all your duties at once and not put them off.

CHILDREN — 495. (Also see Boy, Girl.) To dream you are a parent means you can look ahead to having a happy family.

CHILI CON CARNE — 594. If you dream of seeing or eating this Mexican food, you will be disappointed in your love life and may have other worries too.

CHILL — 509. (Also see Ague.) If you dream of suffering a chill, you will be pressed to pay up your debts.

CHIMES — 459. See Carillon.

CHIMNEY — 954. Smoke coming out of a chimney predicts you will earn more money. If sparks rise from the chimney, you will argue with relatives. If the chimney is cold, you will change your work.

CHIN — 945. If you kiss someone on the chin, your mate will be a critical person. A blow on the chin, whether you give it to another person or you receive it, means you can win when playing cards.

CHINNING — 415. Chinning yourself on a horizontal bar, at home or in a gymnasium, means you will be able to handle new situations as they arise.

CHINESE FOOD — 995. If you eat chop suey or chow mein (or any other Chinese dish) you will be faced with some strange plans which you will be able to solve. Also you must be careful in dealing with insincere but flattering people of the opposite sex.

CHIROPODIST — 534. To dream of having your feet treated by a chiropodist foretells you will find increased satisfaction in work and in money matters.

CHIVALRY — 580. When a man is being chivalrous to the ladies, such a dream portends good luck in business ventures.

CHLOROFORM — 509. See Anesthesia.

CHOCOLATE — 534. If you dream of eating or drinking chocolate, you will go through an illness.

CHOIR — 591. Whether in your dream you listen or partake in singing in a choir, you will do something for other people which will bring you respect from others.

CHOKING — 045. See Suffocation.

CHOLERA — 054. If you dream of this sickness, you will have financial luck provided you do not get recklessly extravagant with the money.

CHOPSTICKS — 504. To dream of people using chopsticks while eating, you will be able to clarify any confused matters in your life. If you eat with chopsticks, you will have disagreements with some close friends.

CHORUS — 405. If you dream of a chorus that sings off-tune, it means someone will have a fatal illness or accident. If the chorus sings on-key, you will find something that is valuable.

CHRIST — 419. Seeing Jesus Christ in your dream is a prophecy of a serene mind which will come to you if you adapt yourself to people and situations in your daily life.

CHRISTMAS — 194. (Also see Yule Log.) Dreaming about the Christmas season predicts higher attainment in work and money.

CHRYSANTHEMUM—584. To pick or wear this flower is a sign of a contented marriage and of meeting interesting people at social functions.

CHURCH—904. (Also see Spire.) To attend church services shows happy conditions in dealing with the opposite sex. To dream of attending social parties in the church foretells you may get into a pessimistic mood about trivial matters. Seeing a church with ivy growing over the outside walls portends you will be loved within family circles. A burning church means you will lose a trusted friend.

CIDER—041. Drinking or serving cider is an omen of happy social times. If you spill cider on your clothes, you will be lucky in a lottery.

CIGARS, CIGARETTES—459. See Tobacco.

CINDER—531. To dream of getting a cinder in your eye, you will hear bad news from a friend. If you sprinkle or shovel cinders, someone who loves you will send you a present.

CINNAMON—351. Using cinnamon in food which is made to taste better by it, is an omen of happy social life. If cinnamon is put in food which does not call for its use, you will suffer disappointment through the one you love.

CIPHER—045. See Code.

CIRCLE—543. If you dream you draw perfect circles, you will find success in following your plans.

CIRCUMCISION—948. Whether you watch another person being circumcized, or you are being circumcized, it is a prophecy of good fortune in work and friendships and health.

CIRCUS—210. To dream you are watching the circus, you will receive satisfying news and will do well in money matters. If you perform in the circus, it is a prediction you may have an automobile accident if you are careless.

CISTERN—904. If you draw water from a cistern, you will get happy news from a faraway friend. If the cistern is dry or has a bad odor, you will get unhappy news.

CITY—041. If you live in the country but dream you are headed for the city, it is a sign of stimulating things going to happen to you with people of the opposite sex.

CIVIL SERVICE—549. To dream you are in a civil service job portends contentment in money matters and in good health.

CLAIRVOYANT—315. See Fortune Teller.

CLAMS—531. Dreaming about clams is a sign of your ability to handle people who may act unfaithfully towards you. If you attend a clambake, you will enjoy social activities.

CLARINET—943. If you play this instrument in your dream, you will receive only mild success in your undertakings.

CLASSROOM—167. See School.

CLEAVER—834. A butcher chopping meat with a cleaver foretells good luck will come to you. If you dream someone is being attacked with a cleaver, business matters will be difficult for you. A person's head being chopped off with a cleaver is an omen of some disaster.

CLERGYMAN—995. (Also see Minister, Priest, Rabbi.) To dream you are a clergyman reveals you will be lucky in family life. Meeting a clergyman is a sign of your being put to embarrassment and having to apologize to others.

CLIMBING—653. Whether you dream of climbing a ladder or stairs or mountains, you will have a chance to improve yourself and your finances.

CLINIC—575. If you dream of going to a clinic for treatment, it is a portent of good health for you.

CLOCK—692. If you dream you wind a clock, you will be lucky in love. To hear a clock tick or strike the hour, means you should not waste time in coming to a decision.

CLOTHES—892. Buying or wearing new clothes is a sign you will meet new admirers and be invited to social events. If you dream you are undressing, you have to watch out against anyone trying to blacken your reputation.

CLOUDS—676. When you cannot see the sun because of clouds, you will find success in your undertakings.

CLUB—901. To join or go to a club foretells you will receive disagreeable news and have petty quarrels with someone you love.

COACH—915. If you ride in a horse-drawn coach, you will have lots of money. If you drive the coach, happiness in marriage will be yours. A coach which overturns predicts change of address and of work.

COAL—984. Whether you buy or deliver or put coal on a fire, is an omen of advancement in work and finances.

COAL MINER—379. If you dream of being a coal miner, you will get higher wages.

COAST GUARD—791. Dreaming of the coast guard prophesies you will get bad news and you will argue with people who live near you.

COAT—483. Wearing a coat that is old and shabby means you will get enough money so you can live on a good scale. To lose a coat means friends and business matters will become difficult for you to handle.

COAT OF ARMS—545. If you dream you have your coat of arms on your stationery or embroidered on clothes or framed on a wall, you are in danger of envious friends because of your own bragging to them.

COBBLESTONES—220. To walk or ride over cobblestones, or to throw one at someone, is an omen that you will experience unpleasantness in dealing with people and with financial matters.

COBBLER—008. See Shoemaker.

COBRA—814. See Snake.

COBWEB—631. (Also see Spider.) If you dream of seeing cobwebs over a bottle of wine, good luck will soon be yours. To see cobwebs over things in daily use (such as toilet articles, books, dishes), you will go through a period of hard luck.

COCKER SPANIEL—237. Dreaming of this breed of dog means you will have an easy life and enjoy good companionship.

COCKTAILS—493. If you mix the cocktails with rum or whiskey, you will have stimulating social life, but if the cocktails are mixed with gin or vodka, you will hear bad news in the family.

COCOA—205. To drink cocoa with friends signifies you will have long-lasting friendships through good and bad days.

COCONUT — 430. If you break open a coconut in your dream, you will find a small amount of money. Eating the coconut shows you will have courage in meeting oncoming difficulties.

CODE — 575. To send a code message in a dream is a word of caution to you not to try to outsmart other people. If you receive a code message, you will find it hard to understand some of the actions of a close friend.

COFFEE — 518. If you dream you make or drink a refreshingly good tasting coffee, you will get helpful news which will surprise you. If the coffee is bad-tasting or weak, one of your companions will prove disappointing. To grind the coffee bean is a sign of happy love relationship.

COFFIN — 309. To dream you are lying in a coffin is a prophecy of a serene life and happiness in the future. If someone else is lying in a coffin, placed on a bier or some type of platform, it means some disaster may occur. If an important personage is lying in a coffin, it is an omen of war.

COGNAC — 678. See Brandy.

COIN — 013. (Also see Money.) To pay with coins for something you received, shows you will find pleasure with those of the opposite sex. If you receive the coins in payment, malicious gossip will be spread about you. A counterfeit coin signifies poor health.

COLD — 940. If you dream you have a cold, try to avoid quarrels with members of the family.

COLD WEATHER — 279. To be uncomfortable because of cold weather, you will be advanced in your job to a higher position.

COLIC — 836. If you dream of having the colic or cramps, someone to whom you were considerate will leave you an inheritance.

COLLAR — 411. Finding it hard to put your collar on means you will have some trouble with the owner of your building.

COLLECTOR — 278. If you dream you are collecting coins, stamps, antiques, or other articles, is a prediction you will meet celebrities.

COLLEGE — 836. (Also see Campus, University.) To dream of going to college predicts a lover's spat. If you dream you are a college professor, you will make new friends with worthwhile people.

COLLISION—411. See Crash.

COLOGNE—278. See Perfume.

COLONEL—318. A man who dreams he is a colonel will achieve heights in business. A girl who dreams she meets a colonel will have many boy friends inviting her out.

COMB—536. If a man dreams he is combing a girl's hair, he may be fooled by a coquettish girl. If you dream you are combing your own hair, you will find easy answers to your problems.

COMEDY—734. (Also see Fun, Laughter.) To dream you are watching a comedy in a movie or theatre means you will be satisfied with new paths which will help you get ahead.

COMET—472. To dream of this sparkling-tailed star streaming across the sky is an omen of sudden good luck in business and love.

COMIC STRIP—017. (Also see Caricature, Cartoon.) If you enjoy reading a comic strip, it predicts financial gain and a vacation for you.

COMMAND—611. If you dream you are giving a command and it is obeyed, you are in line for a promotion. If your command is disobeyed, you will suffer financial loss.

COMMANDMENTS—945. To see Moses in a dream, holding the stone tablet with the ten commandments, is an omen that you will need to guard against any unethical actions.

COMMENCEMENT—306. See Graduation.

COMMITTEE—059. To dream you are on an important committee is a sign of your having to give a donation to some community cause, but if you are the committee's chairman, you may go through some confusion in business matters.

COMMUNION—937. If you dream you are attending communion in a church, you will enjoy life in a calm manner.

COMPACT—618. (Also see Make-up.) If a man dreams he is carrying a compact, he will be embarrassed by his friends. A woman dreaming of using her compact in public will find it hard to understand the man she loves.

COMPANIONS—408. To dream of amicable companionship with

both sexes is a prophecy of your winning out over your untrue friends.

COMPASS — 946. If you dream of a compass which has a defective needle that doesn't point to any direction, you will be worried over situations in family and in your job.

COMPLAINT — 737. A complaint lodged against you shows you will have arguments with members of the family. If you make a justified complaint in your dream, you will meet important new friends.

COMPLEXION — 431. To dream of having a lovely complexion is a sign of being admired by the opposite sex. If blemishes appear on your skin, watch out for people who want to hurt your reputation.

COMPLIMENT — 508. If you pay compliments to another, you will be offered a higher position. To receive a compliment, means you will do well in the job you now hold.

COMPOSITION — 244. To dream of writing a composition, as you did when you were a school child, means you will renew an old friendship.

COMPUTERS — 637. See Business Machines.

CONCEPTION — 241. A married woman dreaming she has conceived a child will form new friendships. A single girl who dreams she conceives will receive a proposal from a new man.

CONCERT — 017. If you dream you are attending a concert, you may have a chance to become a performer. Music which is off-tune and boring means you will argue with relatives.

CONDEMNED — 337. See Judge.

CONDOLENCES — 668. If you dream you offer condolences to someone who has a death in the family, you will clear up some confused matters. Condolences offered to you is an omen of better times for you.

CONDUCTOR — 012. To dream you are quarreling with a conductor on a bus or train means you will have an exciting long trip. If you are the conductor, you will assume a responsible post. If you are conducting an orchestra, you will come into money.

CONE — 534. (Also see Ice Cream.) To dream of any object that is shaped like a cone is a sign of happy times with the opposite sex.

CONFERENCE — 978. To dream you attend a political conference signifies you will work hard and receive little pay. A professional or business conference foretells you will receive beneficial news. If you attend a church conference, you will achieve social acceptance.

CONFESSION — 690. If you hear someone's confession, people will talk behind your back. If you make a confession in your dream, you will soon move to or buy a nice house.

CONFETTI — 317. To dream confetti is being tossed around is a prophecy you will have an exciting experience with someone who is glamorous.

CONFIDENCE — 037. If someone has confidence in you, you will be lucky in business but not too lucky in affairs of the heart. If in your dream you have confidence in someone else, you will form fine friendships with worthy people.

CONFINEMENT — 614. (Also see Childbirth.) A married woman or a widow who dreams of confinement will find happiness. A single girl in confinement may suffer a bad reputation.

CONFIRMATION — 238. If you dream of attending a confirmation in a house of worship shows good relations with friends. If you are being confirmed, you will have peaceful days ahead of you.

CONFUSION — 056. If you undergo confusion of mind and activities, it is an omen of a peaceful life.

CONGENIALITY — 290. To dream you make sure to get along well with others is a sign of being admired and liked by your friends. If others are amiable toward you, it is a warning that you should not talk too much or act in a hurry.

CONGRATULATIONS — 640. To offer someone your congratulations is a sign of success to be achieved by you. If someone offers you congratulations, you will be able to get more money if you want to sell something you own.

CONGRESS — 097. If you dream you are elected to congress, you will lose something of value. To sit as a guest at a meeting of congress foretells you will enjoy a calm and peaceful life.

CONSCIENCE—849. To dream that you are doing good deeds because of dictates of your conscience, foretells admiration from your friends and you will be honored for something good you do for others.

CONSCRIPTION—024. See Draft.

CONSPIRACY—514. See Plot.

CONSTIPATION—595. (Also see Laxative.) If you dream of suffering from this disorder, the prophecy is that you will regret a slight misdeed; also you must guard against too much eating and drinking.

CONTAGIOUS DISEASE—316. To dream of having a contagious disease, is a sign that you will have to be sure about who are your faithful friends.

CONTEMPT—714. If you dream you are showing contempt for someone, you will not be able to do your job well. If someone shows contempt for you, success will come to you through your work.

CONTORTIONIST—741. To watch a contortionist perform his acrobatics, it is an omen you will find difficulty in your work and in friendships and in your love life.

CONTRACEPTIVE—064. See Birth Control.

CONTRACT—993. Signing a contract means you may get a job in civil service. To tear up a contract signifies you may be promoted in your work ahead of others in the same job.

CONTRADICTION—492. To dream you contradict someone means you may have some confusion about business sales. If someone contradicts you, you will not be able to keep an important date.

CONTRIBUTION—089. (Also see Charity.) If you dream you are raising funds and getting contributions, your romantic life will be pleasant. If you make the contribution, you will win respect from others.

CONVALESCENCE—266. Dreaming you are getting well after a sickness is a prophecy you will go on a long and favorable journey.

CONVENT—701. To dream you are staying in or studying in a convent foretells happy friendships and release from worries.

CONVENTION—530. To dream you attend a convention signifies you will have to compromise in coming to a harmonious relationship with others.

CONVERSATION—789. If the conversation is loud and excitable, it means you will be disappointed in some plans and people. A conversation in a language you do not understand foretells you may not receive enough recognition from your family.

CONVERT—227. To dream you converted someone to another religion or political party shows you will not be sure of your own future for some time. If you became a convert, you will meet interesting people in business and will use your mind in a calm manner.

CONVICT—392. If you dream you are a convicted prisoner, you will make a success in some artistic or creative endeavor.

CONVULSION—013. To see someone in your dream who is having a convulsion, is a prophecy that you should take it easy and not rush into any new agreements without studying them. If you are having a convulsion, get sound legal advice on your affairs if they do not seem clear to you.

COOK—100. If you dream you are a cook, you can look forward to good luck and a faithful loving mate.

CORAL—208. If you see or wear pink coral jewelry in your dream, you will find pleasure with the opposite sex. If it is white coral, you will have to work harder and more carefully to attain results.

CORD—455. (Also see Rope.) To tie a parcel with a cord is a sign of you achieving quick results. If you untie a knot in a cord means some tension with one of the opposite sex. To break a cord is an omen of an accident.

CORESPONDENT—617. (Also see Divorce.) If you dream you are named corespondent in a divorce case, you will have to be careful about maintaining your good reputation.

CORK—938. To dream you are uncorking a bottle of beverage is an omen of something strange going on, which you will eventually solve. If you insert a cork in a bottle, you will have a frivolous affair of the heart.

CORKSCREW—244. If you are using a corkscrew, you must guard against hurting someone in a love affair.

CORN—558. Corn stalks in a field foretell good marriage and fine children. Eating corn on the cob means you will make money in your work. To pop corn in your dream shows success if the kernels are white; but if they get burned you may have some worries.

CORNET—261. If you play a cornet in your dream, you will have to be careful in making a new decision.

CORNMEAL—335. If you cook or eat cornmeal, you will have good health and will earn more money.

CORONATION—335. To dream you are being crowned, portends you may earn more money but it will bring you greater responsibilities. If someone else is being crowned, you will travel to a foreign country.

CORPORAL—215. A girl who dreams of socializing with a corporal will be subject of gossip by others. A man who dreams he is a corporal will suffer money worries due to his extravagances.

CORPSE—064. (Also see Morgue.) To dream you see a corpse of someone you do not know, is a sign you will have a long, interesting life. If you dream you are the corpse, you will have good health and will be relieved of worries. If a corpse is being embalmed, you will be made to explain some actions you did not commit.

CORRAL—476. To dream of horses or other animals in a corral is a sign of stimulating activities you will enjoy outdoors in wide open spaces.

CORSAGE—804. See Flowers.

CORSET—918. To see a woman nude except for her corset or girdle, is an omen you will get disturbing news in a letter. If you help a woman adjust her corset, you will soon be rid of money worries.

COSMETICS—676. (Also see Compact, Lipstick Make-up, Rouge.) A woman dreaming of putting on cosmetics at home will find good luck in her future, but if she uses cosmetics in public she will be disturbed about her love life. If a man dreams he is using cosmetics, he may suffer disappointment in business and he may find his friends are maliciously gossiping about him.

COSTUME—243. If you dream you are wearing a fancy costume, you will meet with surprising events.

COTTAGE—964. To dream you live in a cottage is a sign of a good marriage and children.

COTTON—519. Seeing or picking cotton in a field is an omen of comfortable living without money worries. But if you dream someone else is walking with you through the field, you will meet with some disappointments.

COTTON GIN—782. To dream of the seeds-separating machine, you will be promoted to a well-paying position.

COUCH—430. (Also see Sofa.) If you sleep alone on a couch, the sign is good luck in making trades with others. If someone else sleeps with you on the couch, you will have some arguments at your place of work. If you dream you hide under a couch, your new plans will not work out.

COUGH—698. If you dream you are coughing, some accident is going to happen.

COUNCIL—314. To dream of a discussion with others in a council meeting, you will argue with an old friend.

COUNTER—088. If you work behind a counter in a store, the prediction is a good family life and a sound old age.

COUNTERFEIT MONEY—979. To dream about making or passing counterfeit money is a prophecy that someone you trusted will prove false to you. If you destroy the money, you will have good luck.

COUNTESS—001. A countess, who is elderly, is a sign of your receiving social prestige. To dream of a pretty young countess means you will have to make apologies for some of your misconduct.

COUNTRY—473. If you dream of being in the country and the weather is fine, you will find life pleasureable in the near future. If weather is bad, you will have a dispute with someone in business.

COUPONS—308. Saving coupons you get with things you buy, or clipping coupons from bonds, predicts you are being watched by those who are over you in your work.

COURT OF LAW — 502. If you are in court, you will soon need to clarify some of the things you said and did (which others misunderstand).

COURTSHIP — 618. To dream of two people courting portends you will try and succeed at some new things you have in mind.

COUSIN — 312. Dreaming of being on friendly and affectionate terms with a cousin, signifies a life that is free from troubles.

COW — 578. (Also see Calf, Cattle.) If you dream of a cow chewing her cud, it predicts good health to you. An ugly cow is a sign of family arguments. To milk a cow or to drink the milk means you will earn more if you concentrate on your work.

COWARD — 933. If you dream you are a coward, you will show bravery when the time is needed.

COYOTE — 523. To dream of hearing the strange howl of this animal, is a prophecy of relatives showing their displeasure of you. If you kill the coyote, you will succeed in your intelligent plans.

CRABS — 421. If you cook a crab or a crawfish in your dream, watch out for a slight accident. To eat the crab will bring you luck in the chances you take. To dream you fish for crabs is a sign of dissension among your friends and you. -

CRACKERS — 645. Eating crackers in bed signifies family quarrels If you dream you see someone baking crackers, you will have a lot of fun and make more money.

CRADLE — 562. (Also see Crib.) A baby in a cradle predicts good luck in family and business matters. Twins in a cradle mean you will move to a new place. A cradle that is empty is an omen of sickness.

CRAFTSMAN — 212. To dream you are using your hands to make things from wood or stone or metal is a sign of joy in family life.

CRAMPS — 712. See Colic.

CRANBERRIES — 319. Whether in your dream you eat raw or cooked or jellied cranberries, it portends some misunderstanding with legal and political officers.

CRAPE — 575. To see in your dream a mourning crape hanging on a door means you may encounter a few small accidents.

CRASH—753. If you dream of being in an automobile or some other crash, you will have slight annoyances but they will turn out all right.

CRAWFISH—012. See Crabs.

CRAYON—618. Drawing pictures with a crayon signifies you will need to apologize for not fulfilling your promises to others.

CREAM—339. If you dream you skim the cream from the top of the milk, you will be most attractive to the opposite sex. If you spill the cream, you will be disappointed in a new plan.

CREEK—418. To dream you swim in a creek predicts you will be lucky in love and in your work.

CREMATION—671. To watch a body being cremated is a sign of interesting travels for you.

CRIB—329. (Also see Cradle.) To dream of a child sleeping in a crib is an omen of happiness in marriage.

CRICKET—684. If you dream you hear these insects sing, whether in the house or out of doors, foretells long life and good family relationships.

CRICKET MATCH—843. To participate in this game means you will enjoy good health. If you watch but do not play, you may find some of your social companions too uninteresting for you.

CRIME—515. If you dream you commit a crime, it is a warning for you to keep your temper down and not rush into new plans.

CRIMINAL—532. If you dream you captured a criminal, you will be paid money that is owed to you. If you give the criminal shelter, you may be taken advantage of by some insincere people. If a criminal attacks you, you will be pestered by those to whom you owe money.

CROCHETING—323. To dream of crocheting some articles is a sign you will be attractive to the opposite sex. If you make mistakes in your crocheting, you will have dissension with relatives.

CROCODILE—538. To dream of being chased by a crocodile, or killing it, foretells you will be unexpectedly fortunate in your plans. If the crocodile catches you, you will suffer an accident.

CROPS—371. If you dream you reap a big crop, you will succeed in money matters. If your crops are small, you will find it hard to handle some of your business matters.

CROQUET—338. To play this game in your dream portends happy times for you with your intimate friends.

CROSS—372. If you dream of a cross, you will be able to overcome difficulties.

CROSSROADS—599. Dreaming of being at a spot where roads cross predicts you will have to make serious decisions about a change in your life.

CROUP—015. To dream of a child or an adult suffering with croup reveals you will have to get some money in a rush to back up some ideas you have.

CROW—938. If you dream of this bird, you will suffer a set-back in your love life. If you shoot the crow, you will enjoy the pleasure of friendship and affection.

CROWD—251. (Also see Mob.) To dream you are in a crowd that is peaceful means you will be able to advance yourself through new people.

CROWN—676. (Also see Tiara.) If you dream you are wearing a real crown in a royal building, you will encounter some misfortune. If you wear a crown of paper at a party or in a play, it is a warning for you to guard against temptation.

CRUCIFIX—423. See Cross.

CRUELTY—902. See Brutality.

CRUTCH—629. To dream either you or another is using a crutch is an omen of good living in social and financial circles.

CRYING—676. If you dream you are crying, you will be unhappy over another person's bad luck. A baby crying is a sign of you getting interesting information in a letter.

CRYSTAL—895. To see crystal, with the sun shining through it and showing beautiful colors, portends you will be in a social group with attractive and interesting people.

CUCUMBER–626. If you cook the cucumber, watch out you do not make errors in your work. Eating a raw cucumber is a sign of a friend's death.

CUPBOARD–635. To dream of a cupboard being filled with food-stuffs means good luck in your work plans. An empty cupboard signifies bad business conditions.

CURBSTONE–843. If you sit on a curbstone, you will undertake some work which is dangerous.

CURLS–041. To dream you cut off the curls in your hair foretells good days ahead for you. If you or another admires your curls, you must guard against saying or doing things to bring on criticism from your friends.

CURRY COMB–360. To groom a horse with a curry comb signifies success in a new enterprise.

CURSE–403. (Also see Profanity.) To put a curse on a person or a thing is an omen of unpleasant social relationships.

CURTAINS–842. If you draw the curtains over the window it is a sign of disappointment in one of your hopes. To open the curtains wide, you will succeed in your plans.

CUSHION–860. To dream you are sitting or reclining on a cushion shows you will come into money. If you throw or tear a cushion, you will be criticized for something you said or did.

CUSTARD–201. If you eat custard in your dream, you will need to be courteous to some people who bore you. Spilling the custard on your clothes means you will suffer some mild annoyances.

CUT–917. (Also see Gash.) To cut yourself with a knife or other sharp blade portends you will lose an intimate friend or some money.

CYCLONE–780. If you dream of a cyclone, you will need to be cautious about taking chances of any sort.

CYMBALS–603. If you dream of playing the cymbals, you will have a lot of fun with one of the opposite sex.

D

DOG

DACHSHUND—391. To dream of this elongated dog is an omen of good fortune in all areas of your life.

DAGGER—571. If you dream of a dagger you have to be careful not to antagonize anyone of whom you are not sure. If someone is stabbed with the dagger, you will conquer your unfaithful friends if you are cautious not to say or do anything that could be misinterpreted.

DAIRY—939. If you dream of being in a dairy, you will have a home and family life which will make you happy and proud.

DAIRYMAID—761. To dream of an attractive dairymaid is a sign of good luck in health, love, and fine surroundings.

DAIS—805. (Also see Platform.) A dais which appears in a dream foretells you might find happiness in working in the theatre.

DAISIES—868. A field of daisies means you will receive an unexpected present. White daisies show you have a faithful lover. Yellow daisies warn that you may have someone as a rival.

DAM—629. If you dream of flooding water rushing over a dam, you must be cautious about not undertaking rash promises. If calm water goes leisurely over a dam, you will succeed in new plans.

DANCERS, BALLET—750. See Ballet.

DANCING—472. (Also see Ballroom.) If you dream of dancing or watching others dance in a ballroom, you will achieve a happy marriage and home life.

DANDELION—910. To dream of wearing a dandelion is a sign of false friends who will ridicule you. Dandelions in bloom on a lawn mean good luck in love.

DANDRUFF—903. If you dream you see dandruff on your own or someone else's clothes, you will argue with people if you do not stick to ethical behavior.

DANGER—591. If you dream you are in danger, be overly careful in dealing with others in matters of love or finances or your job.

DARKNESS—707. If you dream of an eclipse of the moon or the sun, or if the day suddenly gets dark, it is a prophecy that someone may have a fatal illness or accident.

DARKROOM—263. To dream of being in a photography darkroom is an omen of you being able to clear up something that you misunderstood for a long time.

DARNING—521. If you dream of darning holes in hosiery or clothes, you will meet new people who will be charming and lots of fun.

DART—712. See Archery.

DATES—608. To eat dates is a sign of marriage, for you if you are single, or for a close friend. Dates growing on a palm tree signify you will earn more money.

DATING—987. See Appointment.

DAUGHTER, DAUGHTER-IN-LAW—998. If you dream of either one, you will have to carry the burden of some person who might take advantage of you.

DAWN—216. To see the sun rising and dawn breaking shows you will get a chance to earn more money. If you dream the dawn is cloudy and rainy, you will be disappointed in something you hoped to get.

DAZE—935. To dream you are walking around in a daze, it is an omen that malicious gossip is being spread about you.

DEACON—084. If you dream a deacon is acting in an ungentlemanly manner, some people will disapprove of some of the things you say and do. If the deacon is a quiet and thoughtful man, you will receive praise which is long overdue.

DEAFNESS—490. Dreaming that you are deaf is a happy sign you will be relieved of your worries. If you try to talk to a deaf person, you will meet with many disappointments.

80

DEATH—724. If in your dream a person close to you dies, you will suffer many set-backs in future plans.

DEBATE—951. (Also see Argument.) To dream you are engaging in a heated debate with someone, you will be able to win your aims only if you work hard and keep your friends.

DEBTS—102. If you dream you are in debt, you will suffer business difficulties. If you pay off your debts, you will soon have good luck.

DEBUTANTE—206. Seeing a debutante or being one, in a dream, signifies successful new plans in business and social matters.

DECAY—403. To dream you eat or see rotten food or other decayed matter, shows you will have to tackle some heavy troubles.

DECEIT—381. If you catch someone practicing deceit, you will have financial success in trading. If you dream you are the one who is deceitful, you will undergo some unpleasant situations with others.

DECK—624. Whether you dream you are alone or with a companion on the deck of a ship, it is a sign of good luck coming to you you and you may be able to help others too.

DECORATING—585. To dream you are decorating your home, or some articles of clothing, means you will attend some happy parties, and should also be smart in selling things to others.

DEER—174. (Also see Antelope.) To see a deer in your dream predicts breaking up of personal relationships.

DENTIST—350. To dream you are having a tooth extracted is a sign of a financial loss. If the dentist works on your teeth, you will get a letter which will disturb you.

DENTURES—613. If you dream your dentures are loose, you will go through some disappointments through friends. If you are wearing dentures in your dream, you may suffer disappointment with friends through your own fault.

DEPOT—841. A depot, seen in your dream, is a sign you will move to some faraway place.

DERRICK—765. If you dream of a derrick, you will gain your aspirations and will find life gratifying.

DESERT—763. (Also see Oasis.) To dream of a sun-baked, sandy desert, is a sign of your gaining much knowledge through studying books. A caravan crossing the desert means interesting travel for you.

DESERTER—329. If you dream you are a military deserter, you will be snubbed by people for some error you committed in the past. If you stand before a firing squad, you must move carefully in your next plans.

DESIGNS—064. If you see interesting designs, of all colors and styles, you are going to undertake additional burdens.

DESK—341. To dream of sitting at a desk foretells annoyances through relatives. Clearing out articles from the desk drawers shows you will meet new, stimulating people.

DESPAIR—941. If you dream you are despairing because of financial stress or illness, you will soon have good luck.

DESPARADO—820. See Criminal.

DESSERT—370. To eat a plain dessert in your dream means you will find pleasure in a quiet way of life. A rich dessert shows you will get some luxury you now crave.

DESTRUCTION—599. To dream you see buildings or whole territories being destroyed, you are warned to keep your temper and not let your feelings get hurt too easily.

DETECTIVE—375. If you dream you are a detective, you will have annoying worries. If you capture the criminal, you will be able to handle your troubles and straighten them out.

DETOUR—559. To make a detour while on the road, you can look forward to a new job and added duties to perform.

DEVIL—602. If you dream of a devil with whom you are friendly, you can expect people trying to influence you away from a righteous path, also there may be sudden illness. If you overpower the devil, you will get over worries about insincere friends.

DIAGRAM—371. (Also see Map.) To draw a diagram with pen and ink reveals you will have some difficulty in your love life. To draw a diagram with a pencil or crayon shows you will have good luck.

DIAMONDS–808. (Also see Gems.) To see diamonds in your dream means you will have a happy married life. To wear diamonds foretells a friend is going to be unfaithful and troublesome.

DIAPER–329. If you dream of changing a baby's diaper, you will enjoy a good marriage. To refuse to change the diaper, you will work very hard to earn a living.

DICE–629. To dream of dice being thrown predicts someone in the family may have worries. Throwing a lucky combination means you will have only temporary success.

DICTATING MACHINE–912. See Business Machines.

DICTATORSHIP–017. If you dream of living in a country ruled by a dictator, you will clear up your worries and can look forward to happier days.

DICTIONARY–895. Seeing a dictionary in your dream shows you will have a disagreement with a stubborn person. If you look up a word in the dictionary, you are inclined to show off with what you know.

DIGGING–730. If you dig with a shovel, you will work hard but will be well paid.

DIME–612. If you dream of clean, shiny dimes, someone will say you are stingy. If you give away a dime, you are going to get a surprise present in the mail.

DIMPLES–842. If you see good-looking people who have dimples in their cheeks or chin, you are fickle in affairs of the heart.

DINNER–021. To dine alone with the one you love is an omen of a good marriage. To eat dinner with many friends in a cafe or hotel, it means you are going to have annoying arguments with friends.

DIPLOMA–995. To dream of diplomas being given at a graduation is a prophecy of you reaching a highly respected position.

DIPLOMAT–492. To meet a diplomat in your dream signifies you will be faced with a situation which will necessitate you being tactful with others.

DIRIGIBLE BALLOON–212. (Also see Airplane.) To see a dirigible in your dream portends you will undertake new actions which may entail much danger.

DIRT—351. See Filth.

DISAPPEARANCE—641. If you dream a person or a thing just disappears from sight, you will be faced with personal and financial worries which you will have to solve.

DISAPPOINTMENT—032. To dream you are disappointed in people or things means you will have your hopes rewarded soon.

DISARMAMENT—974. To dream all countries are disarming, is a sign of good fortune in matters of love and accomplishment in work. if only one nation disarms, it means sorrow and bad luck.

DISASTER—310. See Catastrophe.

DISCHARGED—840. When you dream you are discharged from a job, it foretells you will have good luck in your job, if you will work hard to keep it. If you discharge someone who works for you, you will antagonize a person who may be important to you.

DISCOVERY—529. If you dream you discovered a new place or idea, you will receive a legacy.

DISDAIN—818. See Contempt.

DISEASE—352. (Also see Illness.) To dream of illness portends unhappy situations for you and a warning that you can make them better if you try hard enough.

DISGRACE—945. If you dream you did something disgraceful, you will experience some friction in dealing with one of the opposite sex.

DISGUISE—061. If you dream you or someone else is wearing a disguise, someone may be trying to hurt you and you might prevent this by being completely sincere in dealing with others.

DISHES—369. To dream of new dishes is a sign of being lucky in affairs of the heart. Dishes which are dirty and broken are a sign of unhappiness in love.

DISHONESTY—903. To dream of someone else being dishonest means you will have to change to new plans. If you are dishonest, you may suffer illness or accident.

DISINFECTANT—765. To sprinkle or spray disinfectant signifies you will be with someone who has a contagious disease, but you will not become infected if you take care.

DISINHERITED—238. If you dream of you or someone else being disinherited, it portends happy marriage and a lessening of things which cause tension.

DISTANCE—405. To dream that whatever occurs is away off in the distance signifies that things you desire now may be a long time in materializing.

DISTILLERY—736. If you dream you are in a distillery, you will make a worthwhile change in your business.

DISTRESS—910. If you dream you or someone else is in distress, you will turn your failures into successes, and may also suffer a temporary ailment.

DITCH—742. To dream of a ditch foretells you will overcome hardships and increase your earnings.

DIVIDENDS—161. If you receive dividends from stocks, you have to be very careful not to trust everyone who appears to be your friend.

DIVING BELL—984. To be inside a diving bell shows you will not have your love reciprocated. If you dream you see a diving bell, you will suffer stock market losses but will later regain them.

DIVORCE—405. (Also see Corespondent.) If you dream of a divorce, you will have misunderstandings with the person you love.

DIZZINESS—620. (Also see Vertigo.) To dream of being dizzy means you are going on a pleasant trip by airplane.

DOCK—159. (Also see Pier.) To dream of being on a loading dock for ships is an omen of happiness, health and financial reward. To see the dock while you are on board a ship predicts a happy surprise for you.

DOCTOR—631. If you consult a doctor in your dream, you will meet with an accident. To enjoy social life with a doctor signifies good fun and better financial conditions.

DOCUMENT—814. Any legal document in your dream predicts bad news.

DOGS – 756. (Also see Rabies.) A barking dog is a sign you will become good friends with some people you now distrust. A dog biting you means quarreling with your loved one, but if you dream you overcame the dog you will receive good luck. If you are scared by a huge dog, you will be in love with a person of high importance. A friendly female dog shows success to you in your job and your love life.

DOLE – 763. See Relief.

DOLLAR – 329. (Also see Bank Notes.) A silver dollar in your dream means good luck.

DOMINOES – 064. To see dominoes in your dream is a sign of poor investments in stock which you can avoid by being careful.

DONATION – 314. See Charity, also Contribution.

DONKEY – 941. To get a donkey as a gift is a sign of business success. If you are kicked or thrown by a donkey, you will have some quarrels with the one you love.

DOOR – 820. An open door shows your hopes will be fulfilled. A closed door predicts you overlooked an opportunity to get ahead.

DOORBELL – 370. (Also see Buzzer.) If you dream you press a doorbell button, you will have some stimulating adventures with the one you love.

DOOR LOCK – 599. See Padlock.

DOPE – 375. To dream you are taking dope or giving it to someone else is a warning for you to courageously meet challenges in your life or you might otherwise weaken.

DOUGHNUTS – 559. Doughnuts seen in your dream are a prediction you will go on long and pleasurable travels.

DOVE – 602. A white dove is a sign of peaceful family life and good business. A flock of doves in your dream means an airplane trip for you.

DOWRY – 371. To dream of a girl's wedding dowry is a sign of a marriage that will be financially sound.

DRAFT – 880. To dream you are being drafted by the military services portends you will enjoy working at a job where you can use your hands.

DRAGON—329. If you dream of a dragon, you will meet people of high aristocray and will achieve wealth.

DRAGON FLY—629. To dream of this insect signifies a long trip on the ocean.

DRAPERIES—071. To dream of lovely draperies on windows and doors is a sign you will have a life of ease. Old, torn draperies show you will have financial losses.

DREAMS—859. If you have a dream within a dream, your hopes will be realized soon.

DRESS—730. To dream of seeing nice dresses in the window of a shop, or being worn by a woman, signifies you will achieve high position in social and political circles.

DRILLING—612. To see servicemen, in military drill, in your dream is an omen of your getting a chance to qualify for a higher position.

DRINKING—824. (Also see Liquor, Whiskey, Wine.) If you dream someone is drinking, you will have a chance to get higher education. If you are drinking heavily, you will meet some people who might take advantage of you if you are not careful about finances, but if you drink only small amounts in your dream, you will be able to handle a job which calls for use of your brains as well as your hands.

DRIVING—021. To dream you are driving an automobile in leisurely manner portends you will be happy and meet with success in a moderate manner. If you speed on the roadway, or drive the car into something, you will not be too happy in your love life.

DROWNING—995. If you dream you or someone else is drowning, you will be faced with unhappy situations.

DRUGGED—429. To be drugged and unconscious in your dream means someone is trying to hurt your chances of getting ahead.

DRUGGIST—221. (Also see Prescription.) To dream you are a druggist portends you will have to work harder but not make more money.

DRUGSTORE—315. To dream you are buying something in a drugstore means you will get good returns on your investments.

DRUM—614. (Also see Tom-Tom.) A drum which is played in your dream shows you will succeed in carrying out original ideas. If you hear the muffled beat of a drum, someone you love will meet with an unhappy event.

DRUNKARD—032. To dream you see a drunkard predicts financial losses. If you are the one who is drunk, you will have to guard against reckless living if you want to have good luck.

DUCHESS—974. A duchess with a tiara on her head is a sign of social advancement for you.

DUCK—310. Ducks in your dream, especially if they are quacking, predict good things will happen to you.

DUEL—804. See Sword.

DUET—592. To hear vocal or musical duets in your dream is an omen of good times with married friends, also spare time for you to develop hobbies.

DUKE—881. To see or talk to a duke shows you will be raised to a higher position and better social conditions.

DUMP—325. If you dream of a place where trash is dumped, you will have to assume responsibilities for other people.

DUNGEON—592. If you dream you are locked up in a dungeon, you will be visited by rich relatives who usually irritate you.

DUSK—818. To dream that dusk is settling, at the end of the day, predicts disappointment in your work enterprises.

DUST—352. To see dust in your dream is an unpleasant omen. You will have disappointing times with friends, the opposite sex, in-laws.

DWARF—945. (Also see Midget.) Dwarfs appearing in your dream are an omen of your being able to deal with problems, and to enjoy good health. If the dwarfs have over-large heads, someone is trying to hurt you.

DYEING—061. Whether you dream of dyeing cloth or clothes or your hair, you will receive prestige in social life.

DYNAMITE—693. See Explosion.

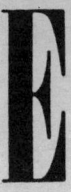

ELEPHANT

EAGERNESS — 039. If you are rushing to do things or get things, in your dream, you will need to curb your enthusiasm and enjoy life with more calmness.

EAGLE — 756. To see an eagle in a high place or flying high predicts good results in business and friendship. If an eagle grabs you and flies away with you, you have to guard against possible accidents. Baby eagles in a nest are a sign of prosperity to come to you through your attention to work.

EARRINGS — 283. If you wear earrings, you will be lucky in a lottery. To see someone else with earrings, you may have a stimulating time with one of the opposite sex.

EARS — 405. To dream of people's ears being conspicuous, you will receive a letter with surprising news. If you pull someone's ears, you will argue with your employer.

EARTH — 736. If you dream of seeing the planet Earth through the lens of a telescope, you will receive a legacy which may take a long time to collect.

EARTHQUAKE — 910. To dream of an earthquake foretells you may lose your job or business but you will conquer your difficulties.

EASTER — 742. To dream of Easter is an omen of a change of work which will be good for you.

EATING — 161. (Also see Appetite.) To eat alone in a dream is a sign of bad luck coming to you. If you eat with guests, your luck will be good and you will enjoy life.

ECHO — 948. If you dream you hear the echo of your own voice, you will have some difficulties with the object of your affection.

ECLIPSE—450. See Darkness.

EDITOR—620. To dream you are an editor means you are frustrated in your work and personal life. If you dream of someone else being an editor, you will have confusion in handling your accounts and living within your budget.

EDUCATION—159. If you dream you have to struggle with your studies, you will be successful in future endeavors but not in educational fields.

EGGS—233. (Also see Omelet.) If you eat eggs in your dream you will enjoy good health. If you find fresh eggs in a hen's roost, you will gain financially through your efforts.

EGOTIST—018. To dream you are speaking to an egotist signifies you will resort to bragging about yourself in order to cover up lack of self-confidence.

ELECTION—439. If you dream you are elected to office, you will suffer set-backs in business. If you attend an election celebration, you may be offered a government job which could turn out to be a big one if you work hard at it.

ELECTRICITY—305. To dream you keep switching the electricity on and off means you will gain recognition from others. If there is a short-circuit in the electric wires, you will lose some property.

ELEPHANT—730. If you dream of elephants, you will prosper in your work and have a happy home life.

ELEVATOR—241. If you ride to the top of a tall building in an elevator filled with people, you can look forward to good luck. If the elevator is headed downward, you will have to watch out for unwise investments and for worries about your love life.

ELK—835. To see or hunt an elk in your dream means you will be attractive to the opposite sex.

ELOPEMENT—329. Whether you or someone else elopes, in your dream, you will have to face facts and not let your imagination get out of hand.

ELOQUENCE—631. If you dream you listen to an eloquent speech-maker or preacher, you must not be influenced by people who pay you compliments but do not mean it.

EMBALMING—757. See Corpse, also Undertaker.

EMBANKMENT—008. To see a high embankment means you should delay new plans for awhile and not let people rush you into them.

EMBASSY—314. See Ambassador.

EMBEZZLER—542. If you dream you or someone else is an embezzler, you will go through confusion about problems and should not discuss them with anyone who does not understand them.

EMBLEM—714. To see or wear an emblem is a prediction of faraway travels for you.

EMBRACE—019. See Hug.

EMBROIDERY—743. If you see someone doing fine embroidery work, you may go through some flirtations and enjoy their stimulation. If you are doing the embroidering, someone you trust is trying to harm you.

EMERALD—952. Whether you see or wear emerald jewelry in your dream, it shows you will come into unexpected money and you will enjoy social life with people of high position.

EMIGRANT—795. If you dream of emigrants coming into this country, you will move to a new place and will have a better life. If you emigrate to another country, you may be in financial stress.

EMPEROR—013. See King, Queen, Throne.

EMPLOYER—671. See Boss.

EMPLOYMENT—876. To dream you are being employed in a new job, or that you are offering employment to others, means you will soon enjoy prosperity.

ENCYCLOPEDIA—592. If you look up some subject in an encyclopedia, you will find it easy to express yourself in writing.

ENDOWMENT—014. To dream you are giving an endowment to a college or other institution, or that you are put in charge of an endowment, predicts you will start new plans which will be too difficult for you to manage yourself.

ENEMY—339. To dream you have made a friend out of an enemy, or that you have succeeded in overcoming him or her, shows you will soon have better luck. If the enemy overcomes you, you may be in some danger and should avoid taking any risks.

ENERGY—125. If you dream you are full of vim, vigor and pep, you may make some foolish mistake because of pride.

ENGAGEMENT—436. To dream you are engaged, or are breaking an engagement, you will not encourage members of the opposite sex to be your close friends.

ENGINE—329. If you dream of an engine, whether it is quiet or in motion, is a sign of your ability to succeed in whatever work you choose.

ENGINEER—086. To dream of being part of the engineering profession is an omen of personal and financial success coming to you if you work hard for it.

ENTERTAINMENT—712. To dream of entertaining people in your home or at some interesting place, is a sign of too much extravagance on your part, which you would do well to curb.

ENVELOPE—757. If you address an envelope, you will soon have a meeting with the person to whom you addressed it. If you seal an envelope, you will have a good marriage.

ENVY—291. See Jealousy.

EPIDEMIC—089. To dream you are caught in an epidemic of disease, it is a prophecy that your health may need looking after by a doctor.

EPILEPSY—098. See Fit.

EPITAPH—289. If you read epitaphs on gravestones, you will be interested in developing your mind through library and research channels.

EQUATOR—538. To dream you are crossing the equator, you will be worried about indecisions which you find hard to solve regarding relatives and money matters.

EQUESTRIAN—334. See Horseback.

ERRANDS—690. If someone sends you on an errand, in your dream, the one you love may leave you if you do not act more unselfishly.

If someone comes to you on an errand, you will want to engage in politics.

ERROR—450. See See Mistake.

ESCALATOR—018. To dream of going up an escalator means you will have new friends, see and do new things. If the escalator goes down, you will have a chance to turn a disappointment into a success if you work hard at it.

ESTATE—374. If you dream of being on or owning an estate, you need to face facts and not keep on deluding yourself with fanciful day dreams.

ETCHINGS—668. To see etchings in your dream is a sign of advancement in your work and social life with people of good taste.

ETHER—711. See Anesthesia.

ETIQUETTE—959. If you disregard the rules of etiquette, you will need to develop more self-confidence if you want to succeed. If you dream you are over-doing your observance of etiquette rules, you will be disappointed in some people you regard as friends.

EUNUCHS—182. To dream of seeing eunuchs in a harem signifies you may break some personal ties with people and will be unhappy about it.

EVANGELIST—469. An evangelist in your dream is a sign of sickness and perhaps mental tension.

EVE—804. See Adam and Eve.

EVENING—604. To dream it is a beautiful moonlight evening, you will be happily in love with someone. To wish on an evening star, in your dream, you can look forward to a pleasurable future.

EVERGLADES—308. If you walk through the everglades, you will suffer disappointment through the one you love.

EVERGREEN—430. To dream of an evergreen tree or shrub is a portent of loyal friendships.

EVICTION—314. If you are evicted from your home, in your dream, you will go through money worries but they will be overcome by you.

EVIL SPIRITS—536. If you dream of evil spirits, you will be faced with difficult situations in putting through your plans, but you will clear this up by trying a new path of endeavor.

EXECUTION—541. To dream of witnessing an execution predicts a disease which you will eventually get over.

EXERCIZE—296. See Gymnasium.

EXILE—620. If you dream you are exiled to a strange country, you will find it hard to make people understand you and you will have to fight hard to overcome troubles.

EXPEDITION—187. To dream of an expedition to faraway lands, you will be engaged in profitable enterprises and will travel a long way.

EXPLOSION—780. If you dream of explosives being used for beneficial purposes, you will be lucky in future earnings and in love. If explosives are used to destroy things or people, you will be worried about finances and love.

EXTRAVAGANCE—801. To spend extravagantly in your dream is a sign of malicious gossip in which you are one of the victims.

EYE—480. Just to see eyes floating around in your dream shows you will be tempted to invest in the stock market and will be successful in a small way.

EYEBROWS—807. Heavy eyebrows in a dream signify you will win the respect of others. Very thin eyebrows show you will have to work hard if you want to succeed in your work and in your relationship with the opposite sex.

EYEGLASSES—604. (Also see Optician.) To see your loved one wearing eyeglasses means you may be separated from that person. If you wear eyeglasses in your dream, good luck will come in new plans you undertake.

EYE PATCH—614. To dream of an eye patch signifies interesting travel in strange countries.

FROG

FABRICS—530. If you dream of seeing and handling lovely materials, you can find pleasure in doing something artistic with your hands.

FACE—298. To dream of your own face in a mirror or other reflection is a sign of unpleasant events. To see a pretty face means interesting new friendships. Ugly faces mean serious accident or other happenings. Washing your face in a dream shows you will seek to make amends for some of your sins.

FAINTING—903. To dream of helping someone who has fainted, or you yourself have fainted, signifies you will choose wrong friends.

FAIRY—692. If you dream you were turned into a fairy, it is a warning that you have to act properly so people will not criticize you. If you have a pleasant dream of seeing fairies, you will find happiness in children around you.

FAITH—541. (Also see Religion.) If you show faith in people, you will realize fulfillment of something you desire.

FAITHFULNESS—129. To dream that your mate (or your sweetheart) is faithful to you, is a sign of a pleasant future and money.

FAKE—415. Whether you dream of a thing or a person being a fake, it foretells you will meet antagonism from friends if you are going to take any chances in your personal or business matters.

FALLING—305. To dream of falling is a prediction of unhappiness in love and perhaps an illness.

FALSEHOOD—621. See Lie.

FAME—508. If you dream you are famous, you will suffer some disappointment in your life. If you see a famous person, good luck will come to you from someone you don't expect.

FAMILY—859. If you dream of a big, joyful family, you will go alone on a vacation. To see a poverty-stricken family portends there will be sudden changes in the political scene.

FAN—384. Any dream involving a fan signifies unpleasant situations in your love life.

FAN DANCER—009. If you watch an exotic fan dancer, you will get what you are after, but it may not be a worthwhile thing.

FANGS—937. An animal's fangs seen in a dream means quarrels with relatives and it might be wise for you to leave the scene.

FARM—998. To dream of a farm that is prosperous is an omen of good health and luck coming to you. If the farm is rundown, you will have financial losses.

FASHION—575. If you dream you are not dressed in style, you will have to work very hard. If you are dressed in high fashion, you will receive social invitations from interesting people.

FASTING—935. If you dream you went on a fast, you will find peace in setting to rights something you did that displeased or hurt others.

FATNESS—307. See Obesity.

FATE—014. To dream that fate has either brought you something good, or was against you, means the same thing. You will be lucky in love and in the things you desire.

FATHER—139. If you dream of your father, you will change your residence. If you dream you are the father of children, you will have a change for the better in your work and in money matters. If you are wrongly accused of being a father, you will have family quarrels.

FAUCET—330. A new water faucet means you will get unexpected happiness. If you dream of a leaky faucet, it is a warning not to betray a secret as that could bring you bad luck.

FAWN—109. To dream of seeing this graceful animal means you will meet with disappointment in the one you love.

FEAR—638. If you dream of undergoing fear, or trying to calm the fears of someone else, you will have to make decisions on how to handle your affairs and to get along with people in order to avoid unhappiness.

FEAST—592. See Banquet.

FEATHERS—937. To dream of feathers flying in the air, or on a big bird, you will fulfill your aspirations and will be financially rewarded.

FEET—069. If you dream of walking in your bare feet, or of seeing many feet walking along, you will undergo disappointments before you achieve what you want. Bathing your feet is a sign of overcoming anxieties.

FENCE—231. To dream of climbing or building a fence is a prediction that you will find satisfaction in your love as well as in work. If the fence falls down, you will quarrel with the one you love.

FERRY—244. If you dream of riding on a ferry boat, you will be well paid for whatever work you do.

FEUD—360. To dream you participate in a feud is a sign of peace and happiness for you.

FEVER—807. To have a fever in a dream is a prophecy of disappointments in the course of true love.

FIELD—231. To see one or more people or yourself running across a field signifies you will be worried and perhaps have legal troubles. If you see animals in a field, you will not have to work so hard.

FIEND—618. If you see a fiend in your dream, it is a warning that you will have to apologize for something you did to hurt another.

FIFE—451. If you dream you play this instrument, you will quarrel with the one you love, but if drums accompany your fife playing, you will be blessed with a clear conscience.

FIGS—932. Whether you pick figs off a tree, or eat them, you will run into social difficulties with people you like.

FIGHT—712. (Also see Quarrel.) If you dream you are in a fist fight, or others are fighting, you will do things to make people respect you.

FIGHTING COCK—392. To dream you are watching a cock fight, some envious person will try to take some things from you. If you put the cock into the fighting ring, you will receive some financial gains.

FIGURES—276. (Also see Accounts.) If you dream of being confused with figures that do not add up, you will compete with someone who will try to win over you.

FILBERTS—513. To eat these nuts in your dream portends you will have harsh words with people who are close to you. To buy filberts means you will go on a short vacation.

FILING CABINET—709. If you dream you are using a filing cabinet in your work, you will have good luck. If a letter or paper is lost in the file, you have to guard against lowering your high standards.

FILLY—102. To see a young horse in your dream is a sign of your being able to have interesting hobbies and perhaps earn extra money in spare time.

FILTH—693. If you dream you are in filthy surroundings, or with peope who have filthy minds, you are warned to be on the lookout for false friends.

FINS—805. To cut the fins off a fish means you will lose a small article and will have to search long to find it. To dream you see a fish waving its fins, you will be rid of some work you do not like.

FINANCIER—132. If you dream you are a financier, you will have to be more cautious in handling your finances. To dream you meet a financier on friendly terms, you will get good results from trading.

FINGER—840. (Also see Thumb.) To cut your finger in a dream, or to point it accusingly at some person, is a sign of discontentment over friends you trusted.

FINGER BOWL—594. If you dream of using a finger bowl after a fancy meal, you will be annoyed at friends who think you are boasting. If you drink from the finger bowl, you will get some unexpected money.

FINGERNAILS—693. To dream you are having a professional

manicure, you will have to cut down on your spending. If you trim your own nails, you will join with others to help the community. If you put red polish on your nails, some people will be scornful toward you. If you cut the nail down to the quick, you will undergo troubles which will work out all right later on.

FINGERPRINTS — 346. If you dream the police are fingerprinting you, you will be unexpectedly befriended in troublesome matters. If you see fingerprints on the wall, you will have money worries.

FIRE — 291. (Also see Arson, Blaze.) To dream you enjoy watching a fire shows you will have bad luck. If you dream you enjoy watching a fire and it does not burn you, you will find life enjoyable.   If you set the fire, you will have a slight accident. To put out the fire shows you will be able to win out over unkind people who want to hurt you.

FIRE ALARM — 930. If you dream you turn in a fire alarm, you will enjoy more money soon.

FIREARMS — 678. See Guns.

FIRE BOAT — 524. If you see the fire boat in action with the water spraying from the hose, you may need to consult a doctor about some tensions you will undergo.

FIRE ENGINE — 450. To see any fire apparatus on its way to a fire, you will have good luck. If the apparatus is returning from a fire, you will have hard luck.

FIRE ESCAPE — 224. If you are on a fire escape, you will be nagged by people to pay back debts you owe them.

FIREFLY — 518. If you dream you see these lit-up insects, you will have to be on your best behavior to avoid others criticizing you.

FIREMAN — 034. If you dream of being a fireman, you will receive honor by some leading people. To dream you are driving some fire apparatus, you will be lucky in overcoming a slight accident.

FIREPLACE — 617. If you sit in front of a burning fireplace, you will have a pleasant home life. But if there is no fire, you may have some disappointment in love.

FIREWORKS — 387. To watch or set off fireworks is an omen of petty annoyances in social life as well as in your work plans.

FIRST AID—561. If you dream you give first aid to someone who is hurt, you will be offered a position which carries prestige.

FISH—492. (Also see Aquarium.) To dream of catching or seeing or eating fish is a prophecy of accident or fatal illness in your family or to a close friend.

FISHHOOK—803. If you dream you are putting bait on a fishhook, you will be lucky in love. If the fishhook catches in your body, you will suffer troubles with relatives and in money matters.

FIT—613. To see a person going through an epileptic fit, or an animal in a fit, portends family annoyances as well as irritability over your work.

FLAG—056. (Also see Half Mast.) Whether you watch the flag flying, or are raising it or saluting it, you will meet with pleasant results in your work and will receive acclaim from others.

FLAMINGO—419. To see this bird flying in your dream means you will go through some pleasant and stimulating occurrences. If the bird is standing or walking, you will have worries.

FLASHLIGHT—738. If you use a flashlight outdoors, you will widen your social circle. If you use a flashlight indoors, you must resist temptation to do things which are not up to highest standard.

FLATULENCE—341. See Belch.

FLEAS—832. If you dream you are bitten by fleas, you will worry about keeping out of debt. If you are a flea and jumping around, you must be cautious about new business matters. To kill a flea means you will have good luck.

FLEET—642. See Battleship.

FLESH—802. To dream of seeing or touching human flesh is a sign of trouble with one of the opposite sex.

FLIRT—261. To dream of meeting an attractive flirt is a prophecy of an exciting but short love affair. If the flirt is not attractive, you will be able to better yourself financially.

FLOAT—480. To dream of stepping from a boat onto a float is a prediction of a friendly settlement of a quarrel. If you dream you are lying on a float, wearing a bathing suit, you will hear unpleasant news.

FLOOD—002. Any dream about a flood is a warning for you to look out for people who might want to harm you.

FLOOR—448. To dream you are sweeping a floor indicates you will go on a pleasant trip. If you lie down on the floor, you will be made unhappy by some person who is close to you. To put a new floor in the house predicts good returns from business.

FLORIST—124. (Also see Flowers.) If you dream you are in a florist's shop, you will go through a love affair which may not turn out well.

FLOUNDER—539. To dream you are catching or eating a flounder, you will be disappointed about some new plans you have in mind.

FLOWERS—096. (Also see Bouquet, Florist, Garden.) To dream of garden flowers is a sign of good luck. If you see wild flowers, it forecasts some stimulating happenings. A bouquet with a lovely fragrance means you will hear from a relative who is away. If the bouquet is old and wilted, it is a sign of serious illness.

FLU—122. See Grippe.

FLUTE—795. If you dream you are playing the flute, you may become involved in an unpleasant situation. The sound of a flute is a sign of a happy home life.

FLY—683. If flies annoy you in your house or outdoors, or are stuck on fly-paper, you will have to be patient and put up with people and situations that are annoying. To kill flies with a swatter means you will have good luck.

FLYING—514. To dream you are flying in the air, like a bird, forecasts difficulty in putting into motion many ideas which are not always possible to fulfill, but if you are flying in an airplane, you will have luck with new plans.

FOG—079. If you dream you are in a fog on land or sea, you will have to go through some troublesome times about yourself and family. If the fog lifts, you will succeed in new undertakings.

FOGHORN—692. To hear a foghorn in your dream is an omen of quickly overcoming any tense situations you may have.

FOLIAGE—268. If the leaves of any growing plants or trees are in green condition, you will find happiness through love, but if the foliage is brown or wormy, your love life will be disappointing.

FOLK SONGS—732. To hear folk songs, sung by others or you, means you will spend happy times with friends and relatives.

FOOD—803. See Frozen Foods, Refrigerator, or various foods listed under their categories.

FOOL—324. To dream you are being a fool is a sign of meeting interesting new friends. If someone else is being a fool, it portends success in your work. If you express your disapproval of someone acting like a fool, you will not be popular with others.

FOOTBALL—619. If you watch a game in your dream, you will need to be careful in picking friends. If you play football, you will get unexpected money.

FOOTLIGHTS—521. (Also see Stage.) To see a row of footlights, either from the audience or in back of them from the stage, you must guard against believing everyone you meet. If the footlights go out, you will meet with a mishap.

FOREHEAD—673. If you see your own forehead in a dream, you will undergo some hardships before things get better. If you smooth someone's forehead, or see a wrinkled forehead, you will find satisfaction in home life and money matters.

FOREIGNER—895. To meet a foreigner signifies good luck in receiving unexpected finance to help you in business.

FOREMAN—703. If you dream you are a foreman in a factory, or on a jury, you can look for good news that could mean more money to you.

FOREST—806. (Also see Ranger.) To dream you are alone, or scared, or lost in a forest, you will be unhappy over broken promises.

FORGERY—973. To dream you are a forger, or someone forged your name to a document, is a warning to beware of strangers.

FORTUNE—014. See Legacy.

FORTUNE TELLER—419. If you have your fortune told in your dream, whether it is a good or bad fortune, you will have success with the opposite sex.

FOUNDLING—351. To dream you find an abandoned baby and arrange to have it cared for is a forecast of your life being peaceful.

FOUNDRY—285. See Factory.

FOUNTAIN—580. A fountain which is squirting water is a sign of a satisfactory marriage. If the fountain is dry, you will meet with disappointments.

FOWL—369. (Also see Hen.) If you dream of any fowl (chicken, duck, goose) you will be able to take your place with people of high prestige. .

FOX—801. To see a fox in your dream signifies you may suffer through false friends. If you are on a horse during a fox hunt, you will soon get invited to a lovely party.

FOX TERRIER—514. If you dream of seeing this dog, you will do well in money matters but may get into a state of worrisome tension.

FRAGRANCE—431. See Aroma.

FRAME—632. To put a picture in a frame is a prophecy of your being able to handle any new job or project you undertake.

FRAME-UP—712. See Pilot.

FRANKFURTER—043. If you eat frankfurters at a picnic, you will succeed in solving your problems. Frankfurters eaten at a roadside stand, or at home, mean you will get into arguments with people you usually like.

FRATERNITY—239. To dream of being a member of a fraternity, sorority, or a similar organization, shows you are going to be with people of high position.

FRAUD—680. If you practice fraud on someone, you are going to lose a friend. If the fraud is practiced on you, you must not be too gullible in trusting others.

FRECKLES—402. To dream you have freckles portends a happy relationship with the opposite sex.

FREIGHT TRAIN—973. If you see or ride in a freight train, your business matters will be easier to handle.

FRICASSEE—217. If you eat fricassee of chicken or veal, you will find it tough going for a while, but all will get better.

FRIEND—665. To dream you are with friends is a sign of good health and money coming to you.

FRIGHT—779. See Fear.

FRITTERS—053. If you eat fritters, you will find stimulating activities with people of both sexes. To dream you are making fritters shows you will undertake more work but not more pay.

FROG—513. To see, hear or eat frogs portends a peaceful and fulfilled life for you, in social and business matters.

FROST—974. To see frost on a window pane signifies you will do things which will make you proud.

FROSTBITE—834. See Chilblains.

FROZEN FOODS—681. If you prepare or eat frozen foods, you will travel to a sunny climate.

FRUIT—311. See various kinds of fruit listed under their categories.

FUGITIVE—971. If you give aid to a fugitive from justice, you will run into financial difficulties. If you dream you are a fugitive, you will have a harsh argument with someone in your family.

FUN—708. (Also see Comedy, Laughter.) To enjoy good innocent fun in a dream forecasts good luck. If the fun is poked at someone, it means problems about health and money.

FUNERAL—306. (Also see Burial, Cemetery, Pallbearer, Undertaker.) To dream of attending a funeral portends death to someone near to you. If you are at your own funeral, there may be some bad happenings in the nation.

FURLOUGH—638. If you dream you have an appointment with someone on furlough, you will enjoy a happy life. If you are on furlough, you will have less to worry about money matters.

FURNACE—114. A furnace with a fire burning in it is a sign of happy social life. If the furnace is cold, you will increase your bank savings.

FURNITURE— 792. See individual articles of furniture in their various listings.

FURROW— 381. (Also see Plow.) If you dream you are planting a straight furrow, it means you will be paid well but will have to work hard. A crooked furrow is a sign that decisions will have to be made.

FURS— 019. If a woman dreams she wears furs, she may be misunderstood by men friends. If a man dreams he wears furs, he is going to enjoy financial profits. If the furs are old and worn out, this means certain recognition and honor will be received.

FURY— 078. See Anger.

FUTURE— 239. If you dream you are planning for the future, you will receive happy news from an old friend.

GONDOLA

GABBING — 680. See Gossiping.

GABLES — 402. To dream of seeing a house with gables means you will travel to new places.

GALE — 973. See Storm.

GALLERY — 217. (Also see Art.) If you dream you are visiting an art gallery is an omen of success in your undertakings. To dream of seeing beautiful old paintings means you will soon meet again an old friend. If the art is modern, you will find new friends a bit disturbing at first.

GALLSTONES — 665. If you dream of suffering with gallstones, you are going to have a happy future even though some worries may crop up.

GALOSHES — 797. (Also see Boots.) To wear galoshes in a dream foretells you will be able to add money to your savings. Galoshes which are too large show financial gain for you. Galoshes which are old and torn show you may be punished for something you neglected to do.

GAMBLING — 053. If you dream of losing money at gambling, you will be able to change your way of life and get into better things. If you win, you will have to be careful not to take unnecessary risks through gambling.

GAMES — 531. See Amusement.

GANG — 311. To dream you are part of a gang, or threatened by a gang, you will find it hard to resist influences which would not be good for you. If you are the head of a gang, your earnings may get lower.

GANGSTER—971. See Criminal.

GARBAGE—807. To dream about garbage is a prophecy that you are going to have big results even though you start out small.

GARDEN—306. (Also see Flowers.) If you dream of a garden blooming with flowers, you will find personal and spiritual happiness. If the garden is full of dead flowers, it means money and social worries.

GARDEN OF EDEN—683. See Eden.

GARDENIA—114. If you dream of this flower, you will be happy with the one you love.

GARGLE—430. To dream of gargling your throat signifies you will have to learn how to get along with certain unpleasant situations and be a sport about them.

GARLIC—729. To use garlic in your food means you will get a letter which will worry you. If you smell the garlic but do not eat it, you will win out above others and take pride in your accomplishment.

GARNET—318. To dream you or someone else is wearing jewelry made of garnets, is an omen of you having to work hard with little pay.

GARRET—018. See Attic.

GARTER—078. Any dream involving a man's or woman's garter is a warning not to take any unnecessary chances.

GAS—319. If you dream you smell gas, keep away from other people's business and stick to your own affairs. If you see a burning gas jet, you may have a love affair with a rich person. To see someone overcome from the gas fumes is an omen of someone trying you in a scandal.

GASH—640. (Also see Cut.) If you dream you or someone else has a gash in the body, you may suffer from hurt feelings and you must guard against losing your temper.

GAS MASK—813. Whether you or another person wears a gas mask in your dream, you will be pestered by people to whom you owe money.

GASOLINE STATION—417. If you buy gasoline in your dream, you will earn more money. If you visit the washroom at the gasoline station, your worries will become less troublesome.

GATE—690. To dream you cannot go through a closed gate means you will be frustrated in new plans, but if the gate is open, you will have good luck in new endeavors.

GAVEL—318. If you or someone else uses a gavel to keep order at a meeting, you must have patience and many small worries will disappear.

GELATIN—296. To eat or see gelatin in any form is a sign of enjoyment of life through the opposite sex and through your work.

GEMS—027. (Also see various gems listed in their alphabetical order.) If you see beautiful gems in your dream, you will have interesting and adventurous events.

GENEALOGY—456. To dream of studying a chart showing your family tree foretells you may be disappointed in the one you love.

GENEROSITY—798. If you dream of being generous to others, you will be raised in your work and you will gain prestige.

GENIE—841. To see any form of a genie in your dream is a prophecy of reward coming to you after you work hard.

GEOGRAPHY—690. Studying books and maps of geography is a sign you will make interesting journeys to distant places.

GERMS—085. (Also see Microbes.) If you dream you fear being contaminated by germs, you will have a visit from someone far away. To study germs through a microscope means you can develop yourself through further studies.

GEYSER—731. If you dream of an active water geyser, you could find interest in some literary work although its rewards might not come too soon.

GHETTO—016. See Slums.

GHOST—194. To meet a ghost in your dream signifies you will have to take a strong stand against people who want to take advantage of you. If you dream the ghost is of a person you know, there may be some slight illness but quick recovery.

GHOUL—797. If you dream of ghouls robbing graves in a cemetery, you will be disappointed in trying to further new plans.

GIANT—892. To dream you are a giant is a sign you must not take chances in investments. If a big giant is hurting smaller people, you will have good news in business ventures.

GIBLETS—403. If you see or eat giblets in a dream, you should seek advice from some wiser and more experienced person than you.

GIFT—934. To get a gift from someone means you will have a happy social life and some luck with money matters. If you give someone a present, you will undertake responsibilities that will turn out well.

GIGGLE—329. If you dream you giggle during serious moments, you will need to guard against going into debt and losing respect from others. If you hear others giggle, you will enjoy interesting social activities.

GIN—614. To drink gin in a dream portends you will get a happy surprise. If other people are drinking gin, you will go through a period of indecision and worry.

GINGER—409. If you dream you smell or eat ginger, you will have some stimulating relationships with people of the opposite sex.

GIRAFFE—680. This long-necked animal, seen in your dream, is an omen of you getting mixed up with the affairs of other people.

GIRDLE—146. See Corset.

GIRL—514. If you dream of a pretty girl, you will find that your love life is not too smooth, but a plain-looking girl in your dream is a sign of you being jilted.

GIRL SCOUT—308. To watch girl scouts going through their activities shows you will soon have your wishes fulfilled.

GLACIER—431. If you see a glacier in your dream, you will take a trip to some cold climate.

GLADIOLUS—786. To dream of seeing this flower means you will consider accepting responsibilities which will mean more money to you.

GLAND—391. If you dream of a swollen gland, you will be annoyed over petty worries.

GLASS—540. (Also see Window.) If you dream you break a glass, your plans of life will undergo change. To see glasses on a bar or a table foretells some flares of temper between you and someone of the opposite sex.

GLASSBLOWER—224. To watch a glassblower means you will rise in your occupation and get more pay.

GLIDER—097. If you dream you are soaring on a glider, you should try to win the confidence of someone in business who can help you to advance.

GLOBE—641. To dream of a globe with a map of the world on it is a sign of interesting journeys for you. If the globe is blank (with no map on it), you will try new hobbies and enjoy them.

GLOVES—419. If you dream of new gloves, you will go on to higher things in your work. Worn, old gloves signify you will need to be careful not to do something embarrassing to yourself.

GLUE—312. To use glue in a dream signifies that many of your plans and work will be temporary. If you spill glude on yourself, you will lose something (perhaps through robbery).

GLUTTON—802. If you dream of someone eating to excess, you will receive many social invitations. If you stuff too much food into yourself, you will meet with success but people might shun you.

GNAWING—310. To dream you gnaw on a bone is a prophecy that you will be your own cause of many small worries.

GNOME—583. If you dream of these unreal little people, you must try to solve annoying problems as soon as possible.

GNAT—672. If you dream of gnats, be overly cautious in new financial investments.

GOAT—012. (Also see Kid.) If you dream of goats grazing, you have to watch out that you do not enter into dealings with anyone who is not of highest morals. To dream of milking a goat means lots of petty annoyances. If you get butted by a goat, you may suffer some gambling losses.

GOATEE—211. (Also see Beard.) If you dream you have a goatee on your chin, you may go through scandalous situations. If someone else has a goatee, be more protective about your health.

GOD—876. To dream you are in the presence of God is a prophecy that you can be of service to others, and will find contentment if you adapt to situations.

GOGGLES—231. If you wear goggles in your dream, you will have some slight arguments with those of the opposite sex.

GOITER—942. If your dream shows you have a goiter, you will suffer annoyances which you can overcome, if you have patience.

GOLD—385. If you are mining gold, you will be annoyed with some family situations. If you see or buy gold in any form, you might lose friends because of your being too stingy.

GOLDENROD—920. If you pick goldenrod in a garden or field, you will learn many fine things from a new friend. To see the goldenrod growing, you must avoid interfering in other people's affairs.

GOLDFISH—498. To dream of seeing goldfish is a warning that some people are trying to meddle in your affairs.

GOLF—418. If you play golf in your dream, you will have a chance to correct some mistake you made.

GONDOLA—396. To dream of a gondola gliding on a canal, you will enjoy traveling with a pleasant companion.

GONG—728. If you hear the clang of a gong in your dream, you might succeed in some former work if you want to go back to it.

GOOSE—342. To dream of a goose, is a warning for you to limit your eating habits so you will not get too fat.

GOSSIPING—503. If you dream of being the object of people's gossiping, or that you are gossiping about someone, you will not have smooth relationships with your friends and will have to guard your temper.

GOULASH—611. To dream you are eating goulash means you will attend a stimulating party.

GOUT—763. If you dream of having the gout, it will be well for you to put off seeing some old friends and to avoid over-indulgence in alcoholic drinks.

GOVERNOR—514. To dream of seeing or meeting the governor of your state, you may buy a new automobile.

GRACE—203. If you say grace before a meal, you will receive a worthwhile gift from an unexpected source.

GRADUATION—387. To be at a graduation in your dream portends you will rise in social and business matters.

GRAIN—918. If you handle bags of grain, you will soon be visited by relatives. If you feed grain to animals, money matters will be eased up.

GRAMMAR—392. To correct someone's use of grammar is a sign of many disappointments, but if you dream someone is correcting your grammar, you will soon have good luck.

GRANDPARENTS—806. If you dream of your grandmother, you will be well off financially. To dream of your grandfather means you will be a respected member of your community.

GRAPES—413. To dream of picking or eating grapes is a sign of satisfaction in your work and being well paid for it.

GRAPEFRUIT—096. To dream of grapefruit signifies you will scatter yourself into too many directions in your personal and business matters.

GRASS—831. If you dream of healthy green grass, you will succeed in finances and in love. If the grass is of poor condition, you will work hard to achieve results.

GRASSHOPPER—071. If you dream of a grasshopper, you will need to seek advice from those who are older and wiser because you will not be able to handle unexpected matters.

GRAVE—669. (Also see Cemetery.) If the grave is covered with fresh flowers, someone is going to break a promise. If the grave is badly tended, you may cause unhappiness to someone by breaking a promise.

GRAVESTONE—332. Any dream of gravestones in a cemetery is a good sign of doing well in work and in friendships.

GRAVY—840. To dream about making gravy is an omen of good luck in a lottery. If you pass the gravy to someone during the meal, you may be careless in overlooking a good chance that could bring you success.

GREASE—733. Whether you get grease over your clothes or other things, or are handling greasy pots and dishes, the prophecy is that you may get impatient and make rash promises.

GREENHOUSE—384. If you dream you are in a greenhouse, your future will be filled with pleasant people and good adventures.

GRENADE—402. See Hand Grenade.

GRIEF—672. If you are stricken with grief, in your dream, you have to be careful about a stomach ailment.

GRINDSTONE—796. To dream you are turning a grindstone means you will have some difficulties in your work, but can overcome them if you apply yourself to solving problems.

GRIPPE—301. If you dream you are ill with grippe, you will soon enjoy pleasant leisurely activities.

GROANING—200. To hear someone groaning signifies your wish may not come true. If you groan, you may have to explain your income tax returns.

GROCERY—128. If you see a grocery in your dream, you will be rewarded for your work and will enjoy a vacation trip.

GROTTO—394. If you dream of a grotto in the earth's depth or in a mountain, or of a religious retreat, you will be able to enjoy good health if you have faith in a cure.

GUARDIAN—087. To dream of being appointed guardian over a young person is a prophecy that you will have financial worries and people will criticize you.

GUEST—602. If you are a guest in someone's home, you will travel to an unfamiliar place. To have guests in your home forecasts you will be rewarded for some high achievement.

GUIDE—542. To dream you are guiding an out-of-town person, or you are being guided, you will have a chance to make money through a new idea.

GUITAR — 450. If you listen to someone playing the guitar, you will be made happy by the one you love. If you play the guitar, you may have your pocket picked if you are not careful.

GULL — 620. To dream of seeing gulls flying at the shore or over water means you will have some pleasant, mild adventures.

GUM — 291. See Chewing Gum.

GUNS — 837. (Also see Revolver.) To dream you aim and hit the mark when you fire a gun, you will succeed in your aspirations. If you fail to hit the mark, you will have difficulties in your plans. If you aim a real or toy gun at anyone, you may have an illness or be unhappy through being jealous of someone. Any other dream of holding or hearing or firing a gun, is a sign of hardship coming your way, if you are not careful in the way you handle your relationship with other people.

GUTTER — 641. If you dream of lying in a gutter, you will have to treat others with consideration in order to avoid dissension. If you clean out a gutter, you will be successful in a new job.

GYMNASIUM — 098. To dream of exercising in a gymnasium, portends you will need to be less fickle in social relationships, if you want your friends to respect you.

GYPSIES — 714. To meet gypsies in your dream means you will have a stimulating love life. Having your fortune told by a gypsy foretells good luck in choosing a mate.

HADDOCK—901. To dream you eat this fish means you may have lovers' quarrels but they will end up peacefully.

HAG—019. If you dream of an old hag, you may have some differences with the one you love.

HAILSTORM—498. A hailstorm in a dream forecasts some unpleasant events.

HAIR—733. (Also see Curls, Permanent Wave, Shampoo, Wig.) If you comb your hair, you will find a way to handle problems. To comb the hair of someone of the opposite sex means that any problems in your love life will soon be settled. If you comb the hair of someone of your own sex, some friend will call on you for assistance. If you get your hair cut, good luck will come to you in some new situation. If you cut someone's hair, you will have to contend with antagonistic people. To braid or set the hair of yourself or another, signifies misunderstanding which will need explanations to get straightened out. If a girl dreams she is dyeing her hair, she will be popular with men, but if a man colors his hair, he will suffer embarrassing situations.

HAIRDRESSER—127. (Also see Permament Wave.) To dream you go to a hairdresser is a warning you must not repeat malicious gossip.

HALF DOLLAR—622. To dream you get shiny new silver half-dollars, you must prepare for disappointments.

HALF MAST—510. If you see a flag at half mast, you will have some unhappy occurrences.

HALITOSIS—099. See Breath.

HALLOWEEN—508. If you dream of having fun on Halloween, you will reach a position of prestige in community activities.

HALLWAY—912. To dream of being alone in a hallway, you will go through worries and pessimism.

HALO—260. To dream you are wearing a halo portends you will go on a long journey. If you remove your halo, you can look forward to good luck in business. If you see someone else with a halo, it is an omen of death to someone you know.

HAM—430. To see or cook or eat a ham, good luck will come to you in business if you work hard.

HAMMER—824. If a woman dreams she is using a hammer, she will find life much easier for her. A man using a hammer should watch out he doesn't meet with an accident.

HAMMOCK—291. To dream of sharing a hammock with someone of the opposite sex is a sign of social activities. If you are alone in the hammock, you may suffer annoyances due to your own selfishness.

HANDS—803. To dream you are holding hands with someone indicates happiness in love and marriage. If you see beautiful hands, or hands that are busy with work, you will enjoy vacationing after hard work. If hands are old and worn, money matters will be easier for you. If hands are waving, that foretells separation from loved ones.

HANDBAG—631. If you dream of a purse filled with money you will soon get more money. If the handbag is being opened and its contents examined, by you or someone else, you may go through some puzzling events but they will be cleared up.

HANDCUFFS—962. To dream you put handcuffs on someone, it foretells a promotion for you. If handcuffs are put on your wrists, you may get criticism from people with whom you work or your own family.

HANDGRENADE—408. If a grenade is thrown in your dream, it is a warning for you to proceed with caution in relationship with people in your work and in personal life.

HANDICRAFTS—390. To dream you are doing skillful work

with your hands forecasts better things are coming to you and you will not have to worry about earning a living.

HANDKERCHIEF—538. To wave your handkerchief at someone is a portent of a pleasant affair of the heart for you. If you wash the handkerchief, you may suffer financial loss. If you blow your nose or wipe your face with a handkerchief, you will earn more money.

HANDSPRING—412. If you dream of turning handsprings, you should concentrate on the work you are doing, also be careful in how you behave in company of the opposite sex.

HANDWRITING—814. To dream you are trying to decipher an illegible handwriting means you will get good results in business.

HANGAR—388. If you are in a hangar that is empty of any airplanes, you will be annoyed at small disappointments. If there are planes in the hangar, your money matters will be bettered.

HANGING—940. To dream you are watching a person being hanged, you will be asked to give someone an alibi in a legal case.

HANGOVER—453. If a single woman dreams she is undergoing a hangover, she should be cautious about dealing with men. If a man or a married person dreams of a hangover, money matters will become less worrisome.

HARBOR—012. If you are on a ship that is leaving a harbor, you will enjoy traveling to a faraway place. A ship coming into a harbor is a sign of your ability to pay back financial or social debts.

HARE—268. See Rabbit.

HAREM—304. If a man dreams he is keeping a harem of women, he will have to face critical gossip from others. If a girl dreams she is a member of a harem, the course of her love may not run too smoothly.

HARLOT—714. See Prostitute.

HARMONICA—291. If you play or hear a harmonica, you will have a happy love relationship.

HARNESS—797. To put a harness on a horse or other animal shows you will be able to succeed in some new ventures.

117

HARP—086. If you dream you are playing a harp, you will find solace through the spiritual part of your nature. To listen to someone playing a harp forecasts you will receive a good favor from a friend. If the wind blowing through the harp strings produces a lovely tune, you will find contentment with the opposite sex.

HARPOON—533. To dream of a harpoon flung at a whale or other fish or animal signifies improvement in finances and way of life. If the harpoon strikes your body, you will suffer financial loss.

HARPSICHORD—819. If classical music is being played on this instrument, you may expect happiness through love. If jazz music is played, you will be confronted with confusing situations.

HARVEST—617. To dream of reaping a plentiful harvest foretells good general conditions in your life. If there is too lean a harvest, you will have business complications.

HASH—891. To make or eat hash is a sign of small unsatisfactory conditions arising in your life, which you can straighten out with patience.

HAT—329. (Also see Cap.) If you dream you wear a hat too big for your head, you are warned to avoid indiscreet behavior. A hat that is too small forecasts disappointment in love. If you dream the wind blows your hat off, you will have small business worries. If you buy a new hat, you will enjoy good luck.

HATCHET—847. To dream of sharpening a hatchet means you will earn more money. If you split logs or cut kindling wood with the hatchet, your family conditions will be made comfortable.

HATE—530. If you dream someone hates you, you will have better rewards for your work and in social matters. If you hate another, it portends you will go through depressing happenings.

HAUGHTINESS—429. If you dream you are being haughty toward anyone, you will have temporary bad luck. If someone snubs you, you will soon have fun-filled times.

HAWK—689. To dream of a flying hawk is a sign of good opportunities coming for your business improvement. If the hawk is not flying, you will be disappointed over some events.

HAY—450. If you dream you are making hay while the sun shines, you will suffer money setbacks. If you make hay during cloudy weather, you will get some unexpected money. To dream of being in a hayloft portends pleasurable love affairs.

HAY FEVER—239. To dream you are a victim of hay fever, you should consult your physician to safeguard your health.

HEAD—096. If you dream you see a head without a body, you will have to use calmness and intelligence to tackle new situations in your life.

HEADACHE—215. To dream of having a headache is a prophecy that you will succeed with new plans, provided you do not tell others about your work or your financial situation.

HEAD HUNTER—193. If you are captured by head hunters, it is a sign that you must avoid friends who are not of highest standard, also you should apologize for anything you feel has hurt another.

HEADLIGHTS—510. To dream that headlights are coming to you, from a car or train, you will have to use great care in deciding how to avoid something that could cause you harm.

HEADSTONE—438. See Gravestone.

HEALTH—220. If you dream you are concerned about your health, or are doing things to maintain good health, you will find happiness in your future.

HEARSE—215. To dream you are inside a hearse, you will soon take a business trip. If you ride with the driver of a hearse, you will need to assume more responsibilities.

HEART ATTACK—418. See Apoplexy.

HEARTH—616. See Fireplace.

HEAT—094. (Also see Steam.) If you are uncomfortable from the heat, in your dream, you will need to make amends to someone you hurt through something you said or did.

HEAVEN—502. To dream you died and went to heaven portends you will have to do new and harder work, but will be better paid.

HEDGES—641. If you dream you are clipping a hedge, you will enjoy better luck in the future. If you jump over the hedge, you will not find things too easy for you until some later time.

HEIR — 937. See Legacy.

HELL — 672. To dream of hell forecasts better days for you as far as income is concerned, but you may not get along too well with neighbors.

HELMET — 812. To dream of wearing a helmet forecasts good health. If you see soldiers wearing helmets, you may need to get medical advice about an ailment.

HELP — 757. If you dream someone is calling for help, you will soon be in a situation where you will ask for help and you will receive it. If you dream you are calling for help, your financial situation will improve.

HEM — 308. To dream you are sewing a hem on a garment indicates you will achieve good results by being a competent worker.

HEMORRHAGE — 941. To dream of excessive bleeding, whether from your body or someone else's, it forecasts you must not work too hard.

HEMORRHOIDS — 748. If you dream you are suffering with piles, you have to be cautious about staying away from anyone with an infectious disease and from any physical danger hazards.

HEN — 390. (Also see Fowl.) If you feed hens, your family life will undergo some annoyances which will be cleared up. To dream you see a hen sitting on eggs means you will be financially better off. To pluck a hen's feathers indicates you will go on a spending spree. If you kill a hen, you can expect a surprise visitor. If the hen is mothering her brood of chicks, you may encounter family quarrels.

HERBS — 679. To plant or smell or eat herbs in a dream is a prophecy of new and stimulating things happening to you and the people you love.

HERMAPHRODITE — 032. See Homosexual.

HERMIT — 394. If you dream of seeing a hermit in his retreat, you will be able to solve annoying problems, but if you are a hermit, you will have to overcome your tendency to raise too much fuss over trifling things others say and do.

HERNIA — 018. See Rupture.

HERO, HEROINE— 226. If you dream of doing some heroic act, you will suffer criticism from others about trivial things you said or did. If you watch someone else perform a deed of heroism, you will profit by new business ventures.

HERRING—691. If you buy salted or smoked herring, you will find some of your friends being suspicious of you. To eat the herring foretells you may incur some criticism because of too much drinking of liquor.

HICCOUGH—008. To dream you are a victim of hiccoughing is a sign you must be more temperate in drinking liquor.

HIDES—127. If you dream about animal hides, you are going to be the guest of a rich person on a vacation trip.

HIEROGLYPHICS—487. If you dream you are deciphering the inscriptions or hieroglyphics on old Egyptian stones, you are capable of coming up with new ideas which will bring you recognition.

HIGH SCHOOL—632. To dream you are attending high school classes, is a prophecy of a stimulating but perhaps not successful affair of the heart.

HILL—531. If you climb a hill, you will succeed in your undertakings. To sit or stand on a hilltop means comfortable financial conditions.

HIPS—739. To dream of seeing the naked hips of someone of the opposite sex forecasts many annoying worries.

HIPPOPOTAMUS—672. If you view this animal in a zoo, you will find some of your friends boring to you. If you see the animal in its native place, it is a warning to look out for possible accidents.

HISS—415. To dream you are hissing a speaker or an actor is a sign of you being treated with disdain by some people. If you are the one who is being hissed, you can look forward to better results with your work.

HISTORY—780. To study history in your dream means you will have a chance to better yourself, if you use your good sense and have patience to wait for the right time.

HITCHHIKING—443. (Also see Thumb.) If you dream of being a hitchhiker, you will be scorned by others, if you are not more independent in looking out for yourself. If you pick up a rider while you are driving on a road, you will have to pay your bills to avoid trouble.

HIVE—757. To see a bee hive in your dream means you will be rid of present worries. If you upset the hive and let the bees escape, you will be beset by new worries.

HIVES—589. If you dream you are suffering with this skin condition, you will be able to get rid of annoying worries if you put your mind to it.

HOARSENESS—603. To dream your voice is hoarse, you are warned against some personal relationship which could become enbarrassing.

HOAX—702. If you play a practical joke on someone, you will have to apologize to someone for an unpleasant thing you said or did.

HOBBY HORSE—480. To dream you are riding a hobby horse means you will find pleasure in pursuing an interesting hobby.

HOBO—933. See Tramp.

HOCKEY—311. To watch or take part in a hockey game means you will be able to go further in your work, if you pay more attention to it.

HOE—219. If you use a hoe in your dream, you will have good luck in selling or trading.

HOG—436. To dream of a hog predicts good luck in a new activity you undertake.

HOLD-UP MAN—831. See Bandit.

HOLIDAY—395. (Also see Celebration, Vacation.) If you dream you are enjoying a holiday, you will earn more money provided you work harder.

HOLLY—615. To dream of hanging holly branches or wreaths on a door or any part of the house portends good luck in finances and friendships.

HOLY COMMUNION—840. If you dream of taking Holy Communion, you will form a lifelong friendship.

HOLY PERSON—335. If you dream of a holy person, you will have good relationships and peaceful life with your family and friends.

HOME LIFE—712. To dream of having a happy home life is a sign

122

of a peaceful life with some money in small sums.

HOME RUN—619. If you dream you make a home run in a baseball game, you will find success in your next business project.

HOMESICKNESS—038. To dream you are suffering homesickness portends you will hear encouraging news from a friend.

HOMINY—983. To eat hot hominy is a sign of some boring companions. Eating cold hominy shows you will have a minor ailment.

HOMOSEXUAL—018. To dream you are a homosexual means you will go through some disturbing situations. If you dream you see or talk to a homosexual, you will need to act more cautiously toward those of the opposite sex.

HONESTY—236. If you dream that some dishonest person you know acts in an honest manner, good luck is coming to you soon.

HONEY—540. If you dream of eating or touching honey, you will have some hard pulling to reach any measure of success.

HONEYMOON—291. If you dream you are on your honeymoon, you will have a good marriage.

HONEYSUCKLE—680. This flower in your dream is an omen of a contented life with your family and neighbors.

HOOD—014. To dream you are wearing a hood shows one of your friends is unfaithful.

HOODLUM—442. If you dream of hoodlums, you may suffer much unhappy criticism from people you know.

HOOF—614. To dream of seeing an animal's hoof means you will be fooled by people in business matters as well as in love.

HOOP—930. To dream you are rolling a hoop predicts you can keep your job permanently.

HOPEFULNESS—887. If you dream you are hopeful, even when things are hard, you will eventually find things working out to your satisfaction.

HORIZON—983. To dream of a horizon that is far distant is a prophecy of good luck in love and business. A horizon that is close by is a sign that many petty annoyances will trouble you for some time.

HORN—617. To hear a ship's horn in your dream means a happy social life for you. The horn of an automobile means you must watch out for possible accidents. A horn played in a band or orchestra forecasts family troubles.

HORNET—764. If you dream this insect stings you, you will succeed in business ventures.

HOROSCOPE—831. (Also see Astrology.) To dream your horoscope is being read portends good luck.

HORSE—436. (Also see Saddle, Stall.) If you dream of breaking in a wild horse, or being kicked by a horse, or two horses fighting, it is a warning to beware of unfaithful companions. To dream you are riding horseback is a sign of success in community undertakings. If you see horses in a paddock, financial betterment will come to you.

HORSE RACE—831. If you dream your horse wins at the racetrack, you will be happy in social and business matters. If the horse loses, or if there is an accident at the racetrack, you will go through a period of discouraging losses.

HORSERADISH—395. To dream you are eating horseradish foretells you will have to be careful about whom you trust as a friend.

HORSESHOE—615. (Also see Quoits.) If you dream you nail a horseshoe over your door or other part of the house, you will meet with success but first will go through disappointments.

HORSE TRADING—840. To dream about horse trading warns you will have to be cautious in business matters.

HOSE—335. If you squirt a water hose on a lawn or over flowers, you will make new friends. If the hose is used to put out a fire, you will have exciting travel to faraway places.

HOSIERY—712. See Stockings.

HOSPITAL—619. To dream you are in a hospital foretells you may meet some difficulties, but you will be able to win out over them.

HOST, HOSTESS—038. If you dream you are having guests at a function, you will enjoy better money conditions.

HOSTILITY—308. See Hate.

HOTEL—814. If you register alone at a hotel, you will be burdened with heavier responsibilities. If you register with one of the opposite sex, you will be faced with an emergency.

HOUNDS—091. (Also see Bloodhound.) If you dream you are riding to hounds, you will have many leisure-time pleasures.

HOURGLASS—706. To dream of sands running through the hourglass shows you may suffer disappointment, if you waste too many opportunities.

HOUSE—527. (Also see Real Estate.) If you dream you are buying a house, you will have a stimulating but short love affair. To build a house shows good luck in your work.

HOUSEBOAT—024. To dream of seeing or being on a houseboat is a sign of a pessimistic outlook about friendship and love.

HOVEL—319. If you dream you live in a hovel, you will be secure in your old age. If the hovel is destroyed by fire, good news is on the way to you.

HOWLING—387. If you hear an animal or a person howling, it forecasts unhappiness and painful illness.

HUCKLEBERRIES—619. To dream of huckleberries portends sickness which will be of short duration.

HUCKSTER—089. If you dream of being a huckster or a peddler, or to buy food from a huckster, you will enjoy good health and worries will disappear.

HUG—784. An affectionate hug means a happy home life. If the embrace is a passionate one, you will enjoy traveling.

HULA HULA—933. To witness this Hawaiian dance means you will have exciting pleasures with the opposite sex.

HUMIDITY—248. If you dream you are uncomfortable with the humidity, you will undergo an embarrassing situation.

HUMILITY—017. To dream you are showing humility means you must guard against being narrow-minded and bossy toward others.

HUMMING—297. If you hear the sound of humming, some embarrassing events may occur.

HUMOR—631. See Fun.

HUNCHBACK—832. To dream of meeting a hunchback foretells good luck in money matters.

HUNGER—314. If you dream you are helping a hungry person, you will inherit some money and will travel. To dream you are hungry means you will have good luck.

HUNTING—995. If you dream you are hunting animals or shooting game birds, you may suffer some accident. If you hunt big game in the jungle, you will have good luck in business.

HURDY-GURDY—679. To dream you are an organ grinder, turning the handle of the hurdy-gurdy, means you will meet interesting people. If you listen to a hurdy-gurdy, you will find new ways to success.

HURRICANE—496. See Cyclone.

HURRY—012. If you dream you are rushing about for some personal gain, you will meet with irritating situations, but if you are hurrying to help another, good luck is on its way.

HUSBAND—714. If an unmarried woman dreams of being loved by a husband, she can look forward to a good marriage.

HUSKING BEE—368. To dream you attend a husking bee is a sign of a pleasant love life.

HYACINTH—296. To see this flower growing in a pot foretells better financial situation. If the flower is in a garden, you will have unwelcome visitors.

HYDRANT—742. If you dream of a hydrant with flowing water, or if the hydrant bursts, you and those close to you will be lucky in finances. To see a fireman attach a hose to the hydrant means you will suffer slight disappointments.

HYDROPLANE—809. To see a hydroplane on or above the water is a prophecy of a quick solution to a disturbing problem.

HYDROPHOBIA—445. See Rabies.

HYENA—213. If you see a hyena in a cage, you will have a skin ailment. If a hyena attacks you, watch out for false friends. If you kill or safely run away from the hyena, your worries will be over.

HYMN—943. To sing or hear hymns sung by others is a sign of good work you will do to help your community.

HYPNOTISM—430. If you dream you hypnotized someone, you will find it hard to pay off debts. If someone hypnotizes you, you will have to be careful in not telling all you know to others.

HYPOCRITE—327. (Also see Liar.) To dream you are being hypocritical is a sign of sickness. If someone is being hypocritical toward you, be patient in dealing with new situations.

HYSTERIA—097. Any dream involving hysterical people forecasts financial and family troubles. If there is mob hysteria, there will be disaster in the nation.

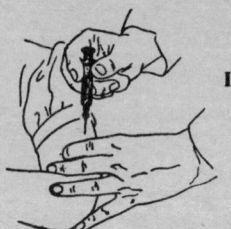

INNOCULATION

IBEX—519. If you dream you see this wild goat in a cage, you will be annoyed by an enemy. If you shoot the ibex, you will have money disappointments. If the ibex is in the field and you do not touch him, you will have better luck.

ICE—762. To dream you slip on the ice, or sit on a cake of ice, you will have a pleasant life and go on interesting trips.

ICE SKATING—565. See Skating.

ICE CREAM—514. (Also see Cone.) If you dream of eating ice cream, your life will be made happier through children.

ICICLE—387. To dream of seeing icicles dripping means you will have to be more thrifty in handling your money. If you eat an icicle, you will have a slight illness.

IDEAS—071. If you dream you get clever ideas, you will enjoy good luck.

IDOL—693. To dream you are worshipping an idol means you will have friction with those who have higher positions than you in your job. If you see someone else worshipping an idol, you can look forward to salary increase.

IGNORANCE—212. If you dream someone shows you up as ignorant, you will get a raise in pay. If you are annoyed with an ignorant person, you will have to apologize for something you did or said.

ILLITERACY—868. To dream you are with an adult, who is unable to read or write, forecasts you will get a higher and more responsible position.

ILLNESS — 634. See Disease.

IMITATION — 242. If you dream something you thought was genuine turns out to be an imitation, you will be disappointed in someone you trusted.

IMMIGRANT — 197. See Emigrant.

IMMODESTY — 317. To dream you or others are dressing and acting immodestly foretells you may make embarrassing mistakes.

IMMORALITY — 894. If you dream you or others are acting in immoral manner, you are warned not to misjudge others and to be careful about your own behavior.

IMMORTALITY — 016. To dream that you will never die is a prophecy of you needing to give more time and thought to your work.

IMPATIENCE — 738. To dream you are being impatient with others means you will meet with disappointment in close friends.

IMPERSONATION — 033. If you dream you are fooled by someone who is doing an impersonation, you will enjoy new social relationships. To dream you are impersonating another character portends you may have to cover up for something you failed to do.

IMPUDENCE — 880. To dream you are being impudent to someone of high esteem, you can look forward to achieving a higher position.

IMPURITY — 786. If you find impurities in food, drink or other things, you will have disappointments through those you love.

INAUGURATION — 315. To dream you are attending a presidential inauguration shows you will have good luck.

INCENSE — 435. To burn incense, or to smell the aroma, you will have stimulating times in traveling and in love.

INCEST — 603. Any dream which has the theme of incest is a warning that you must maintain the highest standards in your way of life.

INCISION — 431. (Also see Operation.) If you dream you are showing your surgical incision to another, you will be promoted in your work because of your efficiency.

INCOMPATIBILITY — 582. To dream of being incompatible in marriage or other relationships, is a warning not to let your temper get out of hand as it might cause great unhappiness.

INCUBATOR—613. If you dream of babies in an incubator, you will enjoy good health. If you see chickens in an incubator, you will be able to keep your promises.

INDEPENDENCE—713. If you dream you are showing an independent spirit, you will have to curb your arrogance in dealing with others.

INDEX—348. To dream you are compiling an index, points to a better position for you. If you are searching for an item in an index, you will come to a more amicable relationship with others.

INDIFFERENCE—411. If you are being indifferent to others, you will suffer financial difficulty. If you dream someone you love is acting indifferently to you, you must strive to better your tact in dealing with others.

INDIGESTION—261. See Constipation.

INFANTRY—432. Dreaming of infantry on the march is a sign of stimulating adventures and fickle love.

INFECTION—893. To dream you have become infected means you will have to avoid taking unnecessary risks.

INFERIORITY COMPLEX—609. If you dream you are lacking self-assurance, you will succeed better if you cooperate with friends.

INFIDELITY—732. To dream you are unfaithful to the one you love forecasts you will have difficulty with the opposite sex, if you are not more careful.

INFLUENZA—024. See Grippe.

INHERITANCE—812. See Legacy.

INITIATION—513. Dreaming of being mishandled by your companions in an initiation ceremony is a forecast of happy friendships and pleasant social life.

INJURY—620. See Accident.

INK—824. (Also see Blot.) To spill ink in your dream is a sign of a calm life. If you dream you are using ink to write to someone, you will need to be cautious about confiding in your friends.

INK WELL—935. If you pour more ink into the well, you will go on a long trip.

INOCULATION—043. To dream of being inoculated with serum is a sign of money matters becoming less hard for you.

INQUEST—802. If you are at an inquest because of someone's death, more responsibility will have to be borne by you.

INSANITY—930. (Also see Maniac.) To dream you are insane is a prophecy of good news. If others are insane, you will quarrel with misunderstanding relatives.

INSECTS—214. (Also see various insects listed alphabetically in their own categories.) If you are annoyed with insects, while you are indoors, you will suffer mild skin ailment.

INSINCERITY—761. If you dream you are not being frank to others, you will have friction with some close friends.

INSOLENCE—097. To dream someone younger is being insolent to you means you have to keep your temper from flaring up. If you are insolent to someone younger or to a subordinate, you will need to defend yourself to someone of high position.

INSURANCE—387. If a salesman tries to sell you insurance, a better job may be offered to you. If you dream you take out an insurance policy, you will have money worries.

INTEMPERANCE—840. See Drinking.

INTERPRETER—402. If you dream you have to use an interpreter to speak to a foreigner, it is a warning for you to be cautious in investments.

INTOLERANCE—899. See Bigotry.

INTOXICATED—842. See Drunkard.

INTRIGUE—808. See Plot.

INVALID—240. To dream you are kind to an invalid forecasts you will receive a letter with pleasant news.

INVENTION—602. To dream you are inventing new things shows you will get what you are hoping for.

INVESTMENTS—587. See Bonds.

INVITATION—671. If you receive an invitation to a function, you will have to bear some unwelcome financial burdens.

IODINE—014. To dream of using this in any form is a prophecy you need to be more optimistic.

IRIS—329. This lovely flower in your dream is an omen of good luck in your personal and working life.

IRONING—085. If you are ironing clothes, you will find peace and better money conditions.

IRRITATIONS—790. To dream you are being irritated by all sorts of petty annoyances means you can overcome troubles, if you work hard enough at doing so.

ISLAND—614. Dreaming of being alone with a member of the opposite sex, on a lonely island, foretells some stimulating happenings for you. If you live on an island, in your dream, you will have to work hard but will win out eventually.

ITCHING—031. If you suffer itching in any part of your body, you will have petty annoyances.

IVORY—296. To dream you are carving lovely things out of ivory is a sign of people respecting you for your deeds. If you dream of hunting ivory in the jungle, you will be helped by rich relatives.

IVY—518. To see ivy growing or if you plant it, you will enjoy good luck. If you rip ivy off the places on which it is trailing, you will have minor worries.

J

JUGGLER **JAGUAR**

JACKASS — 341. See Donkey.

JACKET — 793. If you wear a new jacket in your dream, you will receive an invitation to a lavish social event. If the jacket is old and torn, you will be disappointed in pleasureable pursuits.

JACK KNIFE — 840. See Knife.

JADE — 402. If you buy a beautiful piece of jade, you will entertain unexpected guests. If the jade is set in gold, you will need to contribute money to a worthy cause.

JAGUAR — 899. To dream of this animal is an omen of malicious gossip coming from a false friend.

JAIL — 961. (Also see Warden.) If you are sent to jail in your dream, you have to watch out against being caught in a lie. If others are sent to jail, be cautious about not catching an infectious disease.

JAILER — 087. To dream you are a jailer, or married to a jailer, you will have minor difficulties with a police officer.

JAM — 321. If you dream you are putting up jam preserves, you will find interesting friends in your community.

JANITOR — 540. To dream you are the janitor in a building means you will have to undertake work which is not agreeable to you.

JAUNDICE — 802. If you dream you are having this liver illness, it is a warning for you to take better care of your health.

JAVELIN — 133. To dream you are throwing a javelin at some person forecasts trouble with friends. If you throw the javelin as a sport in athletics, you will have better luck in your work.

JAW — 630. If you dream your jaw stands out from your face, you will go through an embarrassing situation. If you see another's jaw, you will get higher wages.

JAYWALKER—**815.** If you cross the street against the light, or some others are jaywalking, you are warned about arguing with a policeman.

JAZZ—**290.** Whether you hear jazz music or dance to it, you will run into financial difficulty because of your extravagance.

JEALOUSY—**085.** To dream of being jealous or envious of anyone is a warning that you permit yourself to get too pessimistic, and must guard against it.

JELLY—**438.** See Jam.

JESTER—**931.**

JESUS CHRIST—**708.** See Christ.

JEWELRY—**315.** (Also see various jewels or gems listed alphabetically in their separate categories.) To see a display of fine jewelry portends happy social communication with your community. If you dream you buy expensive jewelry, you will have to be careful not to let your private life be known to everyone. If you dream of cheap, flashy jewelry, you will have a minor ailment.

JIG—**699.** If you dance a jig, you will come into an inheritance from an old person.

JIGSAW—**429.** To dream you are cutting something with a jigsaw is an omen of difficulty in your love life.

JILTED—**842.** If you dream you are jilted by the one you love, you will benefit by your investments, but if you are the jilter, you will be disappointed in an important meeting with others.

JITTERS—**753.** If you dream you are afraid to go ahead and feel too nervous, you may be asked to take part in amateur plays.

JIU-JITSU—**537.** See Karate.

JOB—**295.** To dream you lost your job is a warning you have to keep your temper in check. If you get a new job, you may find something of value but will need to return it to its rightful owner.

JOCKEY—**613.** If you dream of a jockey in a horse race, you will be advanced in your job or get a better job.

JOKE — 337. If you laugh at someone's joke, you will receive a visit from someone you do not wish to see. If you tell a joke at which others laugh, you will have good business dealings; but if your joke is met with silence, you will be disappointed in a trusted friend.

JOKER — 841. To dream you are holding the joker while playing cards forecasts you will let a competitor beat you in business.

JONQUILS — 439. If you see these lovely flowers in your dream, you will get a love letter that will thrill you.

JOURNEY — 008. See Travel.

JUDGE — 801. To dream you appear in court before a judge, or that you are acting as the judge, foretells you may go through some embarrassing situations at home and at work.

JUDGMENT DAY — 621. If you dream about this great day, you will be robbed by someone.

JUGGLER — 312. Dreaming of a juggler going through his act is a sign that you will participate in a contest which involves high rewards.

JUGULAR VEIN — 912. (Also see Blood.) To dream of your jugular vein being cut is a prophecy of sickness, and you may need to go to a better climate to recuperate.

JUICES, FRUIT OR VEGETABLE — 001. If you dream you serve juices to your guests means you will be able to help someone in trouble. If you drink the juices, you will get necessary money assistance.

JULEP — 946. See Mint Julep.

JUMPING — 309. If you dream you are jumping over obstacles in your path, you will be able to handle difficult situations and win out.

JUMPING-JACK — Whether a child or an adult plays with a jumping-jack, you will meet new, congenial friends.

JUNK — 043. Any sort of dream about piles of junk means you will meet obstacles in making necessary decisions.

JURY — 619. See Court of Law.

KNIGHT

KANGAROO—314. If you dream of a kangaroo you will soon be traveling. If the kangaroo's pouch contains a baby animal, your trip will be exciting.

KARATE—683. To dream you are participating in the use of karate is a sign of success to you in travel concerning business. If you watch others doing karate, your plans may not work out well.

KEROSENE—286. If you pour kerosene into a stove or fill a lamp with it, you will enjoy long walks with an interesting friend.

KETCHUP—389. To pour ketchup on your food means you will be kept in a state of indecision through someone you admire.

KETTLE—431. A boiling kettle on a stove is a sign of a contented family life. If the kettle boils dry, you will have some sorrows.

KEY—308. To dream you put a key into a keyhole foretells you will be scolded by someone you like. If you hold the key in your hand, you will meet someone who will flirt with you.

KEYHOLE—732. If you look through a keyhole, you will suffer embarrassment in relation to others.

KICK—688. To dream you are being kicked by a person or an animal means you will have to pay more attention to your work to avoid a loss in salary.

KID—278. (Also see Goat.) If you see a young goat, you will be influenced to good thinking by some intelligent person.

KIDNAPPING—902. Whether you dream you are kidnapped or are kidnapping someone else, you will encounter much unpleasantness through social and financial matters.

KIDNEY—412. If you dream you suffer with, or are looking at your kidneys, you will have to be cautious about investments.

KIDNEY STEW—672. To dream of eating kidney stew portends you will suffer a disturbing illness.

KILLING—847. See Murder.

KILTS—097. See Plaid.

KINDERGARTEN—781. Children in a kindergarten are a happy omen of a good marriage.

KING—436. See Queen, also Throne.

KISS—407. (Also see Mistletoe.) To dream you are affectionately kissing someone is a sign of a life of contentment. If the kiss is given hypocritically, you will have a slight illness and social disappointments.

KITCHEN—620. If you are in a clean kitchen, you will entertain pleasant people in your home. If the kitchen is messy, you will have a sudden illness.

KITE—307. To dream of flying a kite, you will undertake work that may prove hard to handle. A kite string that breaks is a sign of business difficulties.

KITTEN—631. See Cat.

KLEPTOMANIAC—312. If you dream you are a compulsive thief of items you do not need, someone you trust is trying to undermine your reputation.

KU KLUX KLAN—870. To dream of seeing people with white hoods over their faces predicts carelessness on your part toward good friends.

KNEE—043. To dream your knees are shaking shows you may need to ask forgiveness for something you did or said. To dream of admiring dimples in a knee means you will meet an attractive stranger.

KNEELING—392. If you dream of kneeling, or seeing someone kneel, in a place that is not a house of worship, you have to watch out you don't do or say things to get yourself in trouble.

KNIFE—841. A knife worn in your belt is a sign of a broken love affair. An open jack knife or a dull knife is a prediction of hard struggle to earn a living. A closed jack knife means someone is trying to cheat you.

KNIGHT—607. See Armor.

KNITTING—431. If you knit in your dream you will be happy with members of your family.

KNOCKING—680. To hear a succession of knocks in your dream, you may meet someone who intrigues you but you will never understand.

KNOTS—197. If you dream you are tying knots in a rope or string, you may have a slight accident by falling off a horse or another height.

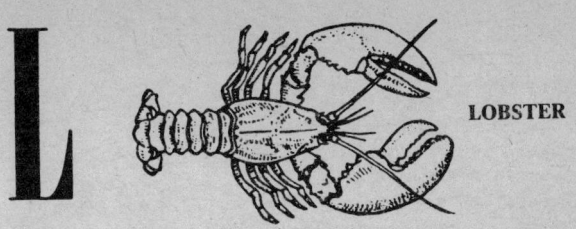

L

LOBSTER

LABORER—697. To dream you work in the construction field is a sign of success in new plans. If you feel belittled because you are a laborer, you will not make the best use of your intelligence. If you dream of being a member of a labor union, you will enjoy better living.

LABORATORY—380. If you dream you work in a laboratory, you will be able to solve a long-standing problem.

LACE—583. To dream of lace trimming on women's things or household articles is a sign of interesting relationships with the opposite sex. Lace on a man's garments is a warning not to become involved in shady financial deals.

LADDER—613. Dreaming of entering a house through a ladder, or if a ladder falls on you, the prediction is that you will be concerned about unfaithful friends. If you climb a ladder and a rung breaks, your money matters will be less worrisome.

LAIR—742. If you find an uninhabited lair in your dream, you will undergo some hardships, but if an animal is in the lair, your worries will soon be over.

LAKE—124. (Also see Pond.) If you are in a boat on a smooth lake, you will meet life's situations with calmness. A boat which overturns into the lake is an omen of quarreling with relatives. If you are on a boat in stormy waters and bring the boat to safety in your dream, you will succeed in your ambitions.

LAMB, COOKED—638. To dream you are eating lamb, your business deals will prosper.

LAMBS—319. (Also see Sheep.) If you see lambs in your dream,

139

you will be able to adjust to life and find peace within yourself.

LAMENESS — 096. To dream you are lame means you have to use caution in furthering new plans. If you feel sorry for a lame person and offer your assistance, you will enjoy good health. To push or hurt a lame person signifies you will incur hard luck.

LAMP — 580. (Also see Lantern.) If you light a lamp (either electric or fuel), you will find cooperation from one you have helped. If you turn out the light, you will go on a restful trip. If you dream you break a lamp, you will have friction among friends. To hang a lamp as a guide is an omen of good luck for you.

LAMP POST — 473. If you dream you are leaning on a lamp post because you have had too much to drink, you will lose some friends. A broken lamp post means some tension in the community.

LANDLADY, LANDLORD — 217. To dream you are being asked for rent by the owner of your building predicts you will make enough money to buy a home.

LANTERN — 939. (Also see Lamp.) If you dream you are signalling someone with a lantern in order to avoid danger, you will meet with insincerity from one of the opposite sex. A lantern which is blown out by the wind means you may have a dispute with a police officer.

LAPIS LAZULI — 614. To dream about this lovely blue gem is a prediction of peace of mind, with a pleasant trip in the future.

LARD — 837. If you dream of lard eaten or used in cooking, you will have to beware of people of loose morals.

LARK — 405. To hear this bird sing is a prophecy of simple, happy pleasures. If you kill the lark in your dream, some unhappy situations will arise in your life.

LARYNGITIS — 501. See Hoarseness.

LASSO — 620. (Also see Rodeo.) If you rope an animal with your lasso, it portends happiness in marriage. If the rope is looped around your body, you will undergo some embarrassment with close friends.

LAST SUPPER — 296. If you dream you are present at the Last Supper, you will form sincere new friendships.

LATHE — 590. To dream you are working at a lathe predicts you will meet with success in working out your new ideas.

LATHER—314. Dreaming about lathering your face before shaving signifies you will find a way out of difficulties. To lather your body with soap while bathing portends an interesting letter coming to you.

LAUGHTER—096. (Also see Comedy, Fun.) Whether you are laughing in your dream, or making others laugh, you will have good luck in money matters.

LAUNCHING—841. If you dream you attend the launching of a ship, you will take part in interesting and successful projects.

LAUNDERING—967. If you dream of laundering clothes in a machine, you will go on a long journey. To dream of washing clothes by hand, you will be a peacemaker in a lover's quarrel. If you send out your laundry to be done by someone else, you may be the subject of malicious gossip.

LAVA—705. See Volcano.

LAVATORY—632. (Also see Toilet.) Dreaming you are in a washroom means you will argue with a salesman. If you slip on the floor of the lavatory, you need to concentrate more on details.

LAW—971. (Also see Judge.) If you dream you are having legal troubles, you will have to work hard in your business. To dream you engage a lawyer in order to sue someone, you have to be more careful in your dealings with others. If you win a lawsuit, you will suffer financial loss.

LAWN—084. If you dream you are mowing or just admiring a green lawn, you will find peace in family life and in your community. If the grass is in bad condition, you will have an illness.

LAXATIVE—793. (Also see Constipation.) To dream you take a laxative is a sign you will be treated well by someone you thought was stingy.

LAZINESS—813. If you dream you are enjoying yourself in lazy manner, you will have good luck. If someone scolds you for being lazy, you will have arguments at home.

LEAPING—049. If you dream you leap over a fence or anything that is high, you can win out over obstacles.

LEARNING—680. Dreaming of acquiring knowledge in scholarly subjects, or learning some new trade, signifies you will be blessed with faithful friends.

LEASE—932. Any dream about a lease being signed is an omen of higher earnings.

LEATHER—557. If you dream of working with leather, you will need to work hard to pay overdue bills.

LEAVE—639. See Furlough.

LEAVES—583. See Foliage.

LECTURE—204. To dream you are giving a lecture means you will take a long journey. If you attend a lecture given by some well-known person, you will have good luck in love.

LEECH—690. (Also see Blood Sucker, Vampire.) Dreaming of a leech sucking your blood is a prophecy of having to meet family obligations.

LEG—012. To dream of seeing just one leg, or breaking a leg, means you will be discouraged over new plans. Lovely legs mean social success. Badly formed legs are a sign of need of funds to go ahead with plans.

LEGACY—326. To dream of getting a legacy from one who is not a relative is a sign of happy times ahead for you. A legacy from a close relative means you will go through some hard times.

LEI—803. A dream about a Hawaiian lei hung around the neck is an omen of success in love.

LEISURE—620. If you dream you use your leisure time in a calm manner, you will get some money and will be well-liked by neighbors.

LEMON—008. Squeezing a lemon in your dream predicts you will have to struggle to overcome obstacles. If you suck a lemon, you will need to use tact in getting along with people of high position.

LEMONADE—454. To mix or drink lemonade foretells you will be respected by friends.

LENDING—037. See Borrowing.

LENTILS—463. Dreaming about lentils is a sign of a happy home life.

LEOPARD — 762. Dreaming of a leopard who attacks you is a prophecy of some tough times you will need to face. If you scare away or kill the animal, you will fulfill your ambitions.

LEPER — 804. If you are in the company of lepers, you will have to work hard to achieve proper goals.

LESBIAN — 937. See Homosexual.

LETHAL CHAMBER — 304. To see another being led to the lethal chamber is a sign of your ability to make money in trading. If you are being led to the lethal chamber, you will need to be careful not to make hasty investments.

LETTER — 446. (Also see Mail, Postcard, Stamp.) If you dream of receiving money or good news in a letter, you will be able to earn more. A letter with bad news means you will need to avoid people gossiping about you. If you dream you are writing a love letter, you may be made to regret some past action. To dream you are mailing a letter to someone portends you will get your wish. If you deliver the letter by hand, you may be bothered by a guilty conscience.

LETTUCE — 943. To eat lettuce means you will enjoy good health. If you plant lettuce, you will have to cover up for a close friend's poor behavior.

LIAR — 561. (Also see Lie, Hypocrite.) If you are called a liar, you will have some arguments with others. If you call another a liar, you will be a victim of malicious gossip.

LIBEL — 018. Dreaming that you are being libeled or you are libeling another, means unpleasant social relationships.

LIBERTY BELL — 619. See Bells.

LIBRARY — 935. (Also see Books.) To dream of being in a library is a sign of being appreciated by others for the work you perform.

LICE — 341. To see any lice on yourself or another person means you will have to deal with some unpleasant people.

LICENSE, CAR — 912. To be asked to show your automobile license to a traffic officer portends a successful love relationship. If you are not able to produce the license, you will participate in relatives' quarrels.

LICENSE, DOG—096. If you dream of getting a license for a dog, you will enjoy peaceful home life.

LICORICE—876. To eat licorice in your dream predicts advancement in business matters.

LIE—692. (Also see Liar.) If you tell a lie in your dream, you will enjoy increased financial and social status. If someone lies to you, you will be hurt either physically or in your business.

LIFEBOAT—859. To launch a lifeboat forecasts you will take chances in new business or love interests. If the boat overturns, you will run into obstacles concerning new plans.

LIFEGUARD—004. To dream of being rescued by a lifeguard foretells stimulating social activities.

LIGHTHOUSE—532. See Beacon Light.

LIGHTNING—664. (Also see Rain, Thunder.) Streaks of lightning in a rainstorm predict some unhappy events. Heat lightning in your dream means happy social times.

LIGHTNING ROD—930. To dream of a lightning rod on a building foretells of unhappiness coming from a strange source.

LILIES—448. To dream about lilies of any variety is a sign of success in love.

LIMA BEANS—631. If you dream of fresh beans, you will gain your ambition. If they are canned beans, you will not be too happy in your work.

LIME—094. See Lemon.

LIMPING—432. See Lameness.

LINENS, BEDDING—127. If you dream of clean bed linens, you will find life agreeable in a leisurely manner.

LINENS, TABLE—378. To dream of clean tablecloths and napkins you will have social prestige.

LINGERIE—933. To dream of pretty underthings means social life with the opposite sex, but you must guard against lax behavior.

LINIMENT—682. If you dream you are rubbing liniment on your body, you can look forward to an inheritance.

LION—409. To dream you are not afraid of a lion, you will be admired by others. If you are attacked by a lion, but are able to save yourself, you will rise higher in your activities.

LIPS—336. (Also see Kiss, Mustache.) To dream of thick lips forecasts love quarrels. If the lips are very red, you may suffer some illness and disappointment about work. If you dream of an old person's lips, you will be faced with unforseen problems.

LIPSTICK—814. (Also see Make-up.) If you dream a girl is using lipstick in public, you will not achieve all you go after. If a man is using lipstick, you will be ridiculed by someone.

LIQUOR—537. Also see Drinking, Whiskey, Wine.) To dream you are imbibing too much liquor is a sign you may regret it if you overindulge in your drinking.

LIVER—672. If you dream you eat liver or are taking cod liver oil, you will be in good health.

LIVER TROUBLE—430. To dream of having a liver ailment portends you will overcome financial woes.

LIVERY STABLE—901. If you see a livery stable in your dream, you will find joy in love and marriage.

LIZARD—793. To dream about a lizard is a warning you must not do something careless to hurt yourself or others.

LOAN—811. If you dream you make a loan to someone, you will make new friends. If you need to make a loan at a bank or other place of money-lending, you will work hard but can succeed in overcoming financial difficulties.

LOBSTER—159. If you eat cooked lobster you will be paid back money that is due to you. Live lobsters predict some minor worries.

LOCK—012. Any dream about a lock is a prophecy of dissatisfaction and embarrassment in whatever you try to achieve.

LOCKET—453. To dream you wear a locket is a sign of an affectionate relationship which will make you happy.

LOCKJAW—695. To dream of having lockjaw means you may not be able to find simple solutions for your problems.

LOCOMOTIVE — 043. Whether you drive the locomotive or ride in the cab, it is a sign you will be promoted in your work.

LOGS — 583. If you dream of sawing logs, or sitting on one, or watching them float down a river, you will have a chance to increase your earnings. If there is a log jam on the river, you will not be able to get all you go after.

LOLLYPOP — 641. If you are given a lollypop by another, you will be chosen to head some group. If you suck a lollypop in a public place, you may be put in an embarrassing situation.

LONELINESS — 570. Dreaming of being lonely forecasts you will be in pleasant social surroundings.

LONGSHOREMAN — 012. If you see these men loading or unloading a ship's cargo, it foretells you will be offered a much better job than you now have.

LORD'S PRAYER — 791. If you dream you are reciting the Lord's Prayer, you will be introduced to interesting people.

LOSS — 557. To dream of losing some article is a sign of annoying troubles. But if you find it, you will have good luck.

LOST — 812. To dream you are lost and cannot find your way is an omen of petty problems which you will soon overcome.

LOTTERY — 908. If you dream you buy a lottery ticket, or win the lottery, you will have to try to avoid tense situations with relatives.

LOUDSPEAKER — 432. Dreaming of a loudspeaker that is annoying is a sign of small worries. If the volume is turned down and is not annoying, you will find satisfaction in cooperating with neighbors.

LOVE — 106. To dream you are sincerely in love foretells a contented life, but if you dream you are insincere in your love, you will have many disappointments. If you dream of watching others make love, your future plans will be successful.

LUGGAGE — 583. See Baggage.

LUMBER — 699. Neat piles of lumber predict good business earnings. If you dream of lumber being scattered about, you will have family quarrels.

LUNCH—123. Dreaming of eating lunch at a restaurant table is an omen of you incurring your employer's dissatisfaction. If you eat at a counter, you will earn more money. Eating lunch outdoors from a basket or box means better health for you.

LUNGS—724. To dream of having breathing difficulty because of a lung condition forecasts you must watch your health as well as your behavior.

LUTE—913. If you play this stringed instrument in a dream, your love life will be happy.

LYNCHING—304. If you witness a lynching, you may get into people's bad graces through something you should not have done or said. If you participate in the lynching, a fatal illness may occur.

MARIONETTE

MACARONI—718. Any dream about macaroni predicts social activities and pleasant family relationships.

MACHINERY—633. (Also see Wheel.) If you dream about machinery that is in motion and in good condition, you will succeed in your job. If machinery is not in motion and is rusty, you will run into disputes with your family and your employer.

MACKEREL—830. Dreaming about fishing for mackerel, or eating it, means you will enjoy traveling.

MADONNA—592. To dream of seeing a statue or a picture of the Madonna means you will be loved by children.

MAGAZINE—811. If you see magazines on a newsstand, you will fall in love with someone who is not from your own city. If you write for a magazine, you will have good luck in your work.

MAGIC—415. (Also see Tricks.) Any dream about magic forecasts you will renew friendship with someone from your past.

MAGISTRATE—609. See Judge.

MAGNET—313. If you dream about a magnet, you will have stimulating times with the opposite sex.

MAGNIFYING GLASS—068. To dream you are looking at things through a magnifying glass, you will come into more money.

MAHARAJAH—732. Any dream concerning a maharajah is a warning for you to use discretion in dealing with the opposite sex.

MAIL—892. (Also see Letter, Postcard, Postman, Stamp.) If you pick up mail at the post office, you will buy new things for the home.

If there is no mail for you, you may be overcharged by a sales person.

MAIL BOX—413. To dream you try to drop a letter in the box but cannot get it in, is a prediction of failure in new plans.

MAJOR—682. To meet a major in your dream is a sign you will be asked to join a community organization.

MAKE-UP—714. (Also see Compact, Cosmetics, Lipstick, Rouge.) If you dream you are making up another's face, you must be careful not to get burned. If you make up for a part on the stage, you will help raise funds for a charity project. To dream you spill powder on your clothes is an omen of disappointment at a social function.

MALARIA—297. If you dream you have this illness, you will soon get á better position.

MANDOLIN—803. To dream of hearing or playing the mandolin is a sign of stimulating wooing and marriage.

MANIAC—291. (Also see Straight-Jacket.) To dream of seeing or being a maniac, you may be the victim of false accusations.

MANICURE—990. See Fingernails.

MANNERS—672. If you dream you are deliberately being good-mannered, your general conditions will be bettered. If you dream of being bad-mannered, you will have slight worries.

MANSION—451. If you dream of luxurious living in a mansion, you will go on a journey with the one you love.

MANUFACTURING—812. See Factory.

MANURE—269. To dream you are shoving manure into piles is an omen of being the subject of others' gossip. If you see garden or farm soil treated with manure, you will receive help from someone to further your plans.

MANUSCRIPT—755. (Also see Writer.) If you dream you are writing or editing a manuscript, you may be called to serve on a jury. To submit the manuscript to a publisher means you may suffer some disappointment.

MAP—954. (Also see Diagram.) If you study maps in a world atlas or on a globe, you may marry someone from a distant place.

MARATHON RACE—336. To dream you are participating in the race portends you may need to apologize for something you did unintentionally. If you watch a marathon race, you will undergo much tension and strain.

MARBLES—204. If you dream you are playing the game of marbles, you will meet someone you loved in the past.

MARDI GRAS—113. To dream you are taking part in the Mardi Gras fun is a prophecy you will sign a legal paper which will bring good luck to you.

MARIGOLDS—844. If you dream of seeing or wearing these flowers, you will buy new clothes.

MARIONETTES—403. Putting on a marionette or puppet show foretells much family happiness.

MARKET—618. Shopping at a market where the foodstuffs are fresh means you will earn more money. If the foodstuffs are spoiled, you will run into some difficult times.

MARMALADE—356. To eat marmalade in your dream is a sign you will get an invitation to visit someone you like.

MARRIAGE—840. (Also see Incompatability, Wedding.) To dream you are happily married forecasts an argument with the one you love. If many people shed tears during a marriage ceremony, someone may get a divorce.

MARS—931. To dream you see the planet Mars through a telescope is a sign of quarreling with business associates.

MARSH—218. See Swamp.

MARSHMALLOWS—087. Any dream about marshmallows means you will meet a good-looking new friend.

MARTYR—136. If you dream you are a martyr to some cause, you will need to watch your diet for health purposes.

MASCOT—782. If you dream you see a mascot (a person or an animal) at a sports game, you will have harsh words with someone in a taxicab.

MASK—609. Whether you or another wears a mask, you will discover one of your friends is unfaithful.

MASQUERADE PARTY—733. To dream of being at a party and

150

having fun forecasts you will have happy surprises through someone of the opposite sex.

MASSACRE—814. If you dream of witnessing a massacre, you will need dental work on your teeth.

MASSAGE—311. To dream you are giving a massage to an ailing person is a sign of good luck to you. If you are getting a body or facial massage, you may lose something of value while attending a party.

MATCH—630. If you dream of striking a match and lighting it, you will be lucky in love.

MATCHMAKER—917. To dream you are a matchmaker is a sign you will have to undertake responsibilities you do not want to handle.

MATHEMATICS—804. If you dream you solve mathematical problems, you will fulfill your plans. If you cannot come up with the right mathematical answers, you will not succeed in new plans.

MATTRESS—680. To dream you are lying on a good mattress means you may not be able to think too clearly about new ideas. If you are on the mattress with someone of the opposite sex, it is a warning for you to be on your best behavior.

MATZOS—123. To dream of eating this unleavened bread portends you will sacrifice your own comforts in order to help others in need.

MAUSOLEUM—830. See Tomb.

MAYONNAISE—607. To dream you make or serve mayonnaise on foods is a sign you may go into the food serving business.

MAYOR—530. If you dream you were elected mayor of your city, you may be called to serve on a jury.

MAYPOLE—336. To dream of dancing around a maypole is a sign of happy marriage.

MEADOW—948. Seeing healthy growing meadow land is an omen of good luck and ability to provide for your future.

MEASLES—450. If you dream you are suffering with measles, you will have to ask someone's pardon for something you said or did.

MEAT — 879. To dream you are buying meat means you will need to work diligently and have no time for relaxation.

MEDALS — 620. To see someone else wearing medals forecasts you will have to curb your jealousy. If you wear medals, you will receive honor for something good you did.

MEDDLER — 497. If you dream you or someone else is meddling into other people's affairs, you must guard against being drawn into quarrels which are not your concern.

MEDICINE — 318. If you take a pill in your dream, you will change your residence. If you swallow liquid medicine, you will enjoy good health. To give someone else medicine or pills means you will suffer slight disappointment.

MEDIUM — 575. See Occult.

MEETING — 914. See Assembly.

MELANCHOLY — 873. (Also see Pessimist.) To dream you are being sad and discouraged is an omen of peace and happiness. If someone close to you is melancholy, you will undergo some business tensions.

MELON — 617. If you dream of eating any kind of melon, you will suffer from indigestion. To see melons growing or selling them in a market is a sign of some changes in your work.

MEMORY — 941. To be able to remember something in a dream, which you forgot while you were awake, you will be offered a better job.

MENAGERIE — 873. See Zoo.

MENDING — 617. (Also see Sewing.) If you dream of mending stockings or clothing, you will find a new way to earn more money.

MENTAL TELEPATHY — 941. See Telepathy.

MENU — 312. To dream of choosing food from a menu in a restaurant forecasts increase in your income.

MERCHANT — 096. See Store.

MERCY — 741. If you dream you show mercy to someone who hurt you, you will have a happy, long life.

MERMAID—215. Any dream about a mermaid means you will go through some disappointments.

MERRY-GO-ROUND—402. To dream you are with children on a merry-go-round predicts lucky changes in your life.

MESSAGE—813. See Letter.

MESSENGER—604. To send someone a letter or package by messenger means you will achieve your plans. If you are a messenger, you may make money through real estate.

METEOR—937. If you see a flashing meteor going swiftly across the sky, you will have temporary good luck.

METER—532. To dream of reading a gas meter or electric meter means you may need to ask someone for sound advice on a problem.

MICROBE—412. (Also see Germs.) To dream of seeing microbes, you need to be careful in an automobile on a wet road.

MICROPHONE—588. See Loudspeaker.

MICROSCOPE—699. If you dream you study objects under a microscope, you may be shocked at the behavior of someone you trust.

MIDGET—134. (Also see Dwarf, Pygmy.) Any dream concerning midgets foretells new friendship with an intelligent person who will prove worthwhile.

MIDWIFE—743. (Also see Childbirth.) If you dream you call a midwife to deliver a baby, you will be in financial difficulty through your extravagances. To dream you are acting as a midwife portends family quarrels.

MILITARY DECORATION—618. See Medals.

MILITIA—940. Dreaming you are serving in the militia forecasts you will be advanced in social and business matters.

MILK (MOTHER'S)—432. Any dream about drinking mother's milk predicts good luck in marriage and social matters.

MILKING—913. See Cow.

MILLIONAIRE—571. If you dream you are rich and spending lots of money, you will unexpectedly get money for something you did long ago. Helping out your friends with money predicts good luck.

MIMIC—811. Whether you or someone else mimic others, it is a sign of some drawbacks in your work and friendly ties.

MINCE PIE—443. To dream of mince pie foretells of arguing with close relatives and unpleasantness from some friends.

MIND READER—718. If you dream someone is reading your mind, you will have to overcome some bad times.

MINER—065. See Coal Miner.

MINES—580. (Also see Torpedo.) If you dream of being on a ship which is blown up by a mine, it is a warning to be careful in dealing with strangers. If you are in a mined area and are scared, you may have some misunderstanding in discussion with others.

MINISTER—931. To dream of talking with a clergyman, you may become interested in doing missionary work.

MINK—532. If you trap minks in your dream, you will receive small earnings for your hard work. To see a woman in a mink coat means you have to beware of false friends.

MINSTRELS—671. If you dream of attending a minstrel show, or of hearing wandering minstrels, you will renew relationship with a good friend.

MINT JULEP—445. Any dream involving a mint julep foretells pleasurable friendships, if you keep a broad-minded attitude toward others.

MIRACLE—892. To dream about a miracle happening is a sign of good luck to you in the future.

MIRAGE—015. (Also see Vision.) To dream of a mirage or of any scene that fades away, portends discouragement in your plans which you can overcome by having more faith.

MIRROR—779. If you see yourself in a mirror, you will be attractive to the opposite sex. To break a mirror in a dream means unpleasantness in your love life.

MISCARRIAGE—813. See Abortion.

MISER—412. Whether you or someone else is being miserly and counting money, you will get more money but you might be embarrassed in the way you get it.

MISSIONARY—697. To dream of a missionary converting you is a prophecy of business success. If you are the missionary, your plans will not materialize to your satisfaction.

MIST—744. See Fog.

MISTAKE—811. If you dream you made a mistake and have apologized for it, you will enjoy good luck. If you blame the mistake on someone else, you will fail in your ambitions.

MISTLETOE—368. (Also see Kiss.) To dream you are hanging the mistletoe, or being kissed under it, you will have a good love relationship.

MISTRESS—533. Any dream about a man keeping a mistress means hardship in financial and social life.

MITTENS—899. To wear mittens in a dream foretells an automobile or machinery accident.

MOANING—067. If you dream you are moaning, you will have to meet your financial obligations. To hear a moaning sound from another, there will be illness in the family.

MOB—412. (Also see Crowd.) To dream you are part of a mob, or being chased by a mob, signifies unfaithful friends.

MOBILIZATION—318. Seeing the mobilization of troops in your dream means you will have money to spend, but you will later be in financial need.

MOCCASINS—708. To dream you are wearing moccasins, you will work as a foreman or manager. If an Indian wears moccasins, you must be careful in picking trustworthy friends.

MOCKING BIRD—905. To see or hear the song of a mocking bird foretells peace of mind and relaxation.

MODEL—430. (Also see Artist.) If you dream you are a fashion model, you will argue with one of the opposite sex.

MODESTY—034. If you or another is acting modestly, you will find matters easing up and your plans succeeding.

MOLASSES — 792. To dream you eat molasses means you will have to take the blame for something you said in haste.

MONASTERY — 126. See Monk, also Nun.

MONEY — 683. (Also see Coin, Counterfeit, Wallet.) If you dream you earned money honestly, you will be in much better financial condition. If you give money away, you will like your job but not get paid much. To dream of finding money means you will need to borrow from others.

MONKEY — 431. Any dream which shows monkeys in it is a prediction of trouble with unfaithful friends and business acquaintances.

MONKEY WRENCH — 899. To dream of using a wrench is a sign of quick solution to a puzzling problem.

MONOCLE — 467. If you wear a monocle in your dream, you will enjoy good fun with others. If you laugh at another who is wearing a monocle, you will be embarrassed through some foolish error you make.

MONSTER — 618. See Ogre.

MOON — 018. To dream of a moon, in a cloudless sky, is a prophecy of good luck coming your way. If the moon is hidden beneath clouds, your efforts will cause disappointment. If you see the moon reflected in water, you will find joy through love affairs.

MOOSE — 531. To dream you shoot a moose, you will quarrel with relatives. If you see a moose running outdoors, you will find new ways of earning money. A baby moose in a dream shows you will go traveling.

MOP — 637. A clean mop in your dream means you will be praised for your good work. If the mop is old and filthy, you have to guard against joining in malicious gossip about others.

MORGUE — 794. (Also see Corpse.) If you dream you are a corpse lying in a morgue, you will have to attend to some tasks you do not like. If you have to identify another's body in a morgue, there may be an accident and you have to take care of your health.

MORNING GLORY — 311. To see this lovely climbing vine in your dream predicts happy vacation days.

MORPHINE—096. See Anesthesia.

MORTAR—814. See Cement.

MORTGAGE—693. If you dream of putting a mortgage on some property, you will have good financial conditions. To dream you pay off a mortgage is a sign of having to work very hard, but if you foreclose a mortgage on another's property, you will have good luck in business.

MOSQUITOES—575. Any dream pertaining to mosquitoes buzzing around or biting is an omen of sad news. If you kill the mosquitoes, you will find peace of mind.

MOSS—931. To dream of soft, green moss is a prediction of a charming romance. If the moss is dark and wilted, you will be disappointed in some of your hopes.

MOTEL—015. See Hotel.

MOTHS—672. To dream of moths in your clothes, it means some family disappointment. If you catch amd kill the moths, you will triumph over those who are unkind to you.

MOTHER—014. If your mother is actually dead, but you dream she is alive, you can look forward to happy times with trusted friends. If you are a child in your dream, and being embraced by your mother, you will find faithful friends in time of trouble. If you see a young mother fondling a baby, you will be able to relax and take it easy.

MOTHER-IN-LAW—549. To dream you are quarreling with your mother-in-law, you will need to be very diplomatic in handling a tense situation. To dream you are a mother-in-law means you will have to guard against saying sarcastic or angry things to others.

MOTION PICTURE—697. See Movies.

MOTOR—411. See Engine.

MOTORBOAT—834. See Boat.

MOTORCYCLE—583. To dream you are riding behind the driver on a motorcycle is a warning for you to be more cautious about your behavior.

MOUNTAIN—692. If you climb a mountain, you will be promoted in your work but will have to work hard toward success.

MOURNING—712. If a dream shows you are in mourning, you will enjoy many happy events. If the whole town is in mourning, sad things will occur but they will eventually work out all right.

MOUSE—490. To catch a mouse in a trap means you will get an unpleasant letter from an annoying friend. If you are scared by a mouse, you will be embarrassed by someone younger than you. If you kill a mouse, you will buy a new wardrobe.

MOUTH—004. If you dream of seeing a lovely mouth you will find happiness through love. If the mouth or several mouths in the dream are ugly, you have to curb your tendency to criticize others.

MOVIES—101. To dream you are enjoying watching a movie, you will get rid of problems that are depressing you. If you find the movie distasteful, you will lose an article you value.

MUSCILAGE—697. See Glue.

MUD—269. If you get mud on your clothes, some evil friend is trying to influence others against you. If you drive a vehicle on a muddy road, people to whom you owe money will pester you for it.

MUFF—413. To dream you are carrying a muff is a sign of disappointment through friendships and love.

MUFFINS—853. To dream you eat or bake muffins shows you will have good family relationships and get some inheritances.

MULE—931. To drive a team of mules, or to be kicked by a mule, means you will have annoyances in social and business matters. If you dream a mule is kicking someone else, you will do much better in business.

MUMPS—471. To dream you are suffering with the mumps is an omen of someone paying for a vacation you will enjoy.

MURDER—168. Whether you dream of witnessing a murder, or committing one, you will not be happy at home or with friends or in your work if you refuse to face facts and take care of things.

MUSEUM—319. To dream of leisurely walking through a museum foretells of nice things happening to you through good friends.

MUSHROOM—804. (Also see Toadstool.) If you dream of picking or eating mushrooms, you will earn more money and meet people who will be helpful to you.

MUSIC—732. (Also see Orchestra, Singing.) To dream you are hearing music or singing that is pleasing to your ears, you will enjoy good luck. If the music is off-key and not pleasant to you, you will go through a disappointment.

MUSICAL INSTRUMENTS—878. See the various instruments which are listed in their individual categories.

MUSTACHE—401. To dream you shave off your mustache forecasts you will break off relationship with one of the opposite sex. To kiss someone who has a mustache, you will become irritated with present surroundings.

MUSTARD—183. If you dream of mustard in any form, you will find love life most satisfying.

MUTINY—216. To dream you are a ship's officer and the crew is mutinying, it is a warning for you to watch out that some people will say you are leading a double life.

MYSTERY—784. If you dream that you are part of some mystery, you will have some trifling problems which will soon be solved.

NECKLACE

NAG—339. To dream you are being nagged by another means you will need medical or dental care.

NAIL—654. See Tack.

NAKEDNESS—093. See Nudity.

NAME—179. If you dream you cannot recall the name of someone you know very well, you will need to cover up for some misdeed of which your family may disapprove.

NAP—349. Dreaming of taking a nap to relax yourself signifies more money coming your way.

NAPKIN—618. Any dream about a napkin predicts you will be able to find satisfaction in your social life and in your work.

NAPOLEON BONAPARTE—938. To see this emperor in your dream forecasts you will not be able to feel relaxed in your new plans.

NARCOTICS—405. See Dope.

NAUSEA—680. To dream you are nauseated means someone will try to blame you for money that is missing, also you have to be on guard against being overly extravagant.

NAVEL—792. If you dream of seeing another's navel, you will meet with a stimulating surprise. To see your own navel means you will be honored by your companions. Dreaming that you have pain in your navel foretells you will visit your childhood scenes.

NAVIGATING—830. Whether you navigate an airplane or a ship, you will succeed in handling problems which may now seem difficult.

NAVY — 311. (Also see Sailor.) To dream you have joined the navy means you will be attractive to the opposite sex.

NECK — 033. (Also see Throat.) If you dream you enjoy seeing someone's lovely neck is an omen of social prestige for you. An ugly neck in a dream foretells financial loss. If you dream of having a painful neck, you will find an indifferent friend suddenly becoming interested in you.

NECKING — 244. See Petting.

NECKLACE — 911. To present someone with a necklace means you will have to apologize for something you said or did. To dream of wearing a necklace forecasts meeting important people socially.

NECKTIE — 077. If you dream you are having trouble in putting on your tie, you will argue with one of the opposite sex.

NEEDLE — 805. Threading a needle in your dream signifies you will enjoy good luck. If you have trouble in threading a needle, you will go through some unhappy situations.

NEON LIGHTS — 540. To see vari-colored neon lights in your dream portends you will find some friends dull and boring. If you smash one of the lights, you will get a raise in pay.

NEPHEW — 213. If you dream that a nephew or a niece asks you for money, you will enjoy amicable social relationships with old and new friends.

NEST — 843. See Bird's Nest.

NEURALGIA — 367. If you dream of having this painful attack, you will quarrel with relatives.

NEWS — 812. To dream of hearing good news forecasts good luck. Dreaming the news you hear is bad, you will suffer disappointments.

NEWSPAPER — 758. If you buy a newspaper, you will have an unpleasant surprise.

NEWSPAPER REPORTER — 977. To dream you are a reporter, you will find good luck in love and business. If you are being interviewed by a reporter, you will go through some trivial disappointments.

NEW YEAR'S EVE—898. To attend a party or in some other way observe the coming new year, you will achieve success in your plans.

NICKNAME—415. If you dream you are calling some important person a nickname, you will receive more money. If you call someone in your family a nickname, you will enjoy yourself at some outdoor function.

NIECE—247. See Nephew.

NIGHT CLUB—613. See Cabaret.

NIGHTMARE—001. If you dream of having a nightmare (a "dream within a dream") you will undergo some unexpected new trouble.

NIPPLE—194. For an adult to dream of drinking from a nipple on a bottle, the forecast is of stress due to money worries.

NOISES—712. To dream you hear noises that are not related to anything at all means you will be made to pay up for overdue bills.

NOMINATION—045. If you dream you are nominated for office, you will meet some hardship in work and family matters.

NOODLES—809. If you eat soft noodles, you will be able to achieve your ambition. If you dream of eating crisp noodles, you will move to a new place.

NORTH POLE—550. See Arctic.

NOSE—672. To blow your nose in your dream is an omen of money problems easing up. If you kiss someone on the nose, you will have family irritations. To pinch someone's nose means happy marriage.

NOTARY PUBLIC—804. If you have a document witnessed by a notary, you will donate to a charity fund.

NOVOCAINE—733. See Anesthesia.

NUDITY—651. To dream of admiring the beauty of a nude body forecasts joy for lovers. If your attitude becomes sensual when seeing the naked body, you will suffer many disappointments. To dream you are nude and are with males and females in one group, you are warned you might be accused of something you should not have done or said.

NUN—521. Seeing or talking with a nun in your dream is an omen of your ability to clear up problems.

NURSE—953. A nurse appearing in a dream foretells good business deals for you. To dream of being a nurse means a good marriage.

NURSING—600. See Milk (Mother's).

NUTS—248. If you dream of eating nuts, you will be influenced by someone who has a dominating personality. If you crack the nut shells, you will succeed in your plans.

NUTMEG—915. To taste nutmeg in your dream predicts you will be in an uncomfortable social position if you break a date. If you grind nutmeg, you will be admired for your congeniality at a party.

NYMPH—412. See Fairy.

OWL

OAK TREE—013. To dream of oak trees forecasts a loving marriage.

OAR—579. If you dream you break the oar while in a row boat, you will encounter some troubles, but your quick mind will overcome them.

OASIS—312. (Also see Desert.) To dream you find an oasis in a hot desert, you will achieve success in something new and unusual you are planning.

OATH—604. If you take an oath in order to aid an innocent person, you will experience good luck.

OATS—619. Any kind of dream about oats (or oatmeal) forecasts success in your work.

OBEDIENCE—049. If you are giving obedience to someone in power, you will come to a mutual agreement with someone you had not trusted before.

OBESITY—318. To dream you are too fat portends you will have many friends and few enemies. It is also a warning for you not to overeat or overdrink.

OBITUARY—607. If you dream you are shocked by reading someone's obituary notice, someone near you will move far away.

OBOE—933. To hear or play an oboe is a sign that you must guard the health of your eyes and ears.

OBSERVATORY—441. To dream of looking out from an observatory and seeing beautiful sights in the land and in the sky is an omen of success in friendship and business.

OBSTETRICS—441. See Birth.

OCCULT—835. Dreaming of attending a meeting of spiritualists or researchers of the occult, you will incur criticism from friends because you are too sensitive.

OCEAN—811. If you see a calm ocean, your money affairs will be good. A stormy sea forecasts disappointment in work. If you dream you swim in this ocean, you will have peace of mind. To dream of an ocean voyage means you will be able to get rid of annoying friends.

OCCULIST—017. See Optician.

ODOR—326. See Aroma.

OGRE—002. To dream of an ogre who frightens you, portends you may suffer a guilty conscience, if you do something that is best left undone.

OIL—778. If you dream of a rich oil field, or if you are oiling machinery parts, you will get better pay and much praise for your work. If you buy oil at a gasoline station, you will get a pleasing surprise telephone call. If you sell oil, you will receive an appeal from some dishonest people who will try to influence you.

OINTMENT—902. To rub ointment on your body or another's body, you will have unfriendliness from the opposite sex.

OLD MAID—286. See Spinster.

OLDER PEOPLE—275. If you dream of your elders, you will be called upon to display your knowledge to others.

OLIVES—415. If you eat ripe black olives, you will enjoy love-making. Green or stuffed olives mean you will meet strangers and will need to be careful of what you tell them.

OLIVE OIL—729. To dream of using the oil to fry food is a sign of happy social times. Using the oil in salad dressing means you will fall in love at first sight.

OMELET—631. (Also see Eggs.) To dream of eating a fluffy, light omelet means happiness in courting and marriage. A heavy, dry omelet forecasts disappointment in love.

ONIONS—295. If you eat boiled or raw onions, you will be in good

165

health. If the onions are fried, you will have an enemy. To dream of crying while peeling an onion, you will go to a carnival or other exciting entertainment.

ONYX—024. To dream of onyx jewelry is a sign of your changing plans in an important matter. If you break the onyx, good luck will be yours.

OPERA—630. If you enjoy listening to an opera, you will be influenced by someone to act badly toward a friend.

OPERA GLASSES—915. To look through the glasses at an important person predicts interesting meeting with people in the theatre. If you use the glasses to spy on someone, you will have to defend yourself against those who say you lie.

OPERATION—015. (Also see Incision, Surgeon.) If you are being operated on, you will be under mental and physical strain through problems. If you dream of watching an operation, you will succeed in an important job.

OPIUM—812. See Dope.

OPOSSUM—550. If you eat roasted opossum, you will attend a celebration.

OPTICIAN—732. To dream of getting eyes examined and buying new eyeglasses, you will have difficulties about your job but you will be able to remedy the situation.

ORANGES—914. Any dream involving oranges forecasts slow but good success in your work and love life.

ORATION—682. See Speech.

ORCHARD—066. To dream of a blooming orchard predicts happy family life and a good income.

ORCHESTRA—978. (Also see Music.) If you hear jazz and swing music you will have enjoyable social life. Symphony music means you will be a guest in a fine home.

ORCHIDS—676. To dream of orchids is a sign of your extravagance leading you into debt.

ORGAN—444. If you dream you are playing an organ, you will be included in a wedding party. Listening to organ music is an omen of true love from one of the opposite sex.

ORGAN GRINDER — 291. See Hurdy-Gurdy.

ORPHAN — 668. To dream you are a child in an orphanage, you have to stop telling your troubles to others as they will find you boring. If you dream you adopt an orphan, you will be made uncomfortable by someone's jealousy of you.

OSTRICH — 089. This bird in your dream forecasts many friends and lots of money.

OUIJA BOARD — 615. If you dream of using a ouija board, you will be betrayed by one of the opposite sex with whom you shared secrets.

OUTLAW — 432. See Criminal.

OVEN — 584. If you use a hot oven for cooking, you will be elected to a high post in the community or your church. A cold oven means you are looking back to old days which will never return.

OVERALLS — 679. To dream of wearing overalls portends you will buy new clothes for evening wear.

OVERCOAT — 123. If you dream of losing your coat, you will have some hard times. If you dream you button up your overcoat in cold weather, you will have business disappointments.

OWL — 043. To dream of an owl forecasts unhappiness through arguing with relatives. If you dream you frighten the owl and it flies away, your living conditions will improve.

OXEN — 940. If an ox or a yoke of oxen appears in your dream, you will enjoy many friends and a simple life without having much money.

OXYGEN TENT — 681. Dreaming you are in an oxygen tent is an omen of being able to put your plans into successful action.

OYSTERS — 722. If you eat fried oysters in your dream, you will need to develop more self-confidence to make people notice you. If you open and eat raw oysters, it is a warning that someone you trust is acting in a tricky manner.

PISTOL

PACKAGE—003. If you dream of wrapping packages, you will succeed in your work. If you carry the packages, you will have to carry family responsibilities.

PADDLE—443. See Canoe.

PADDLE WHEEL—227. Seeing an old-fashioned boat with a paddle wheel is a warning not to take chances in financial matters.

PADDOCK—411. (Also see Horse.) Dreaming of horses in a paddock who are attended by their grooms is an omen of plentiful family finances.

PAGEANT—098. See Mardi Gras.

PAIL—619. See Bucket.

PAIN—730. If you dream you are in pain, watch out that someone will not slander you.

PAINT—314. (Also see Varnish.) If you dream of putting a new coat of paint on something, you are trying to keep secrets from your friends. If you see a house being painted, your friends are keeping secrets from you.

PAINTING—669. (Also see Art.) Beautiful oil paintings hanging on the walls mean you must not get too proud. If you dream of paintings of your ancestors hung on the walls, you will get a surprise legacy.

PAJAMAS—197. Whether you dream of wearing sleeping or lounging pajamas, you will go through some fickle love affairs.

PALACE—760. To dream of living in a palace means someone is going to marry a rich old person who is not long for this earth.

PALLBEARER—088. (Also see Funeral.) If you are a pallbearer at someone's funeral, you will get a better job.

PALMIST—433. To dream of having your palm read predicts worries in family and financial matters.

PALM TREE—799. Any dream about a palm tree means disappointment in business and friendships.

PALSY—014. To see someone who is shaking with palsy foretells you will have a long life.

PANCAKES—347. To see or cook or eat pancakes in your dream is an omen of relaxed home surroundings and a small inheritance.

PANIC—043. If you are in a panic-stricken area, you have to guard against quarreling with your employer.

PANSIES—558. These flowers in a dream portend misunderstanding and disputes with others.

PANTHER—997. To dream of this animal is an omen of troubles coming through a gossiping acquaintance. If you kill or frighten the panther away, you will earn much money.

PANTOMIME—314. If you watch a pantomime performance, or some people who cannot talk making sign language, you will be introduced to people in the theatre.

PAPER—280. (Also see Tissue Paper.) To dream of white paper means you will work hard but you will succeed. Colored paper shows that your efforts will not produce results. Torn or old paper is a sign of good chances coming your way.

PAPRIKA—763. To season your food with paprika predicts quarreling with someone who has a hot temper.

PARACHUTE—673. If you dream of descending and you cannot open the parachute, you will get harsh words from a person you love. If the chute opens and brings you safely to the ground, you will enjoy a peaceful love life.

PARADE—241. To dream you lead a parade predicts your election to office. If you watch a parade, you will get more money soon. If you are just one of the many paraders on march, some relatives will visit and stay too long.

PARADISE—683. See Heaven.

PARALYSIS—019. Dreaming of being paralyzed is a warning for you to guard your health.

PARASOL—714. To carry a parasol in your dream is a prophecy of a charming love affair at a vacation resort. If you open a parasol indoors, you will deposit money in the bank.

PARCEL—312. See Bundle.

PARENT—995. See Father, also Mother.

PARK—261. Any dream involving a park is a happy omen of good luck in love and marriage.

PAROLE—863. To dream you want to be of help to a paroled person who is released from prison means you will get a good job, perhaps with a newspaper.

PARROT—667. To listen to the chattering noise of parrots talking is a prophecy of slanderous people trying to make trouble for you.

PARSLEY—512. If you eat parsley in a dream, you will be happy in pleasant community activities.

PARSNIPS—308. To eat parsnips is to lose a friend.

PARSON—137. See Minister.

PARTNER—453. To dream of a good partner in marriage or in business, you will make money. If the partnership is dissolved, your luck will not be too good.

PARTY—619. (Also see Celebration.) To dream of being at a pleasurable party predicts a happy home life. A dull party means you will be disappointed in friends.

PASSPORT—802. If you get a passport to travel, you will have good financial opportunities. If you dream you lose the passport, you will receive sarcastic remarks from someone.

PASSWORD—695. To be asked to give a password when going into a new place, you will form new friendships.

PASTRY—447. (Also see Cakes.) If you eat rich pastries or pies in your dream, you will not be able to keep an important date.

PASTURE—805. See Meadow.

PATENT—617. Receiving a patent for something you invented is a sign of good luck at the races and in card games.

PATH—285. (Also see Trail.) If you dream of walking on a lovely path, you will have a date with someone you love.

PATIO—931. To eat or drink with others on an outdoor patio foretells a happy party where you will meet glamorous people.

PAUPER—073. (Also see Beggar.) To dream you have to beg from others is a warning for you not to become miserly.

PAWNBROKER—318. See Loan.

PEAS—792. If you dream of shelling peas, you will meet stimulating people. If you pick peas from the garden, you will need to make amends for rudeness to someone. Opening a can of peas predicts a temporary family misunderstanding.

PEACE—064. Dreaming that the world is at peace predicts a spiritual power to enable you to help others in simple ways.

PEACHES—430. If you eat unripe peaches, you will need to apologize for something you should not have done or said. Eating ripe peaches is a sign of a pleasant vacation trip.

PEACOCK—059. Dreaming of a strutting peacock with its tail feathers open is a sign of people becoming annoyed at you for being too proud.

PEANUT BUTTER—812. Eating peanut butter in your dream means you will be sorry because of not telling the whole truth to someone.

PEANUTS—415. To dream of eating peanuts means some new friends will invite you to a party.

PEARS—663. If you eat unripe pears, some malicious gossip will be told to you. To eat fresh pears, or see them with other fruits. means you will go to a party with neighbors.

PEARLS—918. Wearing pearls in your dream portends meeting people of high and noble position.

PEBBLES—085. If you walk barefoot on pebbles, you will have to exercise restraint in not looking for revenge on someone. If you throw pebbles into the water, you must guard jewelry or other valuables, if you are on the beach or at home in your bathroom.

PECAN NUTS—217. When you eat these nuts in a dream you will be invited to an enjoyable dinner.

PEDDLER—319. See Huckster.

PEKINESE DOG—568. To dream of this dog is a sign that some of your neighbors will protest that you are too noisy.

PEN—407. If you write with a free-flowing pen, you may succeed with some literary effort. If the pen spatters ink blots on the paper, you have to choose your friends more critically.

PENANCE—699. See Atonement.

PENCIL—814. If you dream of writing with a pencil that has a bad point on it, you need to use better care in your clothes and grooming. If you break the pencil point while you are writing, watch out to avoid accidents.

PENNY—311. (Also see Cent.) If you dream of giving someone a coin, you will have enjoyable times outdoors.

PENSION—633. To dream you receive a pension predicts you will do new work where you can use your hands as well as your mind.

PENTHOUSE—734. Whether you visit or live in a penthouse, you will be financially embarrassed if you spend extravagantly.

PEPPER—482. If you shake ground pepper on your food and it causes you to sneeze, you must guard against losing your temper and causing misunderstandings thereby.

PEPPERMINTS—512. If you dream of eating peppermints, you will be left an inheritance.

PERFUME—945. If a woman dreams of using perfume, she will meet an attractive new man. A man who dreams of using perfume will have some opposition from friends. If you smell the aroma of perfume, you will find stimulating companions of the opposite sex.

PERISCOPE—086. See Submarine.

PERMANENT WAVE—341. (Also see Hairdresser.) To admire your own permanent wave means you will find social happiness. If you get your hair waved, you will get some money soon.

PERSIMMON—638. To eat a ripe persimmon predicts a happy vacation trip. An unripe persimmon means you will not find some friends enjoyable.

PERSPIRATION—711. See Sweating.

PESSIMIST—540. (Also see Melancholy.) If you dream you are pessimistic, you will assume too many responsibilities of others. If you are with someone who is a pessimist, you will have good luck.

PETALS—961. If you pull the petals of a flower, you will undergo a broken friendship or engagement.

PETTING—337. If you dream of petting someone you love it is a sign of happy social relationships. If you are petting someone you do not love, you must be more discreet in your actions. To dream of petting in public predicts you must be careful not to incur criticism from others about your actions.

PETUNIA—291. To see petunias growing forecasts an invitation to a stimulating party. If you wear a petunia, you will not be too happy with the one you love.

PHANTOM—640. See Ghost.

PHARMACIST—742. See Druggist.

PHEASANT—618. Eating pheasant in your dream foretells more money coming to you. If you hunt pheasants, you will earn more money but you will have to be more thrifty.

PHONOGRAPH—123. See Record Player.

PHOTOGRAPH—058. (Also see Camera.) If you dream of viewing old photographs, you will meet old friends who are now successful. A photograph of someone you loved in the past is a sign of your life being pleasantly happy.

PHYSICIAN—669. See Doctor.

PIANO—408. If you dream that you or someone else is playing the piano beautifully, you will succeed in your aspirations. If the playing is out of tune, your job may not last too long. If you dream of being a piano tuner, you may do some work in the theatre.

PICKEREL — 631. If you dream of catching this fish, you will enjoy attractive people of the opposite sex. If the fish bites you, watch out for a friend who might prove insincere.

PICKLES — 889. To eat pickles shows good luck in your money matters and your health.

PICKPOCKET — 093. To dream you nab someone who is picking your pocket forecasts you will quarrel with someone to whom you owe money.

PICK-UP — 442. To dream of picking up someone of the opposite sex, or of being picked up, means you will have irritating differences with employer and with relatives.

PICNIC — 518. If you go on a picnic, you will have good times with friends.

PICTURE — 632. See Camera, Painting, Photograph.

PIE — 714. See Cakes, also Pastry.

PIER — 532. (Also see Dock.) To see ships tied up at a pier predicts a journey to a faraway place.

PIG — 618. See Hog.

PIGEON — 009. Dreaming of flying pigeons indicates family difficulties. To feed pigeons means upset business conditions. If you dream you receive a message through a carrier pigeon, you will get happy news from an old friend.

PILES — 315. See Hemorrhoids.

PILGRIMAGE — 540. If you or others make a pilgrimage to a shrine or other place, you will be lucky in money and friends.

PILLS — 683. To swallow a pill means you will move to a new place.

PILLOW — 249. If you dream of lying on a comfortable pillow, you will earn a good salary. If the pillow is uncomfortable, you will find it hard to pay off debts.

PILOT — 635. To dream you are piloting an airplane or a ship, your opinions will be respected by older people.

PIMPLES—504. If you suffer with pimples, you will not receive payment from those who owe you money. If you pick a pimple in your dream, you may suffer some illness.

PINS—779. To dream you are pinning up some wearing apparel, you will not be happy at an evening party. To sit on a pin, or hear a pin drop, foretells interesting surprises for you.

PINAFORE—013. (Also see Apron.) To see little girls' pinafores in your dream means you will find life peaceful.

PINCERS—412. If you use a pair of pincers to repair something, you will enjoy better business conditions.

PINCUSHION—937. To dream of a pincushion predicts social invitations from the opposite sex.

PINEAPPLE—691. Any dream about pineapples is a good omen of success in love and work and finances.

PINE CONE—378. To pick up pine cones from the ground is a sign of a long life. If you burn the cones, someone you know will give birth to a son.

PINE TREE—016. A pine tree in your dream signifies good health and contentment.

PING PONG—702. If you dream of a ping pong game, you will earn more money but will assume more responsibilities.

PINOCHLE—918. Whether you win or lose while playing this game, you will enjoy good relationships in social life.

PIONEER—196. If you pioneer in a new country, you will find fulfillment of your ambitions.

PIPE—373. If a woman dreams she is smoking a pipe, she will have to guard against being indiscreet in public. A man smoking a pipe will have a chance to earn better pay.

PIRATES—912. To dream of pirates is a warning that you must drive carefully as you might have an automobile accident.

PISTACHIO NUTS—604. To dream of this little green nut foretells happy friendships and social activities.

PISTOL—724. See Guns, also Revolver.

PITCHER — 123. To pour liquid from a pitcher signifies freedom from money worries. If you break a pitcher, you will have trouble with your feet. If you mend a broken pitcher, you will attend a party where there will be a lot of drinking.

PITCHFORK — 006. To dream you are working on a farm and using a pitchfork is a sign of good health. If you are being chased by a person or the devil with a pitchfork, you will have financial worries.

PITY — 712. When someone pities you in a dream, you will have good business dealings. If you pity another, you may need to share your home with an unwelcome relative.

PLAGUE — 453. If you dream that your town is in the woes of a horrible plague, it is a warning for you to see your physician.

PLAID — 219. If you see a Scotsman wearing a plaid kilt, you will have a stimulating love life. If you are wearing something made of plaid material, you will be visited by an old friend.

PLANS — 097. See Architect.

PLASTER — 638. To mix plaster in your dream foretells winning in a lottery. Plastering the walls is a sign of better earnings.

PLASTIC WRAPPING — 317. To buy or wrap things in plastic is a sign of good health and new friendships.

PLATES — 449. See Dishes.

PLATFORM — 940. (Also see Dais, Stage.) If you dream you are on a platform, you may receive an invitation to make a public speech.

PLATINUM — 313. To get a gift of platinum jewelry forecasts happy romance. If you dream of losing a platinum ring, you will need to make amends for overlooking a duty you should have performed.

PLAYGROUND — 699. Happy children in a playground means you will have a long visit with an old school chum.

PLAYING CARDS — 033. See Cards.

PLEDGE — 418. (Also see Oath.) To dream you made a pledge, signifies you may have to give up something you cherish in order to help someone in the family.

PLIERS—570. See Pincers.

PLOTTING—681. If you find out someone is plotting against you, you will get rid of your debts. If you dream you are part of the plotting, you will experience bad luck.

PLOW—314. (Also see Furrow.) If you dream you use a plow drawn by a mule or a horse, you will have success in work and in love. If you use a tractor plow, you can do well in real estate.

PLUCKING FEATHERS—830. If you dream you are removing pinfeathers from fowl, you will enjoy prosperity.

PLUMS—213. To eat a juicy plum in your dream is an omen of a promotion in your job. Canned plums foretell disappointments.

PLUMBING—793. Leaky plumbing in your dream foretells family quarrels. New plumbing means you will travel.

PNEUMONIA—634. If you suffer with this in your dream, you must be careful about your health and not take unnecessary chances.

POCKET—819. To dream you have a hole in a pocket predicts you will do something to annoy your neighbors. If you find unexpected things in your pocket, you will have a good home life.

POCKETBOOK—559. See Handbag.

POETRY—043. Reading or listening to poetry means you will have honor in your community. To be friends with a poet, shows you will be imposed upon by a friend.

POINTER—708. To dream of this dog in a hunting field, you will receive pleasant news.

POISON—450. (Also see Antidote.) If you take poison, you will be laughed at because of some unusual things you do.

POISON IVY—274. To dream you have poison ivy means you will argue with someone of the opposite sex.

POKER GAME—045. Whether you win or lose at poker, you will enjoy social activities.

POLICE—691. To talk to a policeman means you will visit good friends. If you are apprehended by a policeman or are trying to escape from one, you will have to ask pardon of friends for something you should not have done.

POLICE DOG—733. If you dream of a friendly dog, you should get outdoor exercise. If the dog attacks you, you will be asked to donate to a charitable cause.

POLICE WAGON—219. To dream of others being taken away in the "Black Maria," you will receive sad news. If you are being taken away, you will have good luck.

POLICY NUMBERS—406. If the same numbers repeat in your dreams, you will have good luck in all types of betting.

POLITICS—132. To discuss politics with your own sex you will have better money conditions. Politics discussed with the opposite sex is an omen of family quarrels.

POLKA—412. If you dance or watch others dance the polka, you will find new, fine friends.

POLO—405. Any dream involving the game of polo is a sign you will get an inheritance.

POLYANDRY—247. See Bigamy.

POLYGAMY—619. See Bigamy.

POMEGRANATE—921. Eating or picking the seeds of this fruit predicts pleasant relationship with the opposite sex.

PONCHO—460. To dream of wearing a poncho to protect you against bad weather, is a sign of good friends who will help you.

POND—312. (Also see Lake.) To dream of a pond means you will be successful in work and in meeting people of high position.

PONY—093. See Horse.

POODLE—682. To dream of this dog is an omen of stimulating and good experiences.

POOL, GARDEN—459. A dream about an outdoor pool shows good luck in your love life.

POOL TABLE—998. See Billiards.

POORHOUSE—614. To dream you or someone else is a poorhouse inmate forecasts a pleasant, long life.

POPCORN—013. If you eat fresh popcorn, you will have money and good times. Stale popcorn means you will get an unpleasant letter.

POPLAR TREE—721. To plant or see a poplar tree means prosperity. If you cut down the tree, you will suffer temporary money worries.

POPPIES—698. A field of poppies is a sign of adventurous love. If you dream of picking poppies, your plans will not materialize.

PORCELAIN—513. (Also see Dishes.) To see lovely porcelain objects, or to break one means you will make new friends.

PORCH—680. To dream you sit on a porch foretells you must be careful with the opposite sex. If you sleep on a porch, you will need to apologize for something you did.

PORCUPINE—731. This animal, in your dream, is a sign of a better job, but disappointment in friends.

PORK—419. Any dream about pork means a job promotion but you will have to work hard.

PORTER—881. If a porter carries your luggage, you will go on a successful trip.

PORTFOLIO—620. See Brief Case.

PORTHOLE—234. To dream of looking through a ship's porthole forecasts meeting an old friend.

PORTRAIT—096. To have your portrait painted or photographed is a prophecy of disappointments. If someone else poses for a portrait, you will enjoy an important social event.

POSTAGE—450. See Stamps.

POSTCARD—672. Whether you receive or write on a postcard, you will be worried socially and financially.

POSTPONEMENT—012. If you dream of postponing an important event, you will take a long trip after some delay.

POTS—334. Using or breaking cooking pots in your dream is an omen of upsetting situations with friends.

POTATOES—962. Any dream in which potatoes appear is a sign of good luck in money and personal matters.

POTTERY—837. To dream of seeing pottery means your life will take a turn for the better.

POULTICE—412. To apply a poultice on yourself or another portends good ideas which will prove successful.

POVERTY—504. If you dream of poverty, you will have good luck, but if the poverty is in filthy or vulgar surroundings, you will not fulfill your plans.

POWDER, FACE—961. See Make-up.

PRAIRIE—064. If you dream you are alone on a prairie, you will be troubled with a guilty conscience.

PRAISE—472. To be praised in your dream is a sign of new, successful events.

PRAYER—132. Whether you or another is praying, you will have a peaceful, successful life.

PREDICTION—391. To dream you make a prediction and it comes true, you will be able to give good advice to people.

PREGNANCY—048. See Conception.

PREMATURE BABY—620. See Incubator.

PRESCRIPTION—431. (Also see Druggist.) To have a prescription filled at a drugstore means you must be careful of your health.

PRESENT—806. See Gift.

PRESERVES—642. See Jam.

PRICKLY HEAT—491. To dream of suffering this skin condition is a sign of surgery for you or someone close to you.

PRIEST—388. To dream of a priest is a sign of good luck.

PRINCE, PRINCESS—627. If you dream of meeting one of these, you will be honored in your community, but some people might be jealous.

PRINTER—948. To dream of being a printer predicts you will be admired for your intelligence.

PRISON—541. See Convict, Jail, Warden.

PRIZE—820. If you present a prize to someone, you will get an inheritance. If you receive a prize, your work will prosper.

PRIZEFIGHTER—416. See Boxer.

PRODIGY—738. To dream of a young person who is brilliant in some field portends you will find most people boring.

PROFANITY—546. (Also see Curse.) To hear or utter profanity is a prophecy of bad luck in investments and with the opposite sex.

PROFIT—499. Dreaming of profits in business deals is a warning to you not to talk too much.

PROHIBITION—504. (Also see Teetotaler.) If prohibition against drinking is in force, in your dream, you will have some argument with a police officer.

PROMISE—914. See Pledge.

PROPAGANDA—619. If you dream you influence public opinion on certain subjects, you will not be trusted by some people.

PROPOSAL—046. To receive or make a proposal of marriage predicts attention from the opposite sex, also earning money but spending it extravagantly.

PROSTITUTE—472. (Also see Brothel.) To dream of a bold prostitute foretells a minor ailment. If the prostitute is poor and shabby, you will be able to help those who are needy.

PRUNES—321. Dried prunes in your dream are a sign of moving to a new place. Cooked prunes forecast good health.

PTOMAINE POISONING—225. If you dream of this illness, you are warned to follow a stricter diet.

PUBLICITY—683. See Propaganda.

PUBLISHER—430. To sign a contract with a publisher foretells financial success. If you meet a publisher in your dream, you may suffer money worries.

PUDDLE—891. See Mud.

PUGILIST—432. See Boxer.

PULPIT—805. If you deliver a sermon from a pulpit, you will be accused of double-crossing someone.

PULSE — 774. If you feel the pulse of a sick person, you must be cautious about new friends. If you dream your pulse is too fast, you will have stimulating new activities.

PUMP, WATER — 619. To dream you draw water from a pump predicts good luck in money dealings. If you cannot pump any water, some business deals will not materialize.

PUMPERNICKEL — 410. Seeing or baking or eating this bread forecasts enough money to enable you to shop for new things.

PUMPKIN — 327. Dreaming of a pumpkin is a sign of good living for your family.

PUNCH — 833. To dream someone is punching you means you will have to overcome your sensitivity.

PUNCTURE — 619. To dream you do not have a spare tire to replace a punctured one forecasts you will drive safely with no accidents. If you repair the puncture, you will quarrel with someone close to you.

PUNISHMENT — 478. See Chastisement.

PUPPIES — 003. To dream of lively puppies is a sign of happy life. A dead puppy predicts temporary sorrow.

PURSE — 100. See Handbag.

PUS — 941. To dream of pus oozing from a wound is a sign of an accident which might leave you with scars.

PUTTY — 067. If you use putty on a window pane, or mold putty into sculptured figures, you will have success in your work.

PYGMY — 556. (Also see Midget.) Whether you meet friendly or hostile pygmies in your dream, you will be disappointed in a friend you trusted.

PYRAMID — 953. If you dream of seeing pyramids, you will go on a long journey. If the pyramid is inverted and stands on its point, you will suffer financial loss.

QUAIL

QUAILS—880. To dream you hunt or eat quail, your life will be much happier.

QUAKER—671. If you meet Quakers, you will find living more comfortable and peaceful.

QUARANTINE—035. If you dream you are held in quarantine, you will enjoy good health.

QUARREL—670. Any dream in which there is quarreling predicts good luck in work and living conditions.

QUARRY—074. To dream of cutting pieces of rock from a quarry means you will work hard and earn little.

QUARTETTE—313. If you dream you are part of a musical quartette, you will not be in as high a position as formerly.

QUARTZ—858. If you see a lovely piece of quartz in your dream, be on guard against someone who wants to cheat you.

QUEEN—617. (Also see Throne.) To dream you are a queen or a king, you may be pressed for money you owe to others. To kneel before a monarch is a sign of a better job. To kiss the monarch's hand, means you have to be on guard against political or organizational injustice to you. To see a monarch ride by in a carriage or automobile predicts success to you.

QUESTIONS—523. If someone questions you in a dream and you have no answers, you will suffer bad luck. If you question other people, your luck will be good.

QUICKSAND—043. If you are sinking into quicksand, you must not pry into other people's affairs. If you help someone out of quicksand, you will earn more money.

QUIET—509. To dream you go suddenly from a noisy to a quiet place, you will travel. If you are in a quiet place, you will receive an unhappy shock.

QUILT—341. To dream you are covering yourself with a quilt is an omen of loving relatives and more earnings.

QUINCE—602. If you eat a ripe quince, you will not convince some people of your intelligence. Quince jelly, in your dream, means you will meet people who are mysterious.

QUINTUPLETS—721. To see or have quintuplets in a dream, is a forecast of happiness in love and marriage.

QUIZ—843. See Questions.

QUOITS—317. To dream you play the game of quoits predicts peaceful love and marriage.

QUOTATIONS—667. If you quote or hear quotations from famous people, you will rise in intellectual endeavors.

R

RHINOCEROS

RABBI—012. To dream of a rabbi is an omen of a new friend who will assist you in reaching your aims.

RABBIT—239. If you hunt for rabbits, you will meet interesting people on a trip. To see rabbits roaming around, you will have a good family life.

RABIES—538. (Also see Dogs.) To dream of a mad dog biting you and giving you rabies, means you have a gossiping enemy.

RACCOON—690. Any dream in which you see a raccoon is a sign of good luck.

RACING—318. To dream of watching or participating in any sort of a race, you will be lucky if you concentrate on getting ahead.

RACKETEER—743. To dream of being approached by a racketeer is an omen of bad decisions on your part, also a short illness.

RADIATOR—803. To dream of a cold or defective radiator forecasts some evil people will try to blackmail you, which you can avoid by using sound judgment.

RADIO—530. (Also see Broadcaster.) If you are annoyed by a blaring radio, you will have arthritis. A soft, pleasant radio program means pleasant home life and hobbies.

RADISHES—097. To dream of radishes portends you will meet a beguiling person of the opposite sex.

RADIUM—402. If you dream of holding a tiny piece of radium, you will receive much money but not much peace. To dream the radium burns you, watch out you don't drive too recklessly.

RAFFLE—065. To win something in a raffle is a sign of good luck in games of chance.

RAFT—732. To dream you are on a raft going through swift waters, you will have good luck. If you float on a raft in slow waters, you may not succeed because of your laziness.

RAGS—681. If you dream of wearing ragged clothing, you will come into an inheritance. To see dirty rags means a slight illness. If you dream you are handling clean rags, you will earn more money.

RAID—714. If you dream you are making a raid, you will get a money bonus. If you are in a city during an airplane raid, you will lose something you value.

RAILROAD—979. See Train.

RAIN—885. (Also see Lightning, Thunder.) To get wet in a rain, or watch the raindrops through a window, means you will be disappointed in business and in the one you love.

RAINBOW—631. Any dream about a rainbow means you will achieve much happiness.

RAISINS—729. If you eat raisins, you will be able to resist temptation.

RAKE—085. If you see or use a rake in your dream, you will receive a happy surprise.

RAM—627. To dream you are butted by a ram, or chasing it, you should get rid of some undeserving friends.

RANCH—501. To own or live on a ranch predicts you will meet people in theatre and newspaper work. If you are a guest at a ranch, you will incur criticism by joining others in gossiping.

RANGER—120. If you see forest rangers, you will want to see some old friends for whom you yearn.

RANSOM—932. If you are held for ransom, you will get money from someone who once hurt you.

RAPE—878. Any kind of dream about rape is an omen that you must always be on your best behavior.

RASPBERRIES—641. To see raspberries growing or to eat them, means happy social life.

RATS—519. If you dream you catch a rat in a trap, you will enjoy good luck. If rats are running around, you must guard your health.

RATTLE—583. To dream about a baby's rattle predicts you will be host at a dinner party.

RAVIOLI—060. To dream of eating ravioli is a sign of meeting people in high office from foreign lands.

RAZOR—789. (Also see Shaving.) To dream you are shaving yourself indicates satisfaction in your work and through friends. If you cut yourself while shaving, you will need to apologize for some misdeed. To dream you are using a razor as a fighting weapon, you will suffer financial loss.

READING—130. See Books, also Library.

REAL ESTATE—367. (Also see House.) To dream you buy or sell real estate forecasts you will get a legacy.

RECEPTION—293. To dream you are giving a reception, or attending one, you will be given honor by some groups.

RECIPES—669. To exchange recipes with another person predicts you will be rewarded for a good deed you performed.

RECORD PLAYER—074. To hear or record your voice means you will lose self-confidence in front of others. If you listen to recorded music, you will undergo interesting new experiences.

RECTUM—370. See Buttocks.

RED—641. The color red, which is dominant in a dream, is an omen you will have some minor irritations.

RED CROSS—939. If Red Cross workers are aiding people in distress, you will need to help someone who is close to you.

REFORMATORY—541. To dream of being an inmate in a reformatory, is a warning for you to choose your friends carefully.

REFRIGERATOR—023. If you put food into the refrigerator, you will be the host at several parties. To take food out means you will have a visitor at your home for a long stay.

REFUGEE—281. To see refugees fleeing from a country at war, is a prophecy of trouble in the nation. If you give shelter to refugees in your home, you will be misjudged by some friends for something you said or did.

REGIMENT— 369. If you see a regiment marching, you will succeed in participating in community affairs.

REINDEER—247. To see reindeers roaming free or pulling Santa Claus' sleigh, you will be encouraged in investments.

RELATIVES— 804. See various kinds of relatives in their separate listings.

RELIEF— 780. If you dream you are on welfare relief, better times are coming for you.

RELIGION— 314. (Also see Worshipper.) To dream you are being religious, you will further your interest in helping needy people. If you dream you are anti-religious, you will be criticized by some friends for your indifference to them.

RENT— 692. To dream you are collecting rent from someone, you will have a long visit from an older relative. If you dream you cannot pay your rent, you will be invited to a delicious meal.

REPORTER— 841. See Newspaper Reporter.

RESERVOIR— 993. Dreaming of a reservoir of water means you will buy a new wardrobe.

RESOLUTION— 530. To make and then break resolutions in your dream means you will have to take care of someone who will be very upset.

RESORTS— 079. If you dream of being at a resort, you will have a flirtation with someone of the opposite sex who will then become angry with you.

RESTAURANT—612. Eating a thrifty meal alone in a cheap restaurant predicts you will enjoy happy home life. If you dream you eat with others and share the bill, you will be made uncomfortable by some criticism.

RETAIL STORE— 201. See Store.

RETIREMENT— 681. To dream you retire from work forecasts a raise in pay, but you will need to work very hard.

REUNION—932. Any kind of a reunion in your dream is an omen of cooperation from others in achieving your goals.

REVEILLE—926. (Also see Bugle.) If you hear the bugler in a camp at daybreak, you will win out over others, if you work at it.

REVENGE—491. To dream of taking revenge on someone foretells sickness or an accident.

REVOLUTION—578. To dream of a bloody revolution means you need to straighten out your affairs. A bloodless revolution means you will change your job or residence.

REVOLVER—609. (Also see Guns.) If you shoot a revolver in your dream, you must curb your jealousy as it could bring you and others future unhappiness.

REVOLVING DOOR—807. If you dream you are stuck in a revolving door, you will not have good luck until you learn how to use your abilities more fully.

REWARD—312. To dream you get a reward for some good deed, it forecasts good luck through a surprise. If you offer another a reward, you may lose a legal fight.

RHEUMATISM—045. See Arthritis.

RHINESTONES—618. To see or wear something with rhinestones, you cannot rely on someone to give you necessary good references.

RHINOCEROS—713. If you see this animal in a zoo, you will be attractive to the opposite sex. If you see him in a jungle, you will have to pay your debts.

RHUBARB—301. Any dream involving rhubarb is a sign of good health.

RICE—681. A dream about rice, in any form, forecasts good news about relatives and travel to faraway places.

RICHES—538. See Millionaire.

RIDDLE—613. If you ask-and-answer riddles in your dream, you will find it hard to win the one you love.

RIFLE—407. See Guns.

RING—595. If a ring is placed on your finger by someone of the opposite sex, you will be irritated by the one you love. If you lose a ring, you will be lucky in business. If you find a ring, you will fall in love with someone new.

RINK — 208. To skate on an ice rink is a sign of a party with jolly friends. A roller skating rink foretells petty worries.

RIOT — 796. If you are caught in a rioting mob, you must be more cautious in your manner toward the opposite sex.

RIVER — 439. To watch a river flowing, or being on a river, means you will have more social success if you guard your actions.

ROAD — 718. If you are on a long, straight road, you will find life easier. If the road is winding and rough, you will meet success after some disappointments.

ROAST MEAT — 892. To dream you are carving a roast, you will be invited to a party.

ROBBERY — 315. See Burglars.

ROBIN — 530. To hear a robin sing is a sign of good things coming your way. A robin in a nest forecasts a raise in income.

ROCK — 315. To dream of successfully moving a big rock, your working conditions will be bettered. If you cannot move a rock that blocks your path, you will have hard luck. A falling rock shows you will make a change.

ROCKING CHAIR — 665. If you rock in a chair, you will have an easy life. To rock an empty chair is a prediction of unhappy family affairs.

RODEO — 358. (Also see Lasso.) A dream about cowboys and cowgirls at a rodeo predicts a happy reunion with old friends.

ROGUES' GALLERY — 385. To dream you see your own picture in a police file means you will have to be smart to avoid getting mixed up in a scandal. If you see the picture of someone close to you, you will be criticized by some important person.

ROLLER SKATING — 928. See Skating.

ROLLS — 434. See Bread.

ROOF — 099. If you nail shingles on a roof you will increase your income. To climb on a roof forecasts good relationship with old friends and family.

ROOSTER—676. A man who dreams of a rooster will have good luck, but a woman who dreams of a rooster will need to work hard.

ROPE—414. (Also see Cord.) If you handle a coil of rope, you will form a mutually good friendship.

ROSARY—529. If you count the beads of a rosary, you will find life more peaceful and easier.

ROSES—619. Fresh roses in a dream show a happy love life. Wilted roses foretell you will lose a friend. Artificial roses mean someone you trusted will prove to be false.

ROTTING—257. See Decay.

ROUGE—067. (Also see Cosmetics, Make-up.) Watching girls putting rouge on their faces in public portends trouble coming into your life. To see an old woman who is rouged, you will find life getting easier. A young girl who is rouged is an omen of you being uncooperative and getting scolded for it.

ROULETTE WHEEL—301. If a girl dreams she is playing roulette, she will fall in love with someone who is unworthy. If a man dreams he is spinning the wheel, he will have gambling luck.

ROYALTY—853. See King, Prince, Queen, Throne.

RUBBERS—816. See Boots, also Galoshes.

RUBBISH—476. See Garbage.

RUDENESS—021. See Arrogance.

RUBY—293. A dream involving rubies forecasts romantic love.

RUG—505. To dream of a beautiful rug is an omen of an unexpected legacy. An old and worn rug means money worries.

RULER—903. If you measure things with a ruler or yardstick, you will do some things to displease others. Breaking a ruler means good luck in buying and selling.

RUPTURE—618. To dream you are suffering with a rupture (a hernia) forecasts family difficulties, and warns against too much exertion.

SNAKE

SKELETON

SABER—723. See Sword.

SABLE—085. To see elegant sable furs in your dream foretells meeting an adventurous person of the opposite sex.

SABOTAGE—590. If you dream of participating in breaking up machinery or other articles, you will meet with an accident.

SADDLE—613. If the saddle slips under you, while you are riding on a horse, you must be more efficient in doing your job.

SADNESS—797. See Melancholy.

SAILOR—130. (Also see Navy.) To dream you are a sailor on a ship means an exciting journey. If you are a sailor ashore, you may quarrel with the one you love.

SAILBOAT—298. See Boat.

SAINT—812. Talking to a saint in your dream forecasts you having to confess for a misdeed.

SALAD—014. Eating a salad in a dream, is a sign of going to a party, where you will not know the guests and will appear to be shy.

SALARY—861. To dream you got an increase in pay foretells your salary will be cut. If you ask for a raise, but it is not granted, you will get some additional money.

SALMON—392. If you fish for salmon, you will meet interesting new friends. Eating fresh salmon means a stimulating love affair. Canned salmon foretells a thrilling journey for you.

SALOON—541. See Barroom.

SALT—541. Salt sprinkled on food means you will have a mild attack of indigestion.

SALVE—013. See Ointment.

SALVATION ARMY—244. If a meeting of the Salvation Army is in progress, you will be able to aid someone in need.

SANITARIUM—318. See Hospital.

SAND—664. Any dream which involves sand is a prophecy some hypocritical person will try to influence you against your desire.

SANDALS—730. Wearing sandals is a sign of a romance for you. If the sandals hurt your feet, you will quarrel with someone to whom you owe money.

SANDWICH—012. Dreaming of sandwiches is a warning for you to maintain congenial relationships with friends and avoid taking chances.

SAPPHIRE—699. To see this gem means you will meet someone in high position. If you wear a sapphire, you will be too hasty in actions.

SARDINES—415. Any dream in which a can of sardines appears is an omen of others being jealous of the things you achieve.

SAUERKRAUT—803. Eating sauerkraut or drinking its juice foretells hearing good music and having good health.

SAUNA BATH—421. See Turkish Bath.

SAUSAGE—639. If you see sausages in a butcher shop, your business affairs will get better. If you eat sausage, someone will say you interfere in his or her love affair.

SAVAGE—714. See Cannibal, also Head Hunter.

SAVINGS—001. To dream of opening a savings account is an omen of happiness and peace.

SAW—683. If you use a hacksaw, you will get a raise in pay but will need to work harder. A buzz saw in action predicts you will need to defend your reputation. If you dream of a hand saw, you will be involved in politics.

SAXOPHONE—492. To listen to a saxophone, or to lose one, means you will have good luck and enjoy social activities. If you dream you play the instrument, you will quarrel with a neighbor.

SCAFFOLD—990. (Also see Hanging.) An iron or wooden scaffold on a building forecasts better work opportunities.

SCALES—814. If you weigh yourself on a scale, you will go through small worries. To dream of weighing food means you will be prosperous.

SCALLOPS—664. Eating scallops in your dream foretells change to a new residence and a pleasant vacation.

SCANDAL—312. If you dream you are involved in a scandal, you must apologize for a misdeed. If you talk scandalously about another, you will be criticized by others.

SCAR—004. (Also see Blemish.) To see someone with a scarred face portends difficulty with your employer. If you have scars, you will have to clear your conscience of a misdeed.

SCARF—693. If you wear a bright colored scarf, you will be lucky in love. If you knit or sew a scarf, you may be jilted by someone.

SCENARIO—271. To dream you are writing a movie scenario, you will be interested in acting or writing.

SCHOOL—018. If you dream you are a child in school, you will meet an old friend.

SCIENTIST—450. Whether you dream of being a scientist or watching others do their work, you will meet people of high office or in theatrical groups.

SCISSORS—261. If you cut with a pair of scissors, someone is going to play a practical joke on you.

SCOLDING—778. If you dream your employer or parent is scolding you, you will need to be more careful about what you say to others.

SCOTTISH TERRIER—943. To dream of this lively dog forecasts an invitation to an interesting party.

SCOUT—013. See Boy Scout, also Girl Scout.

SCREAMING—980. If you hear someone scream, you will be able to assist sick, old people in need. If you scream in your dream, you may need to hide a family situation from others.

SCULPTOR—445. To dream of watching a sculptor work predicts you are taking a chance with new ideas. To look at pieces of sculpture means you may try to interfere with the affairs of others.

SEA—690. See Ocean.

SEAL—019. If you see a group of seals, you will be invited on a fishing trip. If you kill a seal, business matters will get worse. A sealskin coat worn by you or another means financial betterment.

SEANCE—328. See Occult.

SEARCHLIGHT—690. (Also see Spotlight.) If the searchlight is turned on, you will need to work hard but you will get your wishes. If the searchlight beams are directed to the sky, beware of false friends.

SEAWEED—721. If you dream of becoming entangled with seaweed, while you are swimming, you will need to fight the influence of someone who is trying to sway you.

SECRET—597. Whether you tell a secret or listen to one, you will become involved with gossiping people.

SECRETARY—381. (Also see Stenographer.) If you dream you are a secretary, or you employ a secretary of the opposite sex, you will have annoying situations with friends and relatives. If you dream of being elected secretary of an organization, your wages will be increased.

SEDUCTION—620. See Adultery.

SENATOR—015. (Also see Politics.) To dream you are a senator means somebody is going to ask you to do a favor.

SERENADE—159. Any dream about a serenade forecasts happy home life.

SERMON—805. See Pulpit.

SEWING—621. (Also see Mending.) To dream another person is sewing, you will need to save money for the future. If you are sewing, you will make a change for the better.

SEX—934. If you dream of watching or participating in a sex act, it actually has no meaning; but you must find the meaning of the other things in your dream.

SHAKES—583. See Palsy.

SHAKING HANDS—224. To dream of a hearty handshake forecasts new friendships. A weak handshake means disappointment over something you will undertake.

SHAME—480. If you dream someone is shaming you, you will be admired by friends and employer. If you shame another person, you may have an automobile accident.

SHAMPOO—619. (Also see Hair.) Whether you are shampooing someone's hair, or your own hair, you will get good news and have fun socially.

SHAMROCK—732. To see or wear a shamrock foretells getting three invitations for parties in one day.

SHAVING—152. (Also see Razor.) Shaving the face or any other part of the body means pleasant dates and meeting rich people.

SHAWL—628. If you wear a shawl in your dream, you must guard against being rude to some people.

SHEARS—795. See Scissors.

SHEEP—880. (Also see Lamb.) To dream you are shearing the sheep's wool, you will have more money. If you count sheep, you will have slight worries.

SHEETS—613. (Also see Bed.) To put clean sheets on the bed is a sign of prosperity. Rumpled sheets or being tangled in a sheet forecasts disappointment in love. To escape from a window by tying sheets together, means you will win out over temporary difficulties.

SHELLS—011. If you gather or see seashells, you will attend an occult seance.

SHERBERT—436. Any dream involving sherbert portends you have to be tactful in dealing with the opposite sex.

SHERIFF—321. To see a sheriff arrest someone, means arguing within the family. If the sheriff is trailing you, you will need to apologize to someone whose feelings you hurt.

SHIP—708. See Boat.

SHIP MODEL—683. If you build a ship model in your dream, you will have a romantic marriage.

SHIRT—219. If you wear a clean shirt, you will enjoy good luck. If buttons are missing on the shirt, you will argue with a relative. Losing a shirt means a time of sadness.

SHIVERING—481. See Ague.

SHOES—382. If you wear new shoes, you will take a trip. If you dream of old shoes, you will be peaceful in friendships and family life. If you throw old shoes after a wedding couple, or lose a shoe, you will have some small worries. If you lose a heel, you will have friction with friends.

SHOEMAKER—079. To see a shoemaker (a cobbler) working is a sign of someone coming to your help in a financial way.

SHORE—432. Walking along the shore of a river or other body of water predicts good luck in new undertakings.

SHOVEL—663. To see or use a shovel in your dream is a sign of added responsibilities.

SHRIMPS—126. To dream of this shellfish, means you will meet people of high position.

SIGN LANGUAGE—318. See Pantomime.

SIGNATURE—091. (Also see Autographs.) Whether you dream of signing a check or a legal paper, it means you will earn a modest living but have to work hard.

SILK—628. Any dream involving silk, whether in yard goods or in garments, foretells good luck in social and business matters.

SILO—983. If you see a silo in your dream, you will have to guard against over-drinking and getting into debt.

SILVER—316. To see silver tableware in your dream portends unwelcome visitors to your home. If you see silver money, you will work hard and be prosperous.

SIN—914. See Adultery, Morality, Religion.

SINGING—583. (Also see Music.) If you dream you sing solo, you will go on a vacation trip by yourself. If you sing with others, you will enjoy meeting old friends.

SISTER—497. Dreaming of a sister in trouble, is a sign of bad luck. If you dislike your sister in your dream, you will antagonize friends by telling lies.

SKATING—015. See Rink.

SKELETON—632. (Also see Bones, Catacombs, Skull.) To dream you find a skeleton foretells you need more courage to take a chance. If you see a skeleton on display, you will meet new friends of high intelligence.

SKIDDING—907. To dream you are in a car that skids, you will have to be careful in making family decisions. If you dream you are able to pull out of a skid, you will make a wise business decision.

SKIING—530. To ski smoothly downhill on the snow means you will receive an unexpected sum of money. If you overturn on the skis and go into a snowbank, you will have some differences with your employer.

SKIRT—633. To dream of seeing a woman in a short skirt, which shows her legs, forecasts financial betterment. If you wear a badly-fitting skirt, you will have some petty arguments with others.

SKULL—585. (Also see Skeleton.) Any dream involving a skull foretells success in some unusual activities.

SKUNK—916. If you see or smell a skunk, you will be disappointed in not being invited to a party. To kill a skunk in your dream means you will be lonely for someone.

SKY—230. A sky that is cloudy and gray is a prophecy of faithful friends. If the sky is colorful and sunny, you will terminate an exciting love affair.

SLANG—045. To dream of you or someone else using slang expressions means you will meet people of high position and glamorous personalities.

SLAUGHTER HOUSE—846. If you work in a slaughter house,

you will have to work harder to please your employer.

SLAVE—608. To dream you are enslaved to someone forecasts temporarary unpleasantness.

SLED—732. (Also see Toboggan.) To dream you are on a sled sliding over the snow, you will take part in stimulating social activities.

SLEEP—512. See Nap.

SLUMS—297. Dreaming of a slum area is a prophecy of loss of your home or other real estate.

SMALLPOX—541. To dream you are suffering with this illness, you will undergo an unpleasant situation which will later be remedied. If you nurse someone who has smallpox, you will enjoy new friendships.

SMOKE—066. If you see smoke from a chimney or a fire, you will earn more money. If you smell smoke, but do not know from where it comes, you will go through some irritating worries.

SMOKING—782. See Pipe, also Tobacco.

SMUGGLER—418. If you dream you or another is a smuggler, you will have to use tact to convince people you are not hiding things from them.

SNAILS—692. Any dream about snails predicts success in family life and in work.

SNAKE—343. To dream of a poisonous snake, you will encounter bad luck. If you kill the snake, you will find a way to solve problems.

SNAKE CHARMER—203. A snake charmer in your dream is a prophecy of an illness.

SNEEZE—815. If you sneeze in a dream, you will have good health and more income. If someone else sneezes, you must guard against infection.

SNOB—595. See Haughtiness.

SNOW—087. To dream you are struggling through heavy snowdrifts is a sign of success after you work hard to get it Snow clinging to tree branches means luck in investments. If you shovel snow, you will have to be cautious about an influential person and his actions toward you.

SNOWSHOES—629. To dream of snowshoes is a prophecy of good feeling toward companions, and a reward for doing something good for another.

SNUB—174. If someone snubs you, you may be criticized for the way you dress.

SOAP—550. If you dream about perfumed toilet soap, you will be happy in love. Strong-smelling or household soaps or detergents forecast hard work for you in order to earn a living.

SOCKS—379. See Stockings.

SODA—718. To drink an ice cream soda means you will meet some glamorous person, perhaps from the theatre.

SODA POP—606. Partaking of soda pop or cola drinks forecasts happy times with those you love.

SOFA—959. (Also see Couch.) If you dream of sitting on a sofa with the object of your affections, you will go on a successful business trip. If the sofa has any broken springs, some hard luck is on its way.

SOLITAIRE—302. If you play this card game in your dream, you will do work that is a strain on you. To win at solitaire, you will get some unexpected money.

SON—071. To dream about your son is a sign of happiness and pride in your child.

SORES—683. Whether you see sores on your body or on another person, you will get unpleasant news.

SORORITY—451. See Fraternity.

SORROW—083. See Grief.

SOUTH POLE—892. See Antarctic.

SPAGHETTI—663. To dream you are getting messed up with spaghetti while eating it, you will have an exciting good time with friends.

SPANIEL—721. Any dream in which a spaniel appears foretells good relationships with relatives, also with schoolteachers.

SPANKING — 423. See Chastisement.

SPARROW — 018. If you dream of these birds in the city, you will have family and money worries. To chase the sparrows away means you will have good luck.

SPATS — 370. To dream of wearing spats over your shoes is a sign of a new job. If you wear only one spat, you may lose your job.

SPEECH — 415. If you make a speech in your dream, you will succeed in work and friendships. To have to listen to a boring speech means you will make some sacrifice to help another's reputation.

SPELLING BEE — 691. If you participate in a spelling bee, you will be asked to compete for a prize. If you spell a word wrong, you will suffer embarrassment.

SPHINX — 406. To see the sphinx means you will meet a mysterious person.

SPICES — 023. If you dream about eating or smelling strong spices, you will take a long journey.

SPIDER — 982. (Also see Cobweb.) To see a spider in a web, you will achieve your ambition through industrious work.

SPINACH — 585. To eat spinach foretells good health and happiness. If there is sand or grit in unwashed spinach, you will meet people you dislike.

SPINE — 684. See Backbone.

SPINSTER — 723. A girl who dreams she is an old maid will get a proposal from an excitable and artistic man.

SPIRE — 575. (Also see Steeple.) A church spire seen in your dream portends love and friendships. If the spire leans to one side, you will work hard to achieve your aspirations.

SPIRIT — 683. See Ghost.

SPITE — 747. To dream you are spiteful toward another, you will undergo severe pain. If someone spites you, you will have to reprimand a friend.

SPITTING — 015. If you see someone spitting, you will find a friend to be distasteful to you.

SPLINTER—673. To get a splinter under your skin foretells family quarrels. If you remove someone else's splinter, you will lose an important paper or letter.

SPONGE—647. Whether you wash yourself, or your car or some other article with a wet sponge, or squeeze the water from a sponge, you will be able to earn more money. If you try to squeeze water from a sponge, you may lose at cards or other games of chance.

SPOON—930. If you dream of eating with a spoon the kind of food which needs a fork, you will be ridiculed by others. If you lose a silver spoon, you will have a financial loss.

SPORTS—278. See Arena, Athletics, Stadium.

SPOTLIGHT—018. (Also see Searchlight.) To dream a spotlight is on you while standing on a stage or platform is a sign of high honor being awarded to you.

SPRAIN—322. To dream you sprain some part of your body means you will be nominated for some office.

SPRINGTIME—447. To dream of beautiful weather and blossoming trees, you will have good luck in love and business.

SPRUCE TREE—203. A dream which shows a spruce tree is a forecast of good health.

SPURS—855. To dream of spurs foretells disagreement with someone who has a higher position than yours.

SPY—412. If you dream of being a spy, you will be asked to run for an office you do not want. If someone spies on you, you will have to be cautious about how you behave.

SQUASH—096. Cooking or eating squash forecasts new opportunities for you to increase your income.

SQUIRREL—761. If you feed nuts to a squirrel, you will enjoy social activities. Squirrels chasing through tree branches are a sign of someone coming after you to pay your bills.

STABLE—047. See Stall.

STADIUM—619. (Also see Arena.) If you watch a sports event in a stadium, you will enjoy stimulating social life.

STAG—387. See Deer.

STAGE—789. (Also see Footlights, Platform.) To dream you are on a stage, you will have a chance to express yourself in some creative manner.

STAGECOACH—521. If you drive the stagecoach, you will go through many exciting incidents. If you are a passenger in the coach, you will have a sentimental love affair.

STAGGER—302. To see a person staggering, you will be asked to help a friend. If you are staggering, you may be won over by someone's flattery.

STAIN—884. To dream of stains on clothing means you need to be careful about your friendships. If someone stains the family name, you will be honored for something you do.

STAIRS—316. If you stumble or fall on stairs, you will have to guard against being led into plots by people you trust. If you sweep or wash the stairs, you will enjoy better living conditions.

STALL—528. (Also see Paddock.) To dream of putting a horse in a stall, you will be better paid for good work. If someone puts you into a stall, you will win in a lottery.

STAMMER—067. See Stutter.

STAMPS—146. (Also see Letter, Mail, Postcard.) Any dream about buying or using or collecting stamps forecasts success in work and better financial conditions.

STAR—023. (Also see Evening.) If you see a bright star in your dream, you will be assisted by one of the opposite sex in gaining your goals.

STARCH—458. To use starch in a dream portends good pay for fulfilling a new project.

STARFISH—319. To see a starfish means you can get good advice and aid from an important person if you use tact in asking for it.

STARVATION—437. Whether you or other people starve, in your dream, is an omen of money worries which may be overcome if you are more thrifty.

STATEROOM—801. If you are alone in a ship's stateroom, a happy adventure will come to you. If you share the stateroom with another, you will be disappointed in some new venture.

STATION—632. See Depot.

STATIONERY—915. To buy office supplies in your dream portends better business conditions.

STATUE—794. (Also see Art, Sculptor.) If you carve a statue, you will get new chances to further your career aims.

STEAK—807. Any dream of eating or cooking steak predicts increase in earnings, also invitation to take part in important community events.

STEALING—541. See Burglars.

STEAM—224. To hear the hiss of escaping steam, or be burned by steam, forecasts you will have differences with people in your work. If you dream you turn off the steam, you will be able to solve a long-time problem.

STEEL—048. To see steel being manufactured in things of peacetime use, you will find reward in your work and in community projects. If the steel is used for destructive weapons, you will have to be wary of unfaithful friends.

STEEPLE—672. (Also see Spire.) Young people who dream of steeples will meet interesting people of the opposite sex. A broken steeple is an omen of disappointment with new plans.

STEEPLECHASE—039. To watch horses in a steeplechase race is a sign of interesting social life. If a horse and rider fall, you will need to pay for people attending a dinner.

STENOGRAPHER—841. (Also see Secretary.) If you dream you are a stenographer, you will have a happy marriage. If you make love to a stenographer in your dream, you will have to apologize for something you neglected to do.

STETHESCOPE—509. A doctor listening to your heart with a stethescope predicts you will achieve something for which you will receive compliments.

STEVEDORE—791. See Longshoreman.

STILETTO—803. See Dagger.

STILTS—315. To walk on stilts, or fall off them, forecasts you will have to be more humble than you now appear to be.

STOCK FARM—926. See Ranch.

STOCKINGS—558. If you darn holes in a stocking, you will work hard and find success but not much money. If you put on your stockings, you will start a new venture which may bring money rewards. To hang up a Christmas stocking means you will have many new friends but a scarcity of money.

STOCKS—016. See Bonds.

STOMACH—620. (Also see Belly.) To dream of having indigestion or sour stomach is a warning for you to curb your jealousy of others. If you have a stomach pain, some friend will betray your confidences.

STORE—814. If you dream of being the owner of a retail store, you will get an increase in money. If you work in the store, it predicts better conditions for you.

STORM—336. If you are caught in a rain or snowstorm, or a storm at sea, you will have temporary worries which you will overcome through control of your emotions.

STORY—406. (Also see Writer.) If you dream you are writing a story you will meet many disappointments. To read a story foretells happier days.

STOVE—793. See Furnace, also Oven.

STRAIT-JACKET—614. (Also see Insanity, Maniac.) To dream you try to get out of a strait-jacket, you will need to pay off money owing to others. If you get free from the strait-jacket, you will have good luck.

STRAWBERRIES—592. To eat strawberries in your dream is a sign of happy times with old friends.

STREETCAR—005. Riding on a streetcar is a prediction of riding in a new automobile very soon.

STRIKE—967. If you join others in striking against your employer, you will get to a higher position.

STRING BEANS—601. If you cook string beans in your dream, you may need to look for another job. To eat string beans means you will meet interesting, unconventional people.

STRIPTEASE—014. See Burlesque.

STUDIO—502. Whatever dream you have, if it takes place in a studio, it means you will associate with people interested in the arts.

STUDYING—314. See Learning.

STUNTS—933. To watch others doing stunts forecasts happy meeting with old friends.

STUTTER—822. If you cannot understand someone who stutters, or if you dream you are stuttering, you will have difficulty with a spiteful relative.

SUBMARINE—619. If you are in a submarine, you will need to apologize for not keeping an appointment. To look through a periscope means you will get a disturbing letter. If a torpedo is fired from a submarine, you will need to clear up misunderstanding with one of the opposite sex.

SUBWAY—244. (Also see Train.) To be in a subway wreck predicts an accident. If you ride in a crowded subway, you will need to control yourself in trying situations.

SUFFOCATION—550. If you dream you cannot breathe, or someone is trying to suffocate you, it is a warning you have to be outdoors to avoid illness.

SUGARCANE—799. To see sugarcane growing predicts financial betterment. If you see the cane being cut, your income will be diminished.

SUITCASE—096. To dream you are packing clothes in a suitcase foretells of a boring person coming to visit your home.

SUNDAE—781. See Ice Cream.

SUN DIAL—963. To see a sun dial and tell time by it, is a sign of your ambitions coming true.

SUNFLOWER—540. If you wear a sunflower, you will be criticized by others because of your casual behavior. To eat sunflower seeds means you will renew old friendships.

SUN LAMP—066. To dream you are under a sun lamp forecasts it is best for you to postpone a contemplated vacation until a later date.

SUNRISE, SUNSET—797. A beautiful sunrise or sunset seen in your dream, shows success in a new enterprise.

SUNSTROKE—682. If you suffer sunstroke in your dream, you will need to carry more family burdens.

SUPERINTENDENT—347. See Janitor.

SURF—298. To watch the surf beating on the seashore predicts you will be appreciated for your good work and you will be lucky in love.

SURFING—340. To dream of surfing on high waves means you will suffer through broken promises of others.

SURGEON—916. (Also see Operation.) If you dream you are a successful surgeon, you may get work on a newspaper.

SURPRISE—710. To be surprised in your dream means you will go through an exciting experience. If you surprise someone, your finances will increase.

SUSPENDERS—538. If a man dreams he loses his suspenders, he will win in a contest. A girl who dreams her boy-friend is wearing suspenders will be critical of him because of his bad manners.

SWAMP—267. To be lost in a swamp predicts money losses and family quarrels.

SWAN—617. Whether the swans are flying, or are gliding on the water, the dream foretells happy family life and good money conditions.

SWEARING—054. See Profanity.

SWEATING—889. To dream you are sweating, you will have to work hard, but will have a good life. If the sweat goes into your eyes, there may be illness in your family.

207

SWEATER — 440. To wear a sweater in your dream means you will be scolded for some unintentional wrong you did.

SWEETHEART — 692. If you dream of being happy with your sweetheart, you will enjoy good luck. If you quarrel in your dream, you will have to apologize for some foolish actions.

SWIMMING — 451. To teach someone to swim is a sign of better financial conditions. If you dream you swim in the nude, you will have good luck with money and social matters. To swim in a bathing suit means you will need to explain why you appeared to snub someone.

SWITCHBOARD — 128. (Also see Telephone.) If you operate a switchboard in your dream, you will meet a new friend who will wait for you to encourage the relationship.

SWORD — 643. If you fight a duel with a sword, you will show poor judgment in quarreling with a good friend. If you wear a sword, you will be offered a high position as an officer.

SWORDFISH — 9957. If you eat swordfish in your dream you will enjoy a vacation at the seashore. If you fish for swordfish, you will win out in your plans over the challenge of others.

SYNAGOGUE — 014. To attend a religious service predicts more knowledge for you through studying. If you dream you see people going into a synagogue, you will have good luck in finances.

SYRUP — 530. If you dream of syrup being poured on food, you will act as a matchmaker for two people in love.

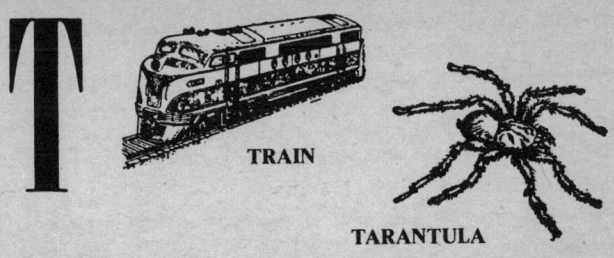

TRAIN

TARANTULA

TABASCO SAUCE—914. If you use this hot sauce on food, you will be adventurous in romance. If you burn your mouth with it, you will suffer through careless acts.

TABLE—362. To dream you are sitting at a table is a sign of good things coming your way.

TACKS—223. To drive tacks or nails with a hammer foretells you will do a good favor for a friend. If you pull out a tack, you will have a disagreement with your employer.

TAIL—619. To find you have a tail, in a dream, you will need to cover up for some misdeeds of your relatives. If you pull an animal's tail, you will have an illness.

TAILOR—432. If you order some clothing from a tailor, you will get an answer to a letter you wrote about a new job.

TAMALE—841. Eating tamales in your dream is a sign of a fishing or hunting trip.

TAMBOURINE—732. If you play the tambourine, you will hear unpleasant gossip. If a dancer plays a tambourine, it foretells you will have to be answerable to your family for some of your trips.

TANGERINE—911. See Oranges.

TANGO—127. To dream you are watching or dancing a tango means you will be extravagant in spending for amusements and drinking.

TAPE RECORDER—013. See Record Player.

TAPESTRY—619. If you see beautiful tapestries in your dream, you will have to be careful about people who gossip about you. Torn tapestry forecasts pessimistic thoughts.

TAPEWORM—483. To dream of having a tapeworm means you will get a legacy.

TAPIOCA—923. To eat tapioca pudding predicts you will be unhappy because of opportunities you ignored.

TAPROOM—619. See Barroom.

TAR—405. If you dream of getting tar on your body or clothing, you will have to be wary about some unfaithful friends.

TARANTULA—671. If you get bitten by this large spider, you will need to guard your health and avoid accidents.

TASSEL—803. To dream of tassels on draperies or other articles, you will work hard, but will not be paid enough.

TATTOO—305. To dream you are being tattooed foretells a long journey. If you see peculiar tattoos on another's body, you will need to keep secrets to yourself.

TAXES—182. To dream of having to pay too many taxes means you will have a chance to earn more money.

TAXICAB—370. See Cab.

TAXIDERMIST—518. If you dream of seeing birds or animals or fish being stuffed by a taxidermist, you will be popular with your friends.

TEA—247. Any dream which shows tea being poured or drunk is a sign of social life and a visitor to your home.

TEACHER—019. If you dream you are a teacher, or studying to be one, you will have many physical and psychological problems. If you meet your old schoolteacher, you will be asked to donate to a worthy charity.

TEAR GAS—833. If you see a crowd dispersed through the use of tear gas, you will worry about a friend who is in need.

TEARS—624. See Crying.

TEASING—915. To dream you are being teased, means you will need to use tact to have people understand your actions.

TEETH—312. See Tooth.

TEETOTALER—625. (Also see Prohibition.) If you dream of a teetotaler refusing a drink you offer, you will be the loser in a family discussion.

TELEGRAM—981. To receive a happy telegram in your dream foretells you will get some money. If you get an unhappy telegram, you may have difficulty with the tax collector.

TELEPATHY—607. To dream you receive a mental telepathy message is a sign of a letter with good news coming to you.

TELEPHONE—451. (Also see Switchboard.) To dream of making a call means you will have a reunion with an old friend. A telephone bell ringing is a sign of worries and illness.

TELEVISION—311. (Also see Broadcaster.) If you dream you watch a public event on TV, you will make more money through working harder. To watch a program that shows death by capital punishment, you will have bad luck.

TEMPER—743. See Anger.

TEMPERATURE—847. See Thermometer.

TEMPLE—660. See Church, also Synagogue.

TEMPTATION—772. To dream you are being tempted by one of the opposite sex foretells you will have to guard your actions and your reputation. If you dream you are able to withstand temptation, you will find life much easier.

TENNIS—812. If you dream you play tennis, whether you win or lose, it means you will be socially popular. If you watch someone play, you will earn more income.

TENT—139. To dream you are in a tent, you will enjoy better social and business matters. If you dream the tent is blown down in a storm, you must guard against an accident.

TEPEE—543. See Wigwam.

TERRIER—806. To dream of any breed of a terrier is a warning you may become too tense about problems.

TERROR—405. See Fear.

TEXTBOOK—983. If you dream of studying a textbook, you will be offered a better position.

THANKSGIVING—078. (Also see Turkey.) To dream of a happy Thanksgiving dinner foretells a better life with more money.

THEATRE—628. A play being produced in the theatre predicts stimulating social activities. If the theatre is dark, you will be bored with existing conditions.

THERMOMETER—307. If you dream you are reading a thermometer, you need to build up self-confidence in meeting the public.

THIEF—449. See Burglars.

THIMBLE—627. To dream of giving someone a thimble as a present portends happiness in love. If you lose a thimble, it predicts a minor accident.

THIRD DEGREE—782. To dream you are given the third degree, in an initiation to an organization, you will form lasting friendships. If you are given the third degree at police headquarters, you should be cautious about whom you pick as friends.

THIRSTY—041. If you quench your thirst at a spring or a well, you will get well paid for your services. If you suffer from thirst in your dream, you will be invited to visit faraway relatives. To drink hard liquor to quench a thirst predicts an accident.

THREAD—935. See Needle.

THRESHING—674. If you see wheat or other grains being threshed, you will enjoy a happy life and more money.

THRIFT—009. (Also see Budget.) If you dream of putting savings in a bank, you will get money through the mail.

THROAT—411. (Also see Neck.) To dream you are aware of the throat of one of the opposite sex forecasts you will be generally dissatisfied with people.

THRONE—618. If you sit as a king or queen on a throne, you will not gain your goals if you hesitate to take necessary risks.

THUMB—731. (Also see Finger, Hitchhiking.) If you dream you have a sore thumb, you will receive some money. If you are thumbing a ride from a passing car, you must be more careful of your behavior.

TIARA—830. (Also see Crown.) If you wear a jewelled crown, you will suffer through envious friends.

TICKLE—830. To dream you are being tickled, or are tickling someone, means you need to be careful in attitude toward the opposite sex.

TIDES—314. To watch the tide go out predicts financial worries. If you dream you see the tide coming in, you will be relieved of money problems.

TIE—745. See Necktie.

TIGER—693. If you are attacked by a tiger in your dream, you will have family arguments. If you kill the tiger, or put it to flight, you will have good luck.

TIME CLOCK—591. To dream you punch a time clock, it foretells you will please your employer with your good work.

TINSEL—003. Any use of tinsel as a decoration, in your dream, means you will need to apologize for something you did not mean to do.

TINTYPE—100. A dream which includes tintypes forecasts a happy married life.

TIRE—685. To dream of a tire blowout or changing a tire or losing a tire, predicts you will have some family and financial irritations. If you buy a tire, you will enjoy peace of mind.

TIREDNESS—792. To dream you are tired predicts good health and increased income.

TISSUE PAPER—812. (Also see Paper.) Using tissue paper to wrap parcels forecasts good luck in investments.

TOAD—368. If you pick up a toad in your dream, you will have a small accident. To step on a toad means you will be able to break up a plot to do you harm.

TOADSTOOL—413. (Also see Mushroom.) Dreaming of eating a raw toadstool means trouble ahead. If you give a toadstool to another, you will need to avoid misunderstanding with friends.

TOAST—530. Eating toast in your dream portends a social invitation. If you butter the toast, you will have to meet added expenses. If the toast is burned, you will have minor troubles.

TOASTMASTER—990. To dream you are the toastmaster at a banquet, you will be respected in your community.

TOBACCO—842. (Also see Pipe.) If you dream you are smoking. you will have a contented life. If you chew tobacco, you will displease one of the opposite sex.

TOBOGGAN—638. (Also see Sled.) To dream you are racing downhill in a toboggan, you will receive a surprise inheritance. If the toboggan turns over in the snow, you will have some unpleasantness with your job.

TOILET—714. (Also see Lavatory.) If you dream you see someone entering a toilet, you will have to give someone money for a needy cause.

TOMATOES—076. Whether you eat tomatoes or drink tomato juice in your dream, you will enjoy much travel.

TOMB—541. To dream you enter a tomb means you will overcome your enemies. If you are locked in a vault, you will suffer an illness.

TOMBSTONE—095. See Gravestone.

TOM-TOM—612. (Also see Drum.) To hear in your dream the beat of a tom-tom forecasts some unpleasant occurrences, which will be difficult to tackle.

TONGUE—934. If you dream someone is sticking out his or her tongue, you will be the topic of malicious gossip by your neighbors. To dream you eat sliced tongue, you will go on a pleasant picnic.

TONSILS—518. To dream of having your tonsils removed foretells you will lose some valued article.

TOOLS—321. If you use tools of any sort, you will get a salary increase. To dream you are searching for a lost tool, you will get a better job if you learn how to control your temper.

TOOTH—066. (Also see Buck Tooth, Dentist.) To suffer a toothache in a dream means upsets in family and business matters.

TOOTHBRUSH—519. See Brush.

TOOTHPICK—271. To pick your teeth with a toothpick is a sign of unfaithful friends who want to hurt you.

TORCH—304. If you dream you carry a lighted torch, you will have troubles in your love life.

TORPEDO—562. (Also see Mines.) If you dream you are on a ship or submarine, and torpedoes are being fired, you will run into social and financial difficulties.

TORTURE—781. To dream someone is torturing you, it means you may become unnecessarily suspicious of people. If you see a person or animal being tortured, you will go through some psychological tensions.

TOTEM POLE—905. Dreaming of a totem pole foretells a happy meeting with a relative from a far city.

TOUPEE—811. See Wig.

TOWEL—422. If you use a cloth towel to dry your face and hands, you will become prosperous. If you use a paper towel, you will suffer money losses.

TOWER—014. To dream you see a tall tower, or look down from one, forecasts false friends may try to cheat you.

TOYS—620. If you dream you present toys to a child, you will win the admiration of friends and relatives. If you play with toys, you will meet new friends.

TRACTOR—405. (Also see Plow.) To drive a tractor in your dream is a sign of a profitable business matter. If the tractor does not run, your lover will prove to be fickle.

TRAFFIC—892. If you watch busy traffic in a city, or drive in a traffic jam, you will need to solve annoying problems in business and personal life. If you dream you drive smoothly through traffic, you will be able to find solutions to pressing problems.

TRAIL—678. (Also see Path.) If you follow a trail on foot or horseback, you will succeed through concentration and hard work. If you lose the trail, you will meet an exciting person of the opposite sex.

TRAILER—953. To dream of living in a trailer forecasts you will change your place of residence.

TRAIN—831. (Also see Freight Train, Subway.) To dream you are on a train means you need to concentrate more on your work to get better results. If you ride in a pullman car, you will earn more money. If you missed the train and it rode past you, you will find a good friend who will be of help to you.

TRAITOR—674. To dream of one who is a traitor to his or her country portends temporary financial strain.

TRAMP—151. (Also see Bum.) To dream you are a tramp, you will soon find life easier. If a tramp asks you for food and you refuse, you will have to work too hard to earn very little. If you give food to the tramp, you will be lucky in real estate.

TRAPEZE—688. To dream of being a trapeze performer predicts happy marriage. If you fall from the trapeze, be careful not to make foolish mistakes.

TRAVEL—890. Any dream which involves traveling predicts money coming to you soon.

TRAY—412. If you carry a tray loaded with dishes, you will enjoy good luck. To drop the tray and break dishes is a sign of troublesome times.

TREACHERY—763. See Traitor.

TREASURE HUNTING—613. To dream of digging for buried treasure portends good health. If you dive in the ocean to hunt for treasure, you will get an expensive present. If you find a treasure without hunting for it, you will have exciting travels.

TREES—309. (Also see various trees listed alphabetically by their names.) To see beautiful trees in a forest, or to plant a tree, signifies happiness in love and marriage. If a tree is cut down, you will be disappointed in love. To cut pieces of bark from a tree means embarrassment with the opposite sex.

TRIAL—841. (Also see Court of Law.) To dream you are on trial, you have to consider the best way to handle problems which might prove serious.

TRICKS—813. (Also see Magic.) To dream you are doing tricks to make people laugh, you will be asked to join an organization.

TRIPLETS—215. To dream you are the parent of triplets predicts you will be the center of social attention. Triplets being wheeled in a large baby carriage are a sign of good luck in card games.

TROLLEY CAR—693. See Streetcar.

TROPHY—413. To dream you win a trophy in an athletic event, you will do well in business deals.

TROPICS—832. If you dream you are in the tropics, you will get gifts of fruit from a friend. To be friendly with those who live in the tropics, you will be fickle in love.

TROUSERS—617. To dream you are pressing a pair of trousers means a raise in salary. If you are in public without your trousers, you will need to apologize to someone toward whom you were rude.

TROUSSEAU—762. If you dream of putting a trousseau together, you will find joy in love and marriage.

TRUANT—415. To dream you are playing hookey from school, forecasts you will find a new friend who will be forever loyal to you.

TRUCK—959. To dream you are a truck driver foretells a happy home life and good income. If you dream you run the truck off the road, you must guard against being held up by a robber.

TRUMPET—803. To dream of blowing a trumpet means you will take pride in a good achievement. If an angel blows a trumpet, you will have an arthritis attack.

TRUNK—542. (Also see Baggage.) If you pack a trunk, you will go on a trip. If you unpack a trunk, it means a change of address. To dream you have to carry a heavy trunk, you will undertake new activities.

TUBERCULOSIS—619. If you dream of having this disease, it is a warning to guard your health.

TUGBOAT—724. To dream of a tugboat on a river, you will work harder and may get into some labor problems.

TULIPS—076. To see tulips growing means much fun with the opposite sex. If you plant tulip bulbs in your dream, you will have some disappointments.

TUNA FISH—291. Eating tuna in a dream foretells you will be bored. To fish for tuna means you will enjoy outdoor activities.

TUNNEL—840. If you go through a dark tunnel, you will gain your ambitions, but will first go through some discouragement.

TURKEY—618. (Also see Thanksgiving.) To kill and prepare a turkey for cooking predicts good luck in money matters. Seeing a flock of live turkeys means you will be asked to speak at meetings.

TURKISH BATH—978. If you take a steam bath, your job may become hard to handle.

TUXEDO—581. To dream you are wearing a dinner suit means you will be asked to give someone money. If you wear a white tie with the tuxedo, you will be the subject of malicious gossip.

TWEEZERS—672. If eyebrows or facial hairs are plucked with tweezers, you will meet interesting people of the opposite sex.

TWINS—086. Dreaming of twins means good luck in family and money matters.

TYPEWRITER—712. To dream you write love letters on the typewriter portends small annoying troubles. If you use a typewriter in your dream, you will get a higher position. If the typewriter is out of order, you will receive unpleasant news.

TYPIST—341. See Secretary.

U

UKULELE

UMBRELLA

UGLINESS—540. To appear ugly in a mirror or to meet ugly people predicts you will have misunderstandings in social and business matters.

UKELELE—65l. Pleasant music strummed on a ukelele is an omen of a sentimental reunion with an old friend. If you dream a string breaks on the ukelele, you will have temporary hard luck.

UMBRELLA—742. Dreaming of an umbrella, carried in the rain, predicts sudden changes for the worse in your general conditions. If the umbrella is carried in sunny weather, you will get sudden news which could change the pattern of your life.

UMPIRE—907. To dream you are an umpire at a baseball game and your decision is being questioned, you may have serious family quarrels. If you criticize an umpire's decision, you are being studied by a skeptical person who may leave you a legacy.

UNCLE—632. See Aunt.

UNDERTAKER—224. (Also see Burial.)

UNDRESSING—579. To dream of one of the opposite sex undressing is a sign you must be skeptical in placing your faith in new people you meet.

UNFAITHFUL—765. See Infidelity.

UNIFORM—013. If you wear any kind of uniform, you will receive public respect for something you do for others.

UNION—981. See Guide, also Wedding.

UNIVERSITY—630. (Also see Campus, College.)

USHER—80l. See Laborer.

VIOLIN
Man Playing a Violin

VACANT HOUSE—595. To dream you are alone in an empty house means you will need to start at the bottom and work your way up to a higher position.

VACATION—833. (Also see Resorts.) If you dream of taking a vacation from work, you will enjoy increased earnings.

VACCINATION—617. To dream of being vaccinated means you will succeed in working at something which expresses your own ideas.

VACUUM CLEANER—938. To use a vacuum cleaner foretells good luck with the opposite sex.

VAGABOND—412. If you dream you are a happy vagabond, you will be able to relax and take a vacation.

VALENTINE—580. If you receive or send a pretty valentine to someone, you will meet someone who will prove fickle. To receive or send a comic valentine means you will have a severe headache.

VALET—667. To dream of being attended by a private valet predicts recognition for you in your community.

VALISE—012. See Suitcase.

VAMPIRE—339. (Also see Blood Sucker, Leech.) If you dream a vampire is sucking your blood, you will undergo unpleasant experiences. To dream you kill the vampire foretells you will be lucky in love.

VAN—087. To dream your furniture is being loaded on a moving van, or you are riding in the van, you will move to a better place and be financially successful.

VANILLA — 697. Enjoying the taste of vanilla in your food means you will be the guest of honor at a party.

VARNISH — 321. (Also see Paint.) If you dream of varnishing a floor or furniture, you will need to apologize for an error you made.

VASE — 800. A vase filled with lovely flowers signifies you have faithful friends. If the flowers are wilted, you will be temporarily sad.

VAUDEVILLE — 253. Whether you watch or take part in a vaudeville show, you will meet interesting people who will be hard to understand.

VAULT — 603. See Tomb.

VEGETABLES — 014. If you raise vegetables, your family will be healthy and happy. To eat vegetables predicts you will be asked to pay up an old debt.

VEIL — 951. Whether you or another is wearing a face veil, or a bridal veil, it means you will do something daring and succeed in it.

VEIN — 087. (Also see Artery, Blood, Jugular Vein.) If you cut a vein, you will get disturbing news from someone you love.

VELVET — 708. To wear velvet in a dream predicts you will need to repent for something you will do.

VENTRILOQUIST — 530. If you laugh at a ventriloquist's performance, you will be the subject of another's sarcasm.

VERMIN — 429. To dream your body has vermin on it, you will not succeed in a new plan.

VERTIGO — 619. (Also see Dizziness.) If you dream of sudden vertigo, you will need to be cautious with the opposite sex.

VEST — 797. Any dream about a vest foretells you will over-indulge in food and drink and displease some people thereby.

VETERAN — 548. To dream about marching war veterans forecasts your being scolded for unfinished tasks.

VETERINARIAN — 326. If a veterinarian is helping a sick animal, you will meet with a slight accident.

VILLAIN—074. If someone calls you a villain, you will go through family irritations. If you dream you call another a villain, you will be attractive to the opposite sex.

VINES—514. If you dream of a building overgrown with vines, you will be made happy by a bearded stranger.

VINEGAR—620. Flavoring food with vinegar portends happy family life.

VINEYARD—068. To dream of vines covered with grapes, you will try out new ideas. If the vines are bare, you are warned not to try anything which may be dangerous.

VIOLETS—912. To pick or wear violets is a sign of going higher in the social scale.

VIOLIN—471. To dream you are playing the violin foretells you will be puzzling to people because of your original ideas, though they will be friendly to you.

VIRGIN—619. If a girl dreams she is a virgin, she will be attractive to the male sex. If a married woman dreams she is a virgin, she will undergo some disappointing events.

VISION—714. (Also see Mirage.) To see pleasant visions means you will be happily surprised. Weird visions predict you will go into debt.

VISITOR—851. If you dream of having a visitor, you will get a welcome gift. If you are visiting some home, you will receive an interesting invitation.

VOICES—622. To dream of hearing voices without seeing the people, you will go through uncomfortable situations about money and health.

VOLCANO—013. To see lava flowing from an active volcano is an omen of some differences with a neighbor, which will be straightened out.

VOMITING—927. Any dream about vomiting is a sign of good luck in your home and business.

VOTE—614. See Election.

WOLF

WADING—409. See Swimming.

WAFFLES—613. To dream of eating waffles, you will part from someone of the opposite sex. If you cook waffles, you will need to take care of a cranky child.

WAGER—738. See Bet.

WAGES—913. See Salary.

WAGON—018. To ride on a wagon in your dream, you will go to an auction sale.

WAITER, WAITRESS—430. If you leave a tip for the one who waits on you, you will lose a small article of value. If the service is slow, you will argue with your landlord. If the waiter spills food on you, you will quarrel with your best friend.

WALLET—992. To dream you find a wallet with money, you will go on a trip. An empty wallet indicates you will be rewarded for something good you do. To dream you lose your wallet, you may be caught in stormy weather.

WALLPAPER—014. If you paper a wall and do a bad job of it, you will have a visitor. To dream of a professional paperhanger doing a good job, you will go to a theatrical event.

WALNUTS—693. A dream in which you shell or eat walnuts is a sign of contentment in love and money matters.

WALTZ—458. If you dream you dance the waltz, you will be faced with a tough decision. If you listen to waltz music, you will meet one of the opposite sex.

WAR—615. See Arms, Army, Battle, Bombs, Mines, Navy, Submarine, Torpedo.

WARDEN—054. A warden in your dream foretells you will have a slight illness.

WART—911. A wart on your body, or someone else's, forecasts you will try to help others, but will end up in an embarrassing situation.

WASHING—690. See Laundering.

WASP—841. To get stung by a wasp in your dream means you will spend money foolishly.

WATCH—385. If you wear a watch in your dream, some important person will help you.

WATER—672. To dream you drink hot water means difficulty in personal and money matters. Drinking cold water predicts good luck. If you throw water on someone, you will annoy friends with your actions.

WATERFALL—014. If you see a beautiful waterfall, you will meet fine people who will be very understanding.

WATERMELON—295. To eat watermelon in your dream predicts a leisurely cruise on a ship.

WATER SKIING—804. If you dream of water skiing, you will be made uncomfortable by a person who does not like you.

WATER WELL—318. To dream of a well which has plentiful water means you will have a comfortable income, though not wealthy.

WAVES—640. If you dream of high waves dashing on the shore, you will be disillusioned about your love life.

WAX—713. (Also see Beeswax.) If you walk on a waxed floor, you will break some important dates.

WEALTH—054. See Millionaire.

WEAVING—691. If you dream you are weaving, you will enjoy peace and prosperity. If you watch someone weaving, you will succeed in your work.

WEB—187. See Cobweb, also Spider.

WEDDING — 509. (Also see Bride, Marriage.) If you dream of attending another's wedding, you will meet new friends. If you go to your own wedding, you will find happiness in love. To eat wedding cake means a long, happy marriage.

WEEDS — 337. Dreaming of weeds in a garden foretells you will need to protect yourself against those who spread gossip.

WEIGHING — 418. See Scales.

WELFARE — 780. See Relief.

WELL — 327. See Water Well.

WHALE — 061. See Harpoon.

WHARF — 804. See Pier.

WHEAT — 630. To dream of a field of wheat forecasts peace and prosperity.

WHEEL — 705. (Also see Machinery.) Turning wheels in a dream predicts hard work for which you will be well rewarded. If you see a wheel on the road, you will be delayed in some of your plans. If a wheel comes off an automobile, you will meet with an exciting event.

WHEELBARROW — 132. To push a loaded wheelbarrow means happy times with the opposite sex. A wheelbarrow turned upside down means many responsibilities for you.

WHIPPING — 619. To whip a person or an animal in your dream, predicts someone will try to disturb your peace of mind.

WHISKERS — 348. See Beard.

WHISKEY — 065. If you dream of drinking whiskey, you will work hard without getting paid enough.

WHISTLE — 739. If you whistle for a police officer, you will not have much money. To whistle for a taxicab means you will enjoy prosperity. If you whistle a tune, you will get something you wished for.

WHITE SLAVE — 318. See Prostitute.

WHITEWASH — 005. To dream you are using whitewash forecasts you will need to help someone who is in trouble.

WIDOW, WIDOWER—614. To dream you are without a mate forecasts a letter which will contain money.

WIG—330. If you dream you wear a wig or toupee, you will get a better job. If the wig is taken off or blown away in public, you will need to answer questions you would rather avoid. ·

WIGWAM—442. To dream you are sitting peacefully in an Indian's wigwam, you will receive a lovely gift.

WIND—699. A gentle wind foretells good luck. A gusty wind means you will work hard to overcome difficulties.

WINDMILL—732. To see a windmill in your dream means you will need to be diplomatic toward people you do not like.

WINDOW—014. (Also see Bay Window.) If you dream of breaking a window, you will encounter bad luck. To open a window means good health. To shut a window foretells you will have a visitor. If you go into a house through the window, you will be slandered by someone.

WINDOW SHADE—173. If you lower the shade, you will fail in a new plan. If you raise the shade, good luck will come soon. If the shade suddenly rolls to the top of the window, you will be happily surprised.

WINDPIPE—267. To dream something is stuck in your windpipe foretells you will need to pay your debts.

WINE—450. (Also see Drinking.) If you dream you get drunk on wine, you will need to be careful not to betray secrets. To drink wine in moderation means you will be influenced by someone in the church.

WING—887. To see a bird with a broken wing predicts disappointment in your aspirations.

WINK—342. If you dream you are winking at someone, you will need to be more discreet in dealing with others.

WISHBONE—873. To break the wishbone, while making a wish, foretells you will receive an inheritance.

WITCH—614. To see a witch riding on a broomstick is an omen of happy social times.

WOLF—608. If you dream of wolves pursuing you, you will need to borrow money. If you kill or scare off the animals, you will have better luck.

WOODPILE—914. To dream of sawing or chopping wood for a woodpile is a prophecy of good luck.

WORMS—285. Dreaming of worms is a sign of good luck, especially to those who do creative work.

WORSHIPPER—451. (Also see Religion.) If you dream of seeing people in a house of worship, you will win advancement through hard work.

WREATH—112. To dream of hanging wreaths of flowers or holly, predicts you will be guest of honor at a function.

WRECK—683. If you dream of being hurt in a wreck, it is a warning to be careful while driving a car. If you witness a wreck, you will be annoyed with business and personal matters.

X

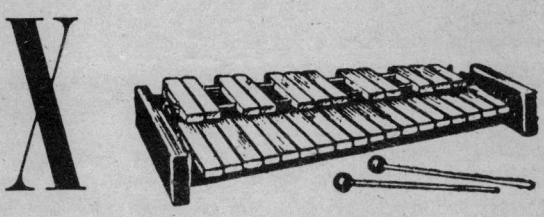

XYLOPHONE

X-RAYS—732. Whether you are having some part of your body x-rayed, or are examining your x-ray picture, you will need to back up some deed which is being questioned.

XYLOPHONE—999. If you play or hear a xylophone which is in tune, you will participate in a celebration. If the instrument plays out of tune, you will meet with a slight accident.

Y

YACHT

YACHT—304. (Also see Boat.) Any dream of being on a yacht is a prediction of luck in love and in business.

YAMS—884. To dream of eating yams means you will gain weight, and this is a warning to go on a diet.

YARD—797. If your backyard is in clean condition, you will enjoy a peaceful family life. If you dream the yard is cluttered with junk, you will need to convince people of your sincerity.

YARDSTICK—615. See Ruler.

YARN—432. To dream of winding yarn into a ball means you will widen your social circle. If you knit or crochet with yarn, you will enjoy happy marriage.

YAWN—016. If you dream you or another is yawning, you must be on guard against an infectious disease.

YELL—016. See Screaming.

YODEL—319. Whether you yodel, or hear another doing so, you will have a peaceful family life.

YOUTH—668. To dream you are young again forecasts a long, good life.

YULE LOG—718. Any dream in which the Christmas log appears is an omen of serene friendships and peaceful living.

ZEBRA

ZEAL—042. If you dream you are working hard and enthusiastically, you will be encouraged in your new plans.

ZEBRA—903. To dream of this striped animal, you will visit friends in a different town. If the zebra is dead, one of your friends may go to jail.

ZERO WEATHER—632. If you dream of suffering in extremely cold weather, you will be presented with new clothes.

ZIPPER—327. A dream in which a zipper is involved is a sign of some friends becoming difficult and you will have to use tact in dealing with them.

ZITHER—880. To play the zither is a prediction of a serene mind and many friends.

ZODIAC—015. See Astrology, also Horoscope.

ZOO—138. To take a child to the zoo means better financial conditions. If you are alone at the zoo, you will go on a long journey.

STUDIES OF SLEEP AND DREAM PATTERNS

Libraries have many books written by and about scientific researchers in this field, which may be of interest to any reader who wishes to devote himself to such literature. This volume, however, brings the subject of dreams and their interpretation to you in a manner that is simple and easily understandable. The way in which these researchers know a sleeping person is dreaming is not only through electronic devices (mentioned in the introduction in this book) but through observing the REM condition of the sleeper. This means "Rapid Eye Movements" and the deduction is that when the sleeping person's eyelids quiver he is having a dream. And when the person (who voluntarily undergoes this testing) awakes, he is asked to immediately tell or write down his dreams. If he says he didn't have a dream, it is either that he doesn't want to admit he dreams or his memory cannot concentrate on its details. The researchers who monitor these sleepers say that everyone does dream.

Young children and babies have also been studied in their sleep, and they also show REM in a pronounced manner, which means they too have dreams even though they may not be able to distinguish between what is a dream and what is reality. Animals, too, have been monitored by sleep-and-dream researchers, and they have REM and often move their bodies in such a way that the observing scientists translate these to mean the animal is having a dream. Of course he cannot discuss the dream, but who knows that the animal does not have a "higher intelligence" wherein he can sense that he is dreaming?

PRECOGNITIVE DREAMS

Psychiatrists and other workers in the field of human behavior usually scoff at the idea that a dream can be a prophecy of something that is going to happen. But those who are interested in the field of parapsychology contend the dreams do predict. This is a long-standing intellectual feud which may never be resolved. But it may interest the reader of this book to know of some cases which have been reported by people who have had precognitive dreams, and the following are some examples of such incidents.

230

The assassination of president John F. Kennedy, which took place November 22, 1963, stirred up a good deal of newspaper and magazine discussion about the warning people got about this unfortunate incident in their dreams, and some were told to him but the president did not heed them. It makes one wonder what might have taken place on that fatal Friday if he had paid attention to these warnings. The most publicized one was that of the clairvoyant, Jeane Dixon, who lives in Washington, D. C. The day after the assassination (November 23rd) this story appeared in the *New York Journal-American*, which quoted her as saying: "The assassination of the President was planned and finalized between 5 and 6 P.M. Sunday. In fact last Sunday I told John Teeter, director of the Damon Runyon Cancer Fund, with whom I had dinner, that I felt a black evil closing over the White House. That I had seen this veil in the past many times—but it is growing closer." Five years previously, in 1958, Jeane Dixon forecast that the president would meet with tragedy, and she again had these same premonitions the week before the Friday when he was shot down.

Another person, who is interested in parapsychology, and had prophetic dreams about John F. Kennedy was Edith Niles, the author of *Astrology and Your Destiny*, and *Palmistry—Your Fate in Your Hands*. This is what she related: "I dreamed this in 1959. was riding on a motorcycle, speeding along the streets in Washington, D. C. Suddenly I felt that danger was going on all around me, and I started to speed up the motorcycle so that I could get away from anything that might take place and prove disastrous. As I increased my speed, I became aware that I was on the highway and it had a white dividing line (which I later recognized in a 1963 newspaper from Dallas as being exactly like the scene of the assassination). I heard shots and saw people falling down to the grass. There was another scene in this dream which followed, and I saw a young man, a commander, being attacked by a short, stocky man. I knew this man was a captain."

On two successive nights, immediately preceding the assassination, Edith Niles had the following dream as she relates it, "Again I saw the young commander in my dream (I had not dreamed of him since that motorcycle dream in 1959). He was a camp counselor and he was leading his people (young adults) out of the woods, into a clearing. Again he was attacked by a short, stocky man. I woke with a feeling of terrible depression, as though wonderful plans would come to nothing because of the event."

That was her dream which occurred twice; she then told, "Later, in a newsreel which was shown on television after the actual assassination took place, I saw Jack Ruby (the one who shot Lee Oswald) and Ruby bore a strong resemblance to the attacker in my dream."

Samuel Clemens (who wrote under the name of Mark Twain) was sensitive in his reaction to dreams and their meanings. Among the stories told about him, is this sad one: As a young man he served on a Mississippi River steamboat, the *Pennsylvania*. On the same boat his brother, Henry, also worked. One night Samuel had a dream that Henry was going to be killed. But he did not want to contemplate such an unhappy thought, and he put the dream out of his mind, nor did he repeat it to Henry as he felt it would disturb him. Samuel Clemens was later transferred to the steamboat, *A. T. Lacey*; but Henry remained in his post on the *Pennsylvania*. The brothers planned they would meet in Memphis, Tennessee where their boats would dock during the river voyage. Henry's boat left two days earlier than Samuel's.

When the *A. T. Lacey* arrived at Memphis, Samuel heard the tragic news that the *Pennsylvania* had suffered a huge fire and that Henry was severely burned in that fire. He suffered for many days, then died as a result of the accident.

The disastrous burning of the ship, the *Yarmouth Castle*, was also foreseen in a dream which Edith Niles (mentioned heretofore) had; she tells of this as follows: "My husband and I took a Caribbean cruise during July 1965. After a pleasant excursion on shore, we returned by tender to our ship. Looking at the brightly lit ships in the harbor the phrase 'a blaze of light' went through my mind; it stuck there, and I just couldn't get it out of my head. It remained there, until finally I fell asleep. While on shore that day, I passed the *Yarmouth Castle*, and felt myself give an involuntary shudder as I looked at that ship. That night I dreamed that a sailor was pushed aside the curtain on the porthole in our cabin. I looked outside, through the porthole, and I saw a ship in the harbor being consumed by flames. I was horrified by seeing that ship afire, yet I was aware that the event I was viewing was not happening now but would happen in the future, and it would affect me anyway. I heard the passengers calling for help, and I still can remember the anguished cries I heard in my dream. I awoke in a cold sweat.

"When we returned home from the trip, I repeated this dream to my housekeeper. Later, in the fall of that year, when the *Yarmouth Castle* burned (in my dreams I did not know the name of the burning ship), she kept the newspaper from me. A friend told me about it, and I obtained a copy of the paper, and then realized why my housekeeper didn't want me to see it. The burning and the people's conversation were exactly what I dreamed and what I had related to her when we got home."

Edith Niles, who so graphically could remember and relate her prophetic dreams, was asked if there were others; she said, "Since this dream about the burning ship, and the one about the John F. Kennedy's assassination, I have had precognitive dreams that foretold events in my own life that were unpleasant. But I remember no previous dreams of this kind, the big disasters! I do recall a dream which was not a tragic precognition, but it is interesting to tell nevertheless. I had gone to a physician for the first time, and we then made an appointment for me to be there the following Thursday. The night before, Wednesday, I dreamed that his nurse called me to say the doctor could not treat me because he had hurt his left ankle. I sloughed the dream off, feeling that maybe it was due to my really not wanting to undergo medical treatment; but I went to keep our 1 P.M. appointment, and as he came into the office I noticed his left foot was limping and he told me that he had sprained his ankle while playing tennis the day before."

Another dream she told about was not hers, but one which her grandmother had when she was hospitalized for surgery. She dreamed she saw an angel who was carrying away her eight-year-old son. The sick woman awoke, screaming, "I know my son is dead, take me to him." Unhappily the boy was dead, as during the night he has suffered a ruptured appendix and arrived at the hospital too late to be helped.

The story is told that Abraham Lincoln dreamed of his own death by violence, and had told this dream to others. Of course, such a dream may have been brought on by the fact that Lincoln received threatening letters from those who wished him evil, and it was only natural for such mail to produce a morbid impression on his mind, rather than for the warning to be an unconscious precognitive dream.

When a war breaks out, the newspapers and magazines are deluged with letters from people who tell they had dreams which had predicted that fighting would break out. Scientists in the field of dream-studying may say these precognitive dreams may not actually have taken place as described by the dreamer, and are not actually psychic warnings, but they may be related by people who are caught up in the emotional hysteria which is engendered by wars and other disasters.

Not all precognitive dreams are those of disaster warnings; some people tell of encountering happy endings which followed their dreams. One case is that of a small boy in a western town who told his mother he had a dream that scared him because it showed that he was buried alive near their house. His mother scolded him for letting his imagination run away with him, she paid no attention to his fears and sent him off to school. When he returned from school he brought along two of his friends; they started to play digging a tunnel in the yard. While digging, the tunnel collapsed becasue the earth had been made soft by days of heavy rainfall. This caused some injury to two of the boys who recovered in a few days. But their digging and showing that the earth was too soft prevented the house itself from sinking into the wet soil (which the building inspector, when called in, told them it would have likely done had the boys not dug first and produced a warning to the owners of the building to properly prop the structure and save damage to property and perhaps to their lives).

A mother who lives in Canada told of a dream which her infant girl had, which was a warning to them that ended well. The child was asleep in her crib, when suddenly she started to toss and violently scream. The mother rushed to the crib and saw that the baby's eyes were still closed and realized she was having a bad dream. She picked up the baby, whose eyes then opened, and to soothe the infant she was taken to the big bed with her parents. In

234

less than five minutes' time the front of their house was struck by an automobile which crashed into it. The body of the driver was thrust through the window, against the crib (where only a few moments earlier the baby was sleeping). The impact of the man's body smashed the little wooden crib to pieces. Of course, the infant could not tell its mother she was having a bad dream; but her parent feels that the child saved her own by a precognitive dream.

DREAMS IN DIFFERENT CULTURES

There is a certain fascination for people of all ages and walks of life to try and find the hidden meanings of their dreams. Often the dreams seem to be so entirely different from the person; for example, a most moral and ethical person might have dreams which don't live up to the high standards of his mind and his way of life. A mature man or woman dreams of being a child. A person who is outgoing, and perhaps even flamboyant, might dream he or she is shy and hesitant and afraid to reach out to others. There is often no relation whatsoever to the person and the theme of his dreams. Such "opposite" dreams might be symbolic of some repression which is being acted out, some wish fulfillment, as expressed by such eminent people like Sigmund Freud, Carl Gustav Jung, Erich Fromm, and others of their stature. To the one who has a psychological interest in scholarly pursuit of dream interpretation, books by these men will prove to be a mine of information.

People are led by their instincts—intellectual and emotional—to look for the meaning of dreams. In ancient times man would think of a dream as a "vision" or as being "possessed" by the people or animals or things he would see in his dream. He would go to an oracle, a priest, or someone in high post, and tell him his dream and rely on the interpretation. Often such interpretations have been the way for some people to gain power over others. In the early times of the talmudic rabbi there was a saying that a dream that is not understood is like a letter not opened; people were warned not to indiscriminately tell their dreams to anyone who was not considered the wise man or the oracle of the time.

235

In the British Museum is a document (the Chester-Beatty papyrus) which is about four thousand years old; it has instructions which tell the Egyptian if he dreams of a moving moon he will receive his god's grace, and if he dreams of crowds in the distance it foretells death.

The Iroquois Indians interpreted dreams to mean they are commands they must follow and obey. Primitive people in the Fiji Islands thought a dream meant the soul is leaving the body. The ancient Greeks not only sought interpretation of dreams from their oracles, but they translated them into ways of healing sick people.

When Europeans (in the 12th to 16th centuries) were beset with fear of witches and demons entering their bodies through their dreams, they were often condemned and burned at the stake by their inquisitory judges who had a book of laws governing the punishment of those accused of witchcraft. In the various religions of the world dreams and their interpretation have played perhaps a more influential part than one cares to imagine.

Today the one who seeks interpretation of the meaning of his dreams, and possibly advice about his behavior as may be expressed in the dreams, does not go to an oracle nor to someone in the field of religion. He goes to a psychiatrist who, even though he may have broken away from or modified basic Freud, is usually still under his influence.

DREAMS FIRE THE IMAGINATION

Among writers of books and poetry and music and plays, dreams have played a large part in sparking the imagination and adding new dimension to the mind. People in various professions and branches of work are often inspired by a dream in broadening their avenues of operation. The timid person may be fired with the desire to achieve more through the prompting of a dream. Sigmund Freud, the Viennese doctor who expounded and developed the theme of man's unconscious called it "a wild beast caged in the heart of a city," and often a dream is the means of opening up the door of the cage and giving the mind and energies the impetus they need toward building a better future. The Swiss psychologist, Carl Gustav Jung, said: "When we lost our way among the endless details and detached events of the superficial world, what would be more natural to expect than to knock on the door of our dreams and ask for views on those problems which could reorient us toward fundamental human facts."

The author, Robert Louis Stevenson, credited his dreams with supplying him with the plot for his book, *Dr. Jekyll and Mr. Hyde*. Richard Wagner dreamed of a flood, and the rushing waters suggested to him chords of music, which he then incorporated in his composition, *Das Rheingold*. William Makepeace Thackeray got the title to his book, *Vanity Fair*, through a dream; and Charlotte Bronte was inspired in the description for the setting of her novel, *Jane Eyre*, through dreaming of such a place.

The song, *Kiss Me Again*, was composed by Victor Herbert through ideas which came to him in a dream. William Archer turned the symbols in one of his dreams into the play, *The Green Goddess*.

In the fields of invention and science, many findings came about through dreams which inspired actual results. A case in point is the sewing machine which was invented by Eli Howe, who told that a dream symbol enable him to solve the problem of threading the needle in the machine.

Dr. Otto Loewi, who won the Nobel Prize in science, was experimenting on the dissection of frogs in order to study their nervous system; he worked at this for many years, until one night in a dream he came across the missing element for which he was searching. He was thus able to complete his experiment on the transmission of the nervous impulse, which won high praise in scientific circles.

When people like these, and others of high achievement, are able to translate some of the symbols in their dreams into productive reality, one must certainly concede that dreams are nothing to scoff at, but could be used by individuals to enrich their minds and to be prepared to face the events of each day.